Pawn Shop Dick

Yeoman Warder Daniel Fear.
This photograph was on the front page of The Tower of London's
visitors' book for many years

Pawn Shop Dick

By

Ray Fear

Published by Ray Fear
39 Hunters Way
Penkhull
Stoke-on-Trent ST4 5EJ
United Kingdom

Date of Publication
Summer 2005

Published by Ray Fear
39 Hunters Way
Penkhull
Stoke-on-Trent ST4 5EJ
United Kingdom

Printed and bound by
Antony Rowe Ltd.
Wiltshire

Typesetting and cover by John Bullock
(www.altaser.com)

ISBN-13: 978-0-9550218-0-0
ISBN-10: 0-955-0218-0-4

Dedicated to Sylvia and to my four daughters;
Jane, Beverley, Lara, and Natasha. The five ladies in my life.

Hoping they won't be too shocked at my past, present and future
illuminating revelations.

My heartfelt thanks to Clive, Anne, and John. Without whose
help this book would not have been possible.

BUCKINGHAM PALACE

16th June, 1997.

Dear M. Fear,

I am commanded by The Queen to write and thank you for your letter.

Her Majesty was interested to hear of your father's service with the Grenadier Guards and as a Yeoman of the Guard, and of your own service with the Grenadiers during the War.

The Queen was amused to read of the childhood incident you recount, and was also interested to learn that your daughter had competed at Badminton and was in Russia with the British Team.

I am to thank you again for your letter, and for the good wishes you have sent to Her Majesty, which were greatly appreciated.

Yours sincerely,

Susan Hussey

Lady-in-Waiting

R. Fear, Esq.

Permission to print this letter was received from Buckingham Palace on the 28th January 2005

32A, OVINGTON SQUARE,

LONDON, SW3 1LR

TEL. 020-7584 1476

FAX. 020-7823 9051

FOREWORD

As you will discover as you read this book, Ray Fear is quite a character and has led and full and colourful life.

He recounts his experiences at the Guards' Depot and later on, with the Grenadiers in the Second World War, with the humour one would expect from him.

As for the rest, you will enjoy his account of his civilian experiences.

Carrington

Lord Carrington

2nd March, 2005.

Readers' Comments

Pawn Shop Dick is a great read, you will enjoy every page.
(Full comments on back cover)

Tony Benn M.P. Ret., London, U.K.

Effortlessly addictive, this book would be a good laugh in any language.

Pilar Cabello, Valencia, Spain

You should never have used those pictures of yourself in this book. I have already had inquiries from the military, civilian and Interpol police asking for your address. I told them I thought you were on the Costa del Flanker, running a retirement home for wealthy bank robbers. Even under duress I did not give you away, even to the Salvation Army, who see you as in chronic need of redemption.

Peter Buxton M.B.E., J.P., Stoke-on-Trent, U.K.

It made me laugh and cry practically at the same time. The author has a unique way of looking at situations and dealing with them in a unique manner. I love the humour he takes to these problems.
All of his life he has never lost who he is as a person. This is a testimony to the best and worst times of his life.

Donna Jones, Birmingham, U.K.

With luck, and the author has plenty, the book sales should offset the costs of libel suits! However, it's a book all ex-servicemen and racing enthusiasts will enjoy, but the legal profession and solicitors will shrink from it in horror.

Dr. J.E. Yardley, Aberystwyth, U.K.

Synopsis

Now in his 79th year, there are not many people who can look back and relive, with such clarity, a life so full and extraordinary. Sometimes bizarre, but never boring. Incidents such as how many people were conceived in The Tower of London these last 600 years, or thrown conkers and bread rolls at the Queen without being incarcerated in some dungeon or other.

His good fortune always revolved around luck, as one would expect of a Sagittarian and an equally lucky Chinese Tiger. Sheer luck meeting so many interesting and unusual characters. A more suitable title for his book 'Pawn Shop Dick' may have been 'Lucky Old Fear'. Being in the right place at the right time influenced his entire life.

Four times married with ten children would make a very interesting tale, but this book relives his whole life from schoolboy, life in a pawn shop, the Brigade of Guards, bookmaker, health shop proprietor, cattery owner and manager of both Britain's youngest Channel swimming team and modern pentathlon champions. To be involved in all this and find time, at 60 years of age, to start marathon running, is no mean feat.

Lucky for him, he now resides on the Costa Blanca of Spain with his lovely young wife, youngest son Dan and 6 year old daughter (yes, you did read correctly, 6 year old daughter), in a modest villa surrounded by his beautiful garden, recently shown on English television's 'Gardens without Borders'.

His ambition is to be the last surviving grenadier of World War II and receive a state funeral.

Contents

Chapter 1

RCSGF

Raymond Charles Sebastian Gigor Fear.

Who is he?

Never heard of him.

Read on, dear reader. You may find the following chapters incredible. That so much could happen in the life of one man. Not big decisions like the evacuation of Dunkirk, or believing the twaddle 'Peace in our time' preached by Chamberlain, but amazing things that happened to 'Lucky Old Fear' with an excellent memory and the ability of being able to relive, with such clarity, the things that happened 70 years ago. Enjoy some of the exploits of 'Pawn Shop Dick', 2624924 Guardsman Fear R., 1st Battalion Grenadier Guards and Honest Ray, Bookmaker Extraordinaire.

I was conceived in The Tower of London and born at Warwick Street, Pimlico, 400 yards from Buckingham Palace. How come? Well, Father was a yeoman warden whose service at The Tower ran from 1916 to September 1926. His name is painted in gold in The Wardens' Tower. I was born in December of 1926, so Ma was humping me about behind those hallowed portals for some 6 months. It would have been very special to have been born there at No. 3 The Casemates, overlooking the lawns and those awesome ravens.

I always referred to my father as a yeoman of the guard. In fact, he was a yeoman warder, or 'Beefeater' who reside in The Tower and have done so since 1078. The Yeomen of the Guard, although dressed the same apart from a gold embroidered cross belt over their left shoulder, live in their own homes and only perform their duties on special occasions, such as coronations, opening of parliament and state visits of foreign dignitaries.

People often ask why the warders are called Beefeaters. Well, it stems from the daily rations of 30 yeomen residing in The Tower in the year 1813:

24 lbs of beef

18 lbs of mutton

16 lbs of veal a day

Between 30 men. Extraordinary. To help wash down the generous helpings each day they received 37 gallons of beer, that is 10 pints each. On special occasions, wine was also served in the same generous quantities. No doubt in Dad's day, the meat allowance had been cut considerably, but I am sure he endeavoured to maintain the standards of his predecessors and consume the daily ration of 10 pints of beer.

Father was born in Aberystwyth from a middle class family of coachbuilders and it was as a coachbuilder that he started work. His ambition was always to join the army, the army that had defeated Napoleon and had helped build the British Empire and reshape the world. Only recently there had been Rorkes Drift, in which the 24th Regiment of Foot - a Warwickshire regiment, but mostly Welshmen recruited from South Wales - where 13 Victoria Crosses had been awarded to those gallant 137 soldiers who defended The Drift against 4,000 Zulu warriors. Episodes like this had fired his imagination, so at 15 he ran away from home and joined the army. On learning this, his mother promptly bought him out and he returned to Aberystwyth and coach building.

His mind was made up and in 1892 at the age of 16, he lied about his age and once more enlisted into the Welsh regiment, this time with his father and mothers' blessing, by which time he had grown the half inch needed to be 5 foot 11 inches, the minimum in those days to join the Guards.

He managed to get transferred into the 1st, or Grenadier Regiment of Foot Guards, the finest battalion in the finest regiment in the world. The Grenadier Guards, who had won fame defeating the French Imperial Guards at Waterloo. It was there that they won the

2

privilege of wearing the 'Bearskin' - an honour that the French Imperial Guards bestowed upon them after their defeat. Besides the usual qualifications to become an NCO, one had to achieve a certain educational level and there were classes the guardsmen could attend to attain this.

However, by the time the 1st Battalion sailed to the Nile Delta on the way to Khartoum, Father was a sergeant. The regiment fought with distinction at the Battle of Omduman where, in one day's fighting, the very small British army defeated the Kaliff and his army of 70,000 - mostly mounted dervishers armed with rifles, swords, and spears. One of the spears went right through Father and severed one of his kidneys. He lay on a waterbed for 90 days hovering between life and death, having contracted malaria to add to his misery. Arriving back in Southampton he was transferred to Netley Hospital where he stayed until his recovery. The dervishers sustained 10,000 dead as their wounded were shot the next day. In a letter to his mother, Winston Churchill wrote 'Today I was ashamed to be a British soldier.'

In the meantime, the Boars had been claiming their rights to South Africa and as a result, the South African War started. In six months, Field Marshall Lord Roberts soon had the war won and returned to England, only for the fighting to flare up again. This time General Kitchener commanded and the war dragged on for another 2 years.

In 1906, with further promotion hard to get (sergeant majors hold their posts forever), Father transferred into the Royal Fusiliers, the City of London Regiment, where he became a sergeant major. Although his 21 years with The Colours finished in 1913, he continued to serve when the Great War started in 1914. Due to his wounds, Father retired and was invited by the governor of The Tower of London to become a yeoman warden. He accepted and became a beefeater in 1916. In 1918, when the RAF was formed from the Royal Flying Corp., they called upon ex-brigade of guards drill sergeants to help start their operation. They wanted to incorporate discipline into this much larger organisation that had previously been sorely lacking in the very gallant flying corp. After the end of hostilities, Father returned to The Tower of London and resumed his duties there.

Ah! What about Mother? Now there is a lady if ever there was one. Born Henrietta Eleanor Harrison in Hereford, she was the only child of aged parents. They had been married for over twenty years before Henrietta was born. Her father was a director of the Great Western Railway, so her parents were very comfortably off. Her father worshiped her, although her mother was as tough as old boots. Hetty was sent off to boarding school when she was 10 years old and learned the art of being a lady. She played the piano, harp, and violin very well and could speak French. Her Latin helped her later in life when she had to seek employment. Her father hunted with the Hereford Hunt and one Saturday afternoon on his return from a day's hunting, he called out:

"Joe" (his nickname for his daughter) "Come and help me off with my boots."

Joe obliged and as she was tugging away, her father fell back off the mounting block suffering a fatal heart attack. He was 75. My mother was broken hearted, as you would imagine.

Her first marriage was to Cyril Badham, a young solicitor. They had three sons - James Roberts (not Robert) born 1914; John Cyril born 1916 and Henry Elton born 1918. It took us a long time to discover why poor Elton was so named. We all called him Elton, which he hated, and as soon as he started work he was renamed Richard. His boss, on enquiring as to his name, said:

"I ain't going to call you bloody Elton, you're Richard from now on." Anyway, Henry Elton was the male version of Henrietta Eleanor. Fancy that Elton John!

Mother always told us that her first husband had a big drink problem and eventually died of alcoholic poisoning. I wonder. She also claimed he had blown her inheritance. It seems from my half brother Jim that she had invested a lot of money in the Castle Nursery, Aberystwyth owned by Randolph Fear, elder brother of Daniel Fear, my father.

It is important to remember this. Why would Hetty invest money behind her husband's back, in a nursery growing orchids, which were sold throughout Europe to enhance the beauty of the rich young ladies of those days, unless Randolph was her secret lover which, from all accounts, it seems he was. Poor Randolph died suddenly after eating parsnips for supper, which Mother always warned us against eating late at night. My guess is that he had been over-indulging in other nocturnal pleasures. Daniel was informed of his brother's death and hastened to Aberystwyth.

According to Mother, she first met Father over the feet of her ex-lover as he lay instate in his parlour. It was love at first sight according to her. Father's first wife had died of cancer; there were five daughters and one son from the marriage. So there we have it, Mother looking for a wealthy husband and Dad looking for a wealthy widow. 'Jackpot', they both thought, and so they became lovers, Mother eventually moving into The Tower. Brother Jim, who was 12 at the time, also lived at The Tower and can remember well his father Cyril Badham calling there on one occasion. According to Mother, he was dead. The plot thickens, for in August 1926, Father retired as a yeoman warden of his own free will.

Before I came to Spain, I had an incline to get a few more details of my father's service at The Tower, so I telephoned and spoke to the governor. He was a perfect gentleman and very helpful. As soon as I mentioned my father's name, he said;

"Oh yes. I see him most days. His photo is in the front of the visitors' book."

We spoke for a few minutes and he said he would get the curator - a Mr. Harrison - to 'phone me that evening, which he did. He had looked up father's records and posted on all the details to me together with a letter confirming dates of his service and which accommodation he changed to and from during his service at The Tower. The one thing he could not answer was why Dad retired.

My brother and I have often spoken on this question and it seems it could have been one of three reasons. Mother complaining that she was not used to living in such miserable conditions (as was the lot of the wardens, The Tower being built some hundreds of years ago), the governor finding out that they were not married, or Father being drunk in uniform on Constitution Hill. I remember well, from the age of 7 or 8, Mother forever complaining to Father during their constant rowing.

"If you hadn't been drunk on Constitution Hill, we would still be comfortably off, instead of this life."

This bewildered me for many years until one day, looking at the London roadmap; I discovered that Constitution Hill ran along one side of Buckingham Palace, so it is my guess that it's there that Pa disgraced himself. The governor of that time would have probably said:

"Now look here Dan, this isn't the first time. Either you retire voluntarily, or we will reluctantly dispense with your services. If you retire, it will be without a stain on your character."

And so, in the middle of the Big 1926 General Strike, Father was out of work along with many millions of other poor souls.

On my birth certificate, he had as his employment 'Storekeeper'. Why, in God's name, couldn't he have put 'Yeoman Warden Retired', as I certainly would have done? But Father had never been in business and didn't understand 'bending the rules a bit'. I think he worked at the Army and Navy Stores in Victoria.

I was born at 117 Warwick Street, Pimlico - now Warwick Way - a stone's throw from Buckingham Palace and Chelsea Barracks. From there our wanderings began, first to Blackpool where Dad got the job as Commissionaire at Blackpool Tower. It was in Blackpool that my younger brother, Daniel, was born on Primrose Day, 19th April 1928, just 14 months after me. Then, it seems, Father made an unforgivable mistake and commuted his pension, that is, he took a lump sum payment and ceased to receive any more monthly contributions. Alas, what a mistake!

With the money, we moved to Bournemouth and he bought a shop dealing in odd bits of second-hand furniture. It seems that at opening times, he stuck a notice in his window to the effect that he would be back in 10 minutes. His habit, in fact, was to retire to the nearest pub for a couple of hours, where he could always get an audience to listen to his war stories. He soon tired of the few hours he did at the shop, and sold out at a big loss.

From there we went to Bagshot in Buckinghamshire, Bagshot Park, where Father took up the position of lodge keeper and security guard. Bagshot Park was the home of the Duke of Connaught, youngest son of Queen Victoria, himself a grenadier and in his late seventies. The estate had a magnificent pair of gates, which were kept shut and only opened on the approach of vehicles. The gates were opened by turning a large wheel inside the lodge. We soon learned the different horns and hooters of the visitors. Princess Alice was the easiest to distinguish, as her chauffeur made a most dreadful noise with his klaxon horn. We called her Miss Winnie.

As the wheel was kept well oiled, Dan and I could manage to turn it quite easily and so let in the distinguished guests. The most important, in Dan's and my own view, was our great Aunt Flo - Nan, as we called her. Nan was Mother's aunt, and a wonderfully kind person she was. She bought up her five boys one way or another. We all loved her dearly. Anyway, she joined us at the lodge, as my two half-brothers James and John (who she had been looking after) had flown the nest and remained in their last place of abode, John in Poole and Jim in London. Elton, who was about 14, came with her, so she had three boys left to look after, as Mother, whilst kind, was not cut out for domestic duties.

I have happy memories of Bagshot, a nice hot summer and helping Nan in the vegetable garden. There was nothing that lady couldn't do. Her cooking was extraordinary and she could make a feast out of the simplest of foods. Every morning before school, we walked to the farm inside the grounds to collect a quart of milk from the Duke's Jersey cows in a highly polished milk churn, and eggs and cheese once a week. I remember well, the Hunt passing the lodge in the winter months and the huntsmen blowing their horns. I used to wonder why some of the field were dressed in pink and the rest in black. Now I know.

We had a large Airedale dog that ate large dog biscuits, which we boys also enjoyed with our cocoa. The dog, whose name was

Major, used to accompany Father around the grounds at night searching for would-be marauders.

Most Sunday afternoons the Duke would call at the lodge and take tea with Father and Mother. We boys would sometimes be invited, and sit as quiet as mice waiting impatiently for Nan's rock cakes to be handed round. The Duke and Father had served in the Sudan conflict and had fought together at Omduman. The Duke was a very fine looking gentleman and very kind in a soldierly fashion. He always gave us a wave when he saw us playing in the grounds. Although the Duke and Duchess employed a staff of 60, we never saw any of them.

Amongst the many frequent guests, were the Duke and Duchess of York. They and their two children, Princess Elizabeth and Princess Margaret, would accompany them. In the grounds was a large, covered-in bandstand, which housed many children's toys like rocking horses, dolls houses, tricycles and the like. During their visit, the young princesses would go to the 'playhouse' - as we called it - accompanied by their nurse, a fearsome nanny dressed like a cross between a nun and Anna May Wong.

One autumn day, Dan and I collected some nice big conkers and crept up as close as we dared and, from behind some bushes, threw the conkers at the young ladies. The nurse was horrified and yelled at us to be off. We beat a hasty retreat and laughed our way back home. We little realised that one day one of the girls we had showered with our conkers would be the Queen and Colonel in Chief of The Grenadier Guards. The nurse must have reported us to Father, for he summoned us before him and asked if we had indeed committed this dreadful offence. His only comment was:

"Did you hit them?"

The Duchess of York had instructed the nurse to tell Father not to be too hard on us. 'They are only boys.'

One day during the hot summer, I remember a heath fire starting on the road to Ascot. The fire engine raced past the lodge and slowed down to allow Elton to board and join the other bunch of volunteers who were off to fight the fire. He returned, black as night, several hours later. Elton also worked part-time at the Pantiles, a country club with a swimming pool. It was only a few hundred yards from the lodge and it was there that he met Douglas Bader, who was courting his future wife. He always gave Elton a sixpenny tip - a princely sum in those days. Douglas Bader, you will remember, was the legless pilot who became a famous fighter ace during the War. When Bader was eventually shot down, it was claimed by the Germans that he was shot down by one of their most famous fighter aces. This had been pre-arranged at Bader's request at his interrogation. He had been told that he had been shot down by an inexperienced sergeant. Bader found that intolerable and claimed he must have been shot down by an officer at least. Now, in 2005, the truth has come to light: He was brought down by Buck Casson, one of his own squadron. It seems that, at certain angles, the Messerschmitt and Spitfire looked very much the same. These days it is called friendly fire. Buck Casson was also shot down in the same action and, like Bader, was a POW for 4 years.

As Douglas floated down on his parachute, he discovered he had left one of his legs behind in the stricken Spitfire. Not to worry, the Huns were very glad to have Bader captive, and allowed one of our planes to drop a new leg. When he had adjusted to his new leg, the first thing he did was try to escape. Now there's a courageous man, and generous too, as Elton will confirm.

These days Bagshot Park is the home of TRH Earl and Countess of Wessex. A couple of years ago I wrote to the Earl of Wessex asking him if my wife and I could visit Bagshot Park with a view to reliving happy memories. I had a very agreeable letter back from the Earl's private secretary, Lieutenant Colonel Sean O'Dwyer, saying a visit would be fine as long as I made contact when next visiting the U. K. so we could make arrangements. Earl Wessex sent his very best wishes.

Unfortunately, very near to our lodge was the 'Cricketers Arms', and it was there that Father would nip of an evening whilst supposedly on duty and, together with Major, would down a few pints. Anyhow, it wasn't long before the bailiff of the estate got wind of these goings-on and reported him. The first we knew about it was a note left from Father to Mother, which read: 'Gone to Falmouth, follow on.' Eventually a card arrived from Father with his new address in Falmouth.

Then came the question of how to raise the fares to get there in the first place. I think Nan gave Mother the money for our three coach fares. Nan returned to London with Elton. I remember distinctly getting on the coach and the long journey to Cornwall. Both Dan and I were very sick on the way. Coaches in those days were not as comfortable as they are now.

We settled into lodgings to start with and eventually moved to a flat in Kimberley Park Road. My only souvenir of that town was a copy of 'The Gorilla Hunters' written by Ralph Ballantyne. It was given to me by a school pal called Ralph. I still have the book which most of my children have also read.

I have memories of mackerel fishing, when you could cast your line and catch a dozen at a time. Eaten straight from the sea they take a bit of beating for flavour and goodness. I won my first running race there at the school Sports Day at the tender age of 6 or 7. The prize was a large bun stuffed with lovely Cornish clotted cream. I remember sharing my prize with brother Dan who was not as lucky as I on the day. I also played in my first football match on a sodden field at the top of Jacobs Ladder. The teacher complimented me on my play and asked the rest of the Cornish lads:

"Why can't you play like this cockney lad?"

I had been very quickly sorted out as a foreigner who spoke with such a strange accent. At times, it was very difficult to understand what they were talking about, but I quickly learned that: 'Ain't it 'andsome' meant 'Isn't it nice', when referring to a Cornish pasty or such. It's quite true, it's only in Cornwall you can get the true flavour of that wholesome dish.

I remember well being paid sixpence by some gypsies. To earn this princely sum, I had to be lowered over a cliff in a basket; the object was to collect the seagull eggs laid on the ledges of the cliff. It was a frightening experience, as once I was over the edge the gypsies could not see me, or I them, and our only means of communication was by shouting. They were very concerned regarding my safety, as no doubt if I had got caught up on some obstacle or other and been hurled to my death, they would have been on manslaughter charges, or even murder. The gypsies, very wisely, did not endanger their own offspring on such a dangerous mission.

I remember collecting over 20 eggs and my employees were very pleased and asked me to return next day. I said I would but, needless to say, I had no intentions of chancing my luck again on such hazardous employment and thought there must be easier ways of earning sixpence then by dicing with death. Periodically the circus came to town and we boys would help the circus staff to erect the big tent and do other jobs such as cleaning out the stables and walking the ponies. Before the first show, the ringmaster asked for a volunteer to help with the elephant act. The other boys pointed at me and said:

"He will do it, he comes from London"

I had to arrive half an hour before the show started and be introduced to Big Jumbo. That was the elephant's name. I was then attired in a very strong, smelly, red jumper, taken into the tent and shown where to sit. I was dismissed with a piece of paper to say that my brother and I were to be admitted free. I was promised sixpence a performance and I thought this was very fair compared with the sixpence earned 'cliff hanging'. Nothing, I thought, could be as bad as that.

By six o'clock, we were seated in the best seats and the performance began in the traditional manner. Half way through the show, it was Big Jumbo's turn to perform. He came out and did a few tricks like standing on his head and taking a penalty shot with a football. Then he pretended to go out of control and his master pretended the animal had gone mad. Jumbo rushed round the ring staring into the crowd; then he suddenly stopped opposite to where I was sitting and, with his long trunk coiled round my body, he whisked me onto his back where, thankfully, there were straps to grasp. The crowd was shocked, as they did not think this incident was pre-arranged.

I was told after that some of the younger viewers cried. I had been told beforehand what the elephant would do, but I didn't expect to be rushed round the ring at such a speed and finally dropped into a bath of water. How the crowd laughed and brother Dan in particular. I think I did about six performances including the grand finale. The ringmaster said I was a very good little lad and on the final night gave me one shilling - double wages, yippee!

Dan claimed half my wages as he had carried my change of clothing there after the first show when I had to return home wet through. I think he was overpaid. Neither of my parents came to the circus to see my exploits on the elephant. Today I find this very strange as if any of my children were doing a similar thing, nothing in the world would prevent me from watching them perform. When my children were in action, I dropped everything to attend their function, but more about that later.

One day, Dan and I were walking home from school when we passed what looked like white icing some 3 metres by 3 metres.

"Let's have a slide" I suggested "You first!"

Dan very bravely ran and attempted to slide on the white surface. Alas, in he went and sunk up to his middle in what turned out to be a lime pit. In those days, it was the usual thing to have a lime pit when constructing houses. Poor Dan was very upset and cried. When we reached home, he told Mother I had pushed him into the lime pit. I was for it and was sent to bed without any tea. Much more effective than a good hiding. I can never ever remember Mother raising a finger against any of her five boys, but she had some very clever ways of maintaining discipline. Dan stood outside our bedroom window wolfing down a cream jam donut.

Father, at this time, did no work and we must have lived on what was left from the sale of the second-hand shop in Bournemouth. But our lovely days in Falmouth were to come to an end and the next thing I remember was returning to London to some rented rooms in Brixton. A nasty place where all the older women looked like prize-fighters.

We were on the first floor and some other tenants lived in the basement. They were always fighting amongst themselves and shouting abuse from morning until late at night - very late, I may add. One day as the lady tenant was about to depart through her front door, I dropped a quart milk bottle on her head. It hit her shoulder and I disappeared inside as quickly as possible. No doubt she had so many enemies she never thought it was little 'Taffy' from upstairs. Yes, 'Taffy'. That's what the other boys used to call us at school because the year we spent at Falmouth had left us with a definite accent, which must have sounded a bit like Welsh.

From Brixton we went to live at Linden Gardens, Chiswick and attended Belmont Infant School. There was an open stove in the classroom and the boys and girls from richer families bought apples to school and were allowed to bake them on the stove in the winter months.

On Sunday afternoons, a man would push a cart along Linden Gardens crying out 'Cockles!'. I think they sold for one penny a half pint and Father would sometimes decide to buy some. We would have bread and jam for tea and some of Nan's delicious rock cakes. I can't recall how long we stayed there, but the next move was to The Avenue, Acton, where we shared a small house with a mad Irishman and his family. The rows in their family were far worse than at Brixton. I remember on Boat Race Day, an ambulance called and with the assistance of a couple of bobbies, our Irish neighbour was entangled in a straight jacket and carted off to God knows where!

We boys, after viewing these goings on, hastened to the nearby River Thames to see the annual boat race. Cambridge won that year and I picked the winner - Dan had Oxford.

While we lived there, Mother started to work for the first time in her life. She worked in a chemist shop at nearby Bedford Park in the dispensing department, making up the different potions and I wonder if it wasn't there that she learned all about poisons.

Brother Elton also started work with United Dairies and it was there that the boss renamed him Richard - a name he has stuck to for the rest of his life. At Christmas, out of his frugal earnings, I remember him buying each of his two younger brothers two large, tin, model aeroplanes made in Japan. They cost sixpence each in

Woolworths. We were overwhelmed at his generosity, but the planes didn't last long, as anything made in Japan was a laugh, not like today when they turn out some of the World's best machinery, when after the Second World War, the Yanks decided to sponsor the Japs as a bastion against poor old Russia.

Elton and Nan stayed behind when we made our next move to Rodney Road, Mitcham, where we were in lodgings. Lots of strange things went on there and the 15 year old daughter of the house used to inspect Dan's and my private parts and wondered why Dan, who was younger than I, had a bigger dongleberry. It's a statement that had me suffering from an inferiority complex for many years. That is, until I discovered that in most cases we men are all about the same and it's the way you use it that counts in the eyes of the opposite sex. More about that later.

The girl's father was always drunk at weekends and created a hell of a noise on his return from the pub every Saturday night. One night my dad could stand this no longer and confronted this much younger man in the front garden. There was a lot of foul language and a fight. Father laid out his landlord in his own front garden and his wife left him there all night for he was still there, sound asleep, next morning.

There was a big pig farm nearby and Dan and I spent many a happy hour helping the farmer. He used to boil up all manner of scraps of food and peelings that, together with the added mash, was called Tottenham Pudding.

On the move again, and this time we stayed at a small boarding house that my eldest brother, Jim, had sorted out for himself at the time. He was working for MacAlpines, the big building concern. He stayed with them for many years and became a close friend of Mr. MacAlpine's son. They had motorbikes and rode round the Wall of Death on several occasions.

Mrs. Parker was the landlady and what a tyrant she was. I recall she liked young Dan but hated me because I blew up some bubble gum and exploded it very close to her face. Part of the bubbles stuck to her beak and she was none too pleased. I was not allowed to view the fireworks let off in the next-door neighbours' garden later that day. Mrs. Parker and Mother never got on as Ma had never peeled a potato in her life, let alone all the other menial tasks a normal housewife would have to undertake when taking a husband. Anyway, we owed so much rent that, in the end, we were turned out. Not a drastic occurrence, as our belongings were few and I suppose we were thinking it quite normal to move house every few months.

Brother Jim, who also lodged there and had paid his own rent, willingly stayed behind. He had fallen in love or got his first perk on with a woman – Mrs. Parker's daughter, Jessie. A total mismatch, which I could see at the ripe old age of 7 or 8. They had four children in quick succession and I am sure, had they stayed together, his offspring would have outnumbered mine. They separated soon after the war ended in 1945, when he met and fell in love with a beautiful divorced Yorkshire lady named Joan.

Chapter 2

Sussex by the Sea

Our next destination was Brighton, Sussex by the Sea and what a wonderful place for us to go. We stayed there for the best part of 20 years, not at the same address, of course, as Dad had hit on a good idea on how to live rent-free.

"I am Sergeant Major Fear, late of The Grenadiers, and we would like to stay with you for a while," he would announce to the boarding house owner. "As my army pension is only paid monthly, I'll settle with you at the end of the month."

In most cases the landladies were overjoyed to have four permanent guests and readily agreed to this arrangement, little realising that there was no pension and no rent forthcoming at the end of the month. When, eventually, we were asked to move, it was easy to find another poor, unsuspecting landlady willing to take us in. We moved all round Brighton. I can remember 46 Queens Park Road, 160 Queens Park Road, 47 St. Luke's Terrace and 160 Freshfield Road, to name a few.

Dan and I went to St. Luke's School, a well-disciplined establishment with a good reputation, where the teachers were held in great respect. We, in the junior school, all had one aim in life and that was to pass our entry exam to either the intermediate school or Varndean, for no other reason than to avoid finishing up in our senior school and coming in contact with the science master.

Both Dan and I failed to pass to either of these two high schools and we often wondered why. We were both quite bright pupils and always finished in the first three in our respective classes. We had exams each term and were placed one to thirty according to our results. I was placed first several times and we both wondered why boys who were near bottom of the class passed to Varndean while we bright boys didn't. The fact we didn't pass probably changed the whole course of our lives - for the better I may add.

Mr. Godfrey, the science master, was the most feared teacher in the school, as he had a shambock made from rhinoceros hide. It was about 2 feet long and he would attack, unmercifully, any boy who upset him for any reason. The cane came very keen on the hand, not to mention the head. He was, however, a fair-minded man and when I finally finished up in his Class 2A, we got on quite well as I was fairly good at sport and played in the school football and cricket teams.

I was the best runner in the school, a sport I had developed in London when running to school and out-pacing the little cockney lads who lay in wait for us Taffies with designs on our apples. Dan, who could not run as fast as I could, often had his apple stolen and I was not very happy when he wanted my 'apple chogg', the core of the apple that more affluent people threw away. In our school, we would have a free-for-all fight for an apple chogg.

In Godfrey's class, one of our first tests was to make a steel yard - an old-fashioned weight machine, still used in abattoirs for weighing large sides of beef, pig, or lamb. I set to my task and I remember melting down some of my old lead soldiers in a cocoa tin, to use as the weight set in the wood at one end of the measure. Very professional. Mr. Godfrey suggested my dad had helped me (which he hadn't) and when I denied this, he gave me a light tap on the head with his shambock and said I must not tell lies. However, I'd made the best steel yard in the class of 30 and won - yes, you've guessed - my usual fee, sixpence.

Later that year war broke out and the Home Guard was formed. Father, with his war record, became sergeant major and Godfrey was in his battalion. One day he called me to one side and asked if Sergeant Major Fear was indeed my father. When I answered in the affirmative, he said:

"How remarkable, he is old enough to be your grandfather" and immediately asked me if I would like to be in charge of the wastepaper collection, as the boy who had been doing the job was not up to it.

Now this job was what we all wanted and it involved bagging up all the waste paper brought to the school by all the pupils on a daily basis to help the war effort. The job ensured that I missed most of the morning lessons. That is, if we were not all in our air raid shelters when the sirens went. The shelters had been hastily dug in our playgrounds as soon as war had been declared. The sirens would sound and all the school would quietly file down to the shelters. They were glorified trenches, zigzagging to prevent blast. They had wooden benches on either side. If we were entrenched for over an hour or two, a teacher would come round and give us all a barley sugar sweet.

As thousands of London evacuees came to Brighton to avoid the blitz, we would only attend school half a day. One week it was mornings and the next week afternoons. The evacuees did alternate weeks. The Londoners who came to our school were from a better class area, Northwood. We got on very well with them, especially the girls.

I remember my very first sweetheart - Betty Verall. We would play games in Queens Park and I know she liked me as when she returned to London she gave me a brown tartan tie, which I kept for many years. I think I gave her a memento but I forget what. I did remember us going swimming in North Road Baths one Saturday. When she came out of the changing cubicle, I thought how big her titties were. Not for long, for after we had dived in and swam to the shallow end I noticed that her bosom had shrunk and one tit was higher than the other. It turned out that to impress me she had stuffed cotton wool into her swimming costume and, of course, once wet it had greatly reduced in size. I often thought about her and wondered what happened to her.

Back to Mr. Godfrey. On leaving school, he asked me if I would like his electric shock machine. It was in a mahogany box with a dynamo inside and two wired cables, which were attached to two brass grips. Someone would turn the handle and the person holding the grips would immediately get an electric shock; the faster the handle was turned, the bigger the shock. I found that after this treatment I could run faster. It's a good job we didn't have doping tests before the races, as no doubt I would have been disqualified for having electrical elements up my arse. Another way my pals helped me train was to tie a rope round my waist with one end attached to their bikes, and I would have to run as fast as they could pedal, or else fall on my face and be dragged along the road. I remember once being pulled over, grazing both hands and knees. Unfortunately, the war affected our sports and I didn't get much chance to show off my prowess until I joined the army.

During our holidays, we were always on the lookout to earn a copper or two. Some of the rougher kids from Whitehawk and Moulscombe would sing under the Palace Pier and the holidaymakers would throw coppers down on to the sand. This was the signal for a free-for-all and the lads dived in like a rugby scrum scratching about for the cash. This was against the law and we had noticed that when the law did appear, the culprits all fled. One day when we were particularly short of money, Dan and I watched the performance from a distance and, when we thought enough pennies had been thrown to the choir, we nipped up from the beach hunting for a policeman. When we spotted one we hastened to tell him:

"They are singing under the pier, Mister!"

"Thank you" said the Bobbie and made his way to the pier.

When the boys saw the policeman, off they ran and Dan and I had a clear field to check for all the hidden coins in the sand. We did very well and didn't have to sing a note.

Our chance to sing came at Christmas time. We would join with a couple of pals and go carol singing. Our main area was around Queens Park, where many of the better-off people lived. I cannot mention Queens Park without remembering 'Old Wanker', who used to frequent the public urinal, standing well back from the wall to show off his penis. He would play with his plonker for hours and endeavour to get us boys to assist him in his task for a small fee. Naturally, Dan and I drew a line there in our efforts to raise money!

On Saturdays, we sometimes got a job with Ernie Waite who did the area with his fruit and vegetables on his cart drawn by a very fat pony. We negotiated wages before the day's work started.

"I'll pay you sixpence a day and you can have all the fruit you can steal," but then he added, "I'll be watching like a hawk."

I hoodwinked him all right, as when we called at a particular friend's house I would dump bananas and oranges in my friend's front garden and collect them on the way home at the end of the day.

Two or three years before the war started, Dan and I had a wonderful period of our lives, hiking with our gang to Devils Dyke, Newmarket Copse and the windmill at Rottingdean, all 8 or 10 miles away. We made these trips during our school holidays and at weekends. Our gang leader was Eric Feast who claimed the position because he was a year older than any of us, and tougher. His pa was a captain in the Merchant Navy, so he lived in one of the nicer houses in Freshfield Road. We would get a few pence from Mother and off we would go to the butcher for some sausages and eggs. We always made sure there was two pence left over for a twopenny packet of five Woodbines.

Newmarket Copse was my favourite venue as it nestled on the South Downs, a nice valley filled with mole hills and rabbit warrens and, of course, gorse bushes, and at the top of the valley the big wood which always felt a bit creepy and mysterious. On leaving Woodingdean Road, there was a dewpond and Feasty would make us run round 100 times before we could light our fire for the much awaited fry-up.

The youngest member of our gang was Bernard Killick, a big lad for his age. We decided that we would train him as a gladiator so he could be our champion and fight our battles against other gangs who may decide to invade our territory in and around Newmarket Copse. His training included making him eat all leftovers when he was full up and running round the dewpond 500 times. He was a mild, likeable, character, who never complained at our barbaric treatment, especially when Feasty, to 'toughen him up' as he said, beat him with a stick. At one time I protested at this treatment of poor Bernard and for my mutinous attitude, Feasty stuck my hand in the hot fat that had been frying our sausages. Very painful, but being a son of a grenadier, I didn't revolt.

One day during our game of 'release', I fell on some broken glass, which sliced a lump out of my leg three inches long by quarter inch deep. It was an ugly wound and even our gang leader was a little scared. However, we bound up my wound with my vest and walked the eight miles back home. Ma was worried I would get lockjaw (tetanus), and said I must go to hospital to be stitched and injected. I refused to go and ran out of the house. I stayed away for some time until it was too late to be stitched. Ma was furious but Father didn't seem to mind and I fancy he was proud of my brave stand, little realising I was terrified of being stitched up. However, all's well that ends well and the wound healed. For years after, I confirmed the scar was gained by shrapnel from a German 88mm at Goch in the Reichswald Forest on the border of Germany and Holland.

Feasty joined the parachute regiment when old enough and finished up a sergeant. As one would expect. Bernard joined the RAF and also did very well. Both of them put their ages up to gain admission to the services. I never saw Feasty again, although I heard he had joined the police force, no doubt doing well and finishing up as chief interrogator and torturer of innocent suspects.

Bernard, on the other hand, kept in touch at Christmas. Because of our intense training of him, he grew and grew and nearly became a giant. He very wisely left the country and became a lumberjack in Canada. He married Maria, who still writes me a letter once a year. They lived in Cambridge, Ontario. Back in 1960, he wrote to me from Canada to say he was coming back to England for a holiday and he would like to visit me. 'Fantastic', I replied. 'It will be like old times.' As it happened, brother Dan was staying with us at Foxdale, Wetley Rocks and we thought of a joke to play on our old pal we had not seen for over 20 years.

Come the day of his arrival at Stoke Station, I went alone to meet him and Maria. They had no children. I recognised him immediately, this giant of a man with his Spencer Tracy hard-boiled face. His broken nose - which gave him the appearance of a prize-fighter - had not changed and he wasn't the sort of guy you would choose to fall out with.

"Hello Bernard my old friend, how are you?" He stared at me with a slightly fuddled look.

"Hello Dan, or is it Ray?"

"No, I am Dan" I replied, quite innocently.

"Where is Ray?" he asked,

"He is at home preparing lunch." I replied. When we got home, he rushed at my brother Dan and very confidently shouted out:

"Hello Ray, how are you old son, you haven't changed much in all these years!" I could hardly keep a straight face. Our deception went on for several days until we told him our real identity. He didn't seem surprised.

"I thought so, as I'd told Maria, Ray is the better looking."

They visited us every five years until he died in his fifties. He was a nice person.

In the mid-thirties, we heard all about Adolph Hitler and Joseph Stalin and at weekends in the East End of London, the fascists would have big punch-ups with the Reds. I always supported the Reds. I remember the Russians declaring their five-year plans, which our politicians thought quite beyond their reach, and how everyone was surprised when they achieved their targets in 4 years, including the Dnieper Dam, which was the biggest hydroelectric power station in the world.

In 1941, when the Huns invaded Russia, the Red Army was quite happy to blow up the dam rather than let the Germans reap the benefit of its power. After the war it was rebuilt in record time. We all remember too, Neville Chamberlain returning from Munich and his meeting with Adolph Hitler.

"Peace in our time" he declared from the doorway of his aircraft. "...an honourable settlement." Fiddlesticks.

It turns out, and confirmed by Anthony Eden, our Foreign Secretary, that Chamberlain sold out poor little Czechoslovakia.

"You can have Czechoslovakia" he declared to Hitler

"But the Czechs have an alliance with France" Hitler replied.

"Forget that," said Chamberlain. "France will not make a move without us. Help yourself"

Now isn't that scandalous? No wonder Eden resigned as foreign secretary. He was ashamed. It was publicly announced that he was a sick man. Sick indeed. Sick of that scoundrel Chamberlain. Hitler thought of Chamberlain as a joke and often mimicked him at his tea parties.

The Spanish Civil War began on the 18th July 1936. Both Hitler and Mussolini recognised Franco's regime on the 18th November of the same year. Chamberlain recognised Franco's fascist government on 27th February 1939, one month before the end of hostilities on the 1st April 1939. Just five months before, Hitler invaded Poland, triggering the start of World War II.

When war was declared on 3rd September 1939, we were just leaving church where Dan and I, for the princely sum of three shillings and sixpence a quarter, sang in St. Luke's church choir. I remember the reserves that had been called up, mustering at the pepper box ready to depart to their appointed destinations. The sirens sounded and we all hurried home expecting to be blown sky high at any moment. 'False alarm'.

Soon after the start of hostilities, the pride of the British fleet, The Royal Oak, was sunk off Scarpa Flo, with the loss of 900 lives including a lad from our choir. Our vicar, Mr. Brookes, was a very brave and exciting man, but his curate, Mr. F----, was a clown. He was a miserable article who was forever after the hides of the junior members of the choir. Soon after the war started came the Harvest Festival at St Luke's.

The week after the harvest, as I was going into the vestry, I spied a rotten marrow in the rubbish bin and thought of a good idea. I got the curate's cassock, tied one end of his sleeve with string, and stuffed the remains of the marrow down the opening. The curate arrived late, as usual, and grabbed his cassock from the hanger; he plunged his arm straight down the sleeve into the mashed-up smelly remains of the marrow. He was hopping mad and his eyes strayed round the choirboys who were enjoying the goings on. When he focused on me, he immediately threw off his cassock, came straight across, gave me a resounding whack on the ear, and sent me home. Later that evening he arrived at our home to explain to my parents why I was being expelled from the choir. Ma, who could never think her boys would do such a thing, quickly assured the curate that we had no intentions of staying at his lousy church, and as we were moving to a better area of Brighton, we would be going to St. Nicholas. So we moved from 160 Queens Park Road to Wykeham House, Wykeham Terrace, 100 yards from the clock tower and the centre of the town. Dame Flora Robson lived at Wykeham House for the latter part of her life.

With the war starting, Dad was in his element. He was the welfare officer of Sussex and had the rank of captain. He was a company commander in the Army Cadets and sergeant major in the Home Guard, which meant he had three uniforms - quite unusual you will agree. He earned a wage and Wykeham House was rent-free, so we were now solvent. Dad did very well as welfare officer, distributing comforts for the troops, which included thousands of handmade socks, jumpers, and balaclava helmets, the hard work of many kindly ladies of the area. These were packed together and sent to the serving sailors, soldiers, and aviators of Sussex. Servicemen on leave, and their dependents, could also call and be handed out such comforts as they required.

Dad had two collecting boxes in his office, one for the 'comforts of the troops', and one for 'Dan Fear'. He produced the former collecting box to the poorer callers and Dan Fear's box to the more prosperous looking members of the community. Needless to say, both boxes had the same label - 'For the Fighting Men of Sussex'. No doubt, in his wisdom, father thought this a good time to get back a few pounds that the country owed him for past services rendered to King and country.

Besides clothing, all manner of goodies came to his office in Queens Square; snooker tables, fishing rods, golf clubs, cricket bats, footballs and all the games one plays. On the odd occasion, I saw Pa heading for the local pub with a fishing rod under his arm and wondered how the hell he could be going fishing, when all the piers, grones and beaches were barb-wired off to prevent the Huns from having easy access to our beloved town. Besides, it was pitch dark outside. No doubt, he had a willing buyer to keep supplementing his craving for drink. I suppose his love of beer and whisky arose from his career in the army where much liquid was consumed in the sergeants' and officers' mess each and every day. A lifetime habit one could claim.

During my last year at St. Luke's, the headmaster thought it a good idea to hold a scripture competition for the whole school, the questions dependant on the age of the pupil. First prize was five shillings; a very good incentive considering we only got three shillings and sixpence for three months singing in the choir - two practices a week and two services on Sunday.

We had some idea as to the questions as they came from the lessons we had learned. One question I guessed they might ask was 'Abraham had 6 sons by his Wife Ketjrah. Name them'. This thought haunted me for some time, as most of the sons' names were unpronounceable. I had recently seen a film with Will Hay called 'Boys will be Boys'. Hay was headmaster at a crazy school. When they sat their exams, all manner of cheating went on. I remember one of the boys had written answers to some of the questions on a paper clipped to the inside of his school tie. What a splendid idea I thought and before our final exam, I wrote down the names of Abraham's six sons and clipped them inside my tie. As a choirboy, most of the religious questions were quite easy and I was overjoyed that my prediction was correct. The last question read 'Name Abraham's six sons'. The lad sitting next to me was quite a duffer by the name of Dunk and I showed him my answer to the final question. A while later the headmaster, Mr. Raisbeck, sent for us both.

"One of you two is a cheat. You are the only two in the school to get the final question right and you sit next to each other."

I didn't rat on him and he didn't admit copying my paper, so it was left to the head to decide who was the most likely to give the correct answer. As I achieved 98% and poor old Dunk less than 40%, and after the Head had consulted with Mr. Pollard and Mr. Godfrey, Dunk was declared the cheat and got a good caning. With my 98%, I was awarded first prize and given a voucher to spend in the town's most famous bookshop. I went to the shop and got a very good stamp album and the headmaster inscribed, signed, and stamped the front page.

'Winner of the Scripture Prize 1940 - Raymond Fear'

I reckon justice was done and cheats never prosper, for in 1990, fifty years later when the album was stuffed with stamps, it was stolen from our villa when thieves broke in here in Spain. I didn't complain and claimed £800 from the insurance company for my album.

Come the end of the summer term the headmaster suggested that any of us who had a job to go to could leave before our 14th birthday. Fantastic, I thought. No more school. I rushed home to tell Mother and Father. Ma pointed out that Mr. Rose, the pawnbroker, wanted a school leaver.

"I don't want to work in a pawn shop" I wailed.

"It's a good job," said Ma and Pa, "I'll take you along." said Father.

As one of their customers, they thought Mr. Rose would give me the job, and so it turned out. At the tender age of 13 years 8 months, I became a pawn shop assistant.

Thomas Donald Rose (TDR), the pawnbroker, was a real gentleman. Disciplined, but a fairer man you could never meet. It was said that he was a great, great grandson of George IV, who was having as much sex as he could manage amongst the serving staff of the Royal Pavilion. So be it, Mr. Rose looked like a king and behaved like one. I think the 3 years I spent there was as good, if not better, than any university education.

To start with, my duties were to open the shop at 9 am. This involved pushing up six heavy roller shutters with a long pole and carrying into the shop 4 side shutters. They seemed very heavy at first, but I soon got used to carrying them. At 1 pm we had an hour for dinner, which meant putting down the shutters, and at 2 pm it was up with the shutters. At 5 pm we closed. All very well, but when the sirens sounded at the approach of enemy aircraft, I had to rush out

26

with the side shutters and then pull down the six rollers. The shop remained open, although during the early raids few people came in.

I remember that one day the sirens sounded at 4.30 pm. 'Good-o', I thought. 'I won't have to close up again today'. How wrong I was. The all-clear' sounded at 4.50 pm and I looked at his majesty. He didn't say a word, just nodded his head in the affirmative. So I pushed up the shutters, waited about 5 minutes and pulled them down again. I didn't dare complain. Now that's discipline if you like.

The shop at 123-4 Queens Road was two large double-fronted shops joined together as one and with two entrances. The top shop was where the wealthy customers went and where one could buy exhibits on sale in the windows and showcases. The lower shop (and rightly labelled) was for the poorer people of the locality. It had two departments, one where you could pawn jewellery and the like, and one where you could buy the assortment of articles in the window. All manner of things like binoculars, fishing rods, ivory chess sets, microscopes, watches galore and wedding rings, most of them pledges under £2 which had become the pawnbrokers property after twelve months.

Articles pawned over £2 were in for 6 months only and at the end of 6 months had, by law, to be offered in auction. Mr. Rose never took possession of the goods after the six months and always gave the customer a chance to redeem their goods weeks after the time stipulated on the ticket. If, for instance, a Rolex watch pawned for £3 was sold at the auction for £6, a record was kept of the transaction and the customer could claim the difference from the pawnbroker, less the interest due on the full time it had been in the pawnbroker's possession. I forget the time limit by which a customer could take advantage of this ruling. Not many people ever came back for this offer as it was in very small print on the back of their pawn ticket. The interest, as I remember, was halfpenny for every 2 shillings for every calendar month, plus a small fee for the ticket. So if you borrowed £1 for a month, it cost you £1 and fivepence to redeem your goods. Cheap, but if it was left for a year, it was £1 five shillings - 25 %. Not bad, and that is why most pawnbrokers were very wealthy men.

With the introduction of the welfare state, many pawnbrokers closed their doors, but I understand they are coming back into fashion now, as the government clamps down on the big handouts of the past. If I were younger it is a business I wouldn't mind undertaking and 100% better than bookmaking, where as a credit bookmaker, you had to win your money twice, once with the result and second, getting the money from the client. Thankfully, after 40 years experience, I had accumulated many wonderful betting clients who won with a smile and paid me with grace.

When I first started at TDR, there was a staff of four. Besides Mr. Rose, there was Miss Dorothy Lucy Nelson, Mr. Fred Wiltshire, and Harry Brown. Miss Nelson was second in command and was a very intelligent lady with a thorough knowledge of pawnbroking. She could value anything from a diamond ring to a violin. She always cycled to work in all weathers from her home in Ditchling Road.

Fred Wiltshire looked like Al Capone with his jet-black hair and pockmarked face that looked as though it had been carved out of granite. He looked right out of place as a pawn shop assistant. He taught me to swear and cheat at cards. Our card sessions took place when we were fire watching, which was organised by the ARP (Air Raid Precautions). All the shops in Queens Road had their staff enlisted and we had to offer our services twice a week. We were lucky and fire watched on 'Jays' the big furniture store and consequently we had very comfortable bunk beds to sleep on. We would play cards - mostly pontoon or brag, from 9 pm until 4 am. I sometimes won, but never lost much thanks to the schooling from Mr. Wiltshire.

Another guy in our group was Harold Benzie who worked next door to me. We were good pals. Later he joined the Royal Navy like his pa. I remember when I was demobbed he bought my double-breasted brown pin striped suit for £3. After I left for Stoke-on-Trent, I never saw him again. I often wondered what happened to him and if he still wears the brown suit as his 'Sunday Best'.

The last member of staff was Harry Brown. He used to bully me but not for long as he was called up for the RAF. I got my own back on him by dropping nose-bogies into his tea, which I had to make for the staff.

As Mr. Wiltshire worked in a non-essential job, he was called up at 39 years of age to work in a munitions factory. I was sad when he left, as I liked the man. I never saw him again, but his face remains clear in my memory.

My duties, after opening up, were to sweep through both shops. I would sprinkle wet sawdust for the poor quarters, which laid the dust. A couple of days after starting work I found a shilling on the floor of the top shop. As I thought this had been laid there deliberately by Mr. Rose to test my honesty, I quickly returned it to His Lordship. When I told Father, he said:

"Typical Jew" and he pierced a hole in a shilling and gave it to me together with a hammer and nail. "If he tries that trick again, nail this shilling to the floor."

My protests were in vain. A couple of days later, there in the top shop was another bright shilling. I did as Father instructed and nailed our shilling to the floor and pocketed the one TDR had set up for me. I felt very uneasy for the rest of the day and fully expected a reprimand. Nothing was said and next day the shilling and nail had disappeared. Nothing was ever mentioned over the incident.

After sweeping through and cleaning the windows, I had to stack the warehouse. This was a mammoth task - easier said than done. The warehouse was a large storeroom with five alleyways with racks from floor to roof. It had places for suits, waistcoats, trousers, skirts, dresses, sheets, blankets, and every conceivable article of household items. It was stacked in such a manner that when Mrs. 'Whoever' came in to redeem her husband's suit, which had been in pawn for 6 months, one could go directly to where it was stacked and quickly deliver it to the counter. As most garments were under £2 they were kept in the warehouse.

I liked working in the warehouse as it was very peaceful and I could have my daily wank undisturbed. One day, however, I had been in the shop all day and had no chance to relieve myself. No customers came in to redeem their goods, which would have given me the chance

I had been waiting for. My luck changed late in the afternoon, when Mrs. Bloggs came in to redeem her old man's suit. I dashed to serve her and rushed to the other end of the warehouse, where a large sink was situated and out came my dongleberry, which seemed very delighted to see daylight. No doubt because of the circumstances, I took longer than usual to hurl my sperms across the sink. What joy! Job done, now I must seek the suit and return it to the customer. She must have complained to Mr. Rose that I was a long time coming. He, to keep her sweet, reprimanded me on my return to the shop.

"Mrs. Bloggs says you have been a long time coming"

I made some excuse or other, but thought to myself 'So would you with so many distractions'. What would Mrs. Bloggs have said if she had know that the bright-eyed little lad before her had, with the aid of her husband's 'whistle and flute' saved the life of 'poor little Pawn Shop Dick'?

In the cellar were a cold storeroom, for fur coats and the like, and a couple of floor-to-ceiling safes, to house all the many articles of jewellery and other valuables. When sheets, blankets or clothing were brought into pawn, they were wrapped in a remnant and pinned together with large pawnbrokers' pins. The ticket was pinned at the front end. When an article was accepted, its description was entered three ways. There were three pens attached to one pen handle and three inkwells. This enabled us to write the description of the article being pawned and the amount loaned, as well as the name and address of the customer; the pens wrote on two tickets and the accounts book. One ticket went to the customer and the other was attached to the pledge. At the end of the day, it was easy to add up what had been loaned and we had to get the till correct before we left the shop after business finished.

It seems that the nightly air raid sirens and the occasional bombing of Brighton began to get Mrs. Rose down, particularly when her son was reported missing, presumed dead, when the cruiser Gloucester was sunk in Greek waters. There were two sons and the other was a captain in the Royal Artillery who survived the war.

30

Mr. Rose said to me one day that he would like me to sleep on the premises, as he would be travelling nightly with his wife to Balcombe. This village was on the London line and was on what was called the 'slow train' stopping at all the minor stations from Brighton to London. As his shop was only about 400 yards from the station, getting aboard presented no problem. Thinking I would be duly rewarded, I gladly accepted his offer.

My bed consisted of an army camp bed and was situated in a large attic over the warehouse. The floor was bare boards and apart from a chair, there was no other furniture. I was given a stirrup pump, some buckets of water and sand bags to put out any fires started by the Huns. It seems the insurance company insisted that someone should be on the premises at all times; otherwise there would be no payout if there were a break-in or fire. I wonder if they would have been very happy had they known the security guard and fire fighter was a 14 year old lad. Would you believe it, I was never paid a penny for this nightly service. I did get paid for fire watching at Jays and would stay and play cards then nip up the road to take up guard at the pawn shop.

Having the keys to the shop was very useful, for on Sundays I was able to enter and borrow Mr. Rose's two bicycles. I was able to let my less fortunate pals who didn't own a bicycle borrow these for the day on our excursions to the beauty spots of Sussex where we knew we would find mushrooms or would go scrumping for apples and plums.

One day Doug Williams was larking about and caught his pedal in Mr. Rose's front wheel, breaking several spokes. Now what shall I do? God help us. Come Monday morning I took the bike to Halfords and asked them to repair the damage. They had this done in no time and before TDR had missed his bike. I told him later that I had had an accident in the warehouse and that the stacking ladder had fallen on to his front wheel.

"That's alright", he said and I heard him telling Miss Nelson later "That boy will go a long way, uses initiative. Took my bike to be repaired without even asking me. He's a good lad."

The Canadian Army was stationed all over Sussex during the war and as would be expected they all headed for Brighton for their Saturday night frolics. They were a friendly lot and seemed all to be 6 foot or more. The material of their battledress seemed to class them all as officers, unlike the khaki of the British Army. For many, their first port of call was TDR to hock their watches. Rolex, Bulova, Westfield, and all the best-known waterproof makes. Mr. Rose, in his wisdom, instructed us not to buy their watches but to allow them to hock them. His reasons were pawn by all means. This way they could always get them back next payday.

"What's the good of a watch? We are going to get killed anyway." some would say.

Unfortunately, many of their predictions came true. However, Mr. Rose was adamant and would never buy a watch. Neither would he do business with any soldier who was under the influence of drink. The maximum he would lend on any watch was two or three pounds. I had different ideas and when I had the opportunity, I would quietly tell the soldier:

"I'll buy your watch for a good price. Meet me in the paper shop in Air Street just across the road about ten minutes past 5 o'clock."

So every Saturday I would leave work and hasten to Air Street, where several Canadians had gathered awaiting yours truly. I paid them £4-£5 a watch, which they gladly accepted, and made their way to await the opening of their favourite pub. I in turn rushed down to Mr. Burly at 9 Duke Street who, although closed to the public, awaited my weekly visit and greeted my secret knock on his door.

"What have you this week Ray?"

Mr. Burly had a very nice jewellery shop in Duke Street dealing mainly with new merchandise. I fancy he had an outlet for high-class watches. I would make a nice profit, in the region of £10 a week, which subsidised my paltry wage of £1 or so a week.

I started with 15/- a week, that's 75 pence in new currency. Mr. Rose gave me a 2/6 rise every 3 months, which meant that after working for 2 years my wage had increased to £1.75. So my illicit dealing greatly increased my weekly earnings, bringing my wages in line with a Member of Parliament of those days, but as I worked much harder than those gentlemen, I think it only fair.

Mr. Burly sang in the choir at St. Nicholas, the mother church of Brighton. I wonder if his prayers on a Sunday included a further batch of Rolex watches from young Ray. To think that today, those self same watches fetch over £1,000.

Mr. and Mrs. Burly were very nice people. I remember her jet-black hair very vividly. What I am about to say would normally be included in my next volume 'Dick in Spain', but I feel it is appropriate to include it now. In 2001, I took my wife and Natasha, my daughter, on a visit to the UK. It was my only visit in ten years. During our stay with Beverley and Steve, it was decided to have a day in Brighton. It turned out to be the highlight of our holiday.

We were strolling through the lanes and came across Duke Street. There facing me was F. Burly, Jewellers 1873. The same shop I used to take my Rolex watches to over sixty years ago. 'I wonder if Mr. Burly's grandchildren are running the shop now.' I pondered. We entered and there standing behind the counter was none other than Fred Burley himself, ready to serve me.

"Hello Ray" he declared. "You haven't changed much. How's Dan?" (My brother) "We all used to sing in St. Nicholas Church choir... No we didn't" he continued, "Dan used to fling" and he went through the motions of one troughing the incense.

Which was true, as Dan had been promoted to altar boy. What a memory to remember all this. It came as no surprise to me that this man, still running and serving at the counter, was 95 years old. We recalled our business deals when, as a 14/15 year old lad, I would take a handful of watches to 9 Duke Street and receive a handsome profit. I reminded Mr. Burley of the one-pound notes he always gave me when I visited him on leave. However, he countered my extended hand with the words;

"You aren't in the army now."

In a few years time you will pick up your daily newspaper and see a photo of Mr. Burly opening his shop, one hundred years old!

About this time I met, for the first time, my step sister Dolly. She was the youngest daughter of the four daughters and one son of Father Fear. She was a great personality, nearly 6 foot tall with an Eton crop. She had been a great sprinter in her time and represented Great Britain in the 1936 Berlin Olympic Games, reaching the final in the 100 metres.

Her first marriage had been to a professional jockey a foot shorter than her. This ended in divorce and her second husband had the biggest nose I had ever seen. Talk about Cyrano De Bergerac the famous dualist. They seemed a very happy couple but when talking to him I couldn't take my eyes off his beak. One day she said to me,

"I want to sell my ex-husband's engagement ring." I looked at it with my experienced eye and thought that perhaps it would fetch £15. I asked Dot how much she wanted and she said anything over £10 I could keep. Yippee, I thought, great. I am in for a profit here.

Next day after work, I hastened to Mr. Burly to sell the diamond ring.

"I've so many rings," he said. "You had best go to Mr. ..." but I can no longer remember the name. "You'll find him over the garages behind the Hippodrome Theatre."

I made my way to the garages and climbed the wooden stairs to the doorway described to me. I knocked and to my surprise, a shutter opened and an evil looking person enquired as to what I wanted.

"The boss" I said.

The shutter slammed in my face. A few moments later 'evil face' reappeared.

"Come in."

The scene before me was something out of a Las Vegas gambling den. There were many tables where men were busily engaged playing cards. I was shown to a large round table, where about eight gentlemen were playing poker. After a while, the boss man held up play and asked what I wanted. I produced my sister's ring.

"I want to sell this, Sir."

"Is it hot?" Was his first question to me. My reply brought the house down.

34

"Well sir, it's been in my pocket and is a little warm"

"What a card. How much do you want kid?"

"£15" I said.

"I'll tell you what," said the head of the Brighton Mafia "I'll give you twenty quid for making us laugh. Come back in 5 years time. I'll give you a job"

I rushed back home and told the family the good news, that I had sold the ring for £15. Dot was overjoyed and said:

"You have earned £5"

"No" I replied. "I only want £2.50, you can have £12.50"

You are a good brother, she said. So she was happy, I was happy and Mafia man had a good laugh and, no doubt, made a profit too.

During this period, the Nazis bombed London nightly. We in Brighton had the usual alert sounded to announce the arrival overhead of the Germany bombers on their way to the capital. Sometimes on their return, if they had not unloaded their bombs on the besieged city, they would jettison their load of bombs on our town. In fact, of all the towns with non-military targets, Brighton had the most casualties.

We were lucky at Wykeham Terrace as, one night, a stack of bombs was dropped on Upper North Street. The fifth bomb dropped on No.9, the home of Mr. & Mrs. Burchett who were luckily on duty with the ARP. The sixth bomb, destined to blow us to kingdom come, landed in the graveyard only 10 yards from our front door. Due probably to the soft soil in which it landed, the bomb failed to explode. How lucky can you get?

Another incident worth recording. A German fighter was shot down overhead and the pilot parachuted down, landing in the trees of the graveyard, only 100 yards from our house. Brother Dan and I had been observing the goings on and when we saw the parachute descending in our direction, we were ready to go and as we raced to the spot where the pilot had landed. Dan shouted out;

"He's dead" and before I had gathered my wits, he was up the tree like a monkey. In no time at all, he returned with a Mauser pistol and a very nice watch. I enquired if he had any rings on.

"This will do me, never had time to search for rings"

Almost immediately, the ARP, police and fire brigade arrived to investigate the incident. Dan and I beat a hasty retreat back home.

A pal of ours was working as a clerk and one day a hit and run German bomber dropped a bomb on his office. He was working in the second floor. The building, including his office was cut in half. Fortunately, the half he was working in was intact. He was typing at the time and half the office disappeared. Later that day he met us at the drill hall where he announced;

"I am joining the rifle brigade, it's safer than being a solicitor's clerk."

He did join the rifle brigade and on his first leave, we were overjoyed to see he had already been promoted to lance corporal.

Listening to Mr. Winston Churchill's speeches fired all us young lads' imaginations and we rushed to join the Naval Cadets, Army Cadets, or Air Cadets. Because of our military background, Dan and I joined the Royal Sussex Army Cadets. It was a highly efficient band of young men with the officers who were mainly veterans from the First World War. We had four companies stationed in and around Brighton. The first company was stationed at the drill hall in St. Nicholas Road, and it was there that we drilled and weapon trained three times a week. Our object was to earn the 'War Certificate A' which would enable us to become officers if we so wished. Father Fear was company commander of 'C Company' stationed at Park Street. He always claimed his company was the best. I doubt it as I was a sergeant and brother Dan, a corporal, thought that 'A Company' was the best.

Our company sergeant major was a chap called Scroggins, a much better disciplined person than myself. However, we didn't hit it off and so we agreed to fight each other in the boxing ring. The hour arrived and the ring set up.

"Box" said the ref. and in about one minute, more blows were struck than in any professional fight of today. With no real boxing training, we both just dived in throwing punches from all directions. At the end of the first round, Scroggins' father said;

"That's enough boys, shake hands and be friends."

36

This is indeed what happened, but Mr. Rose was none too pleased when I arrived next day with two black eyes and a very swollen mouth and nose. I did no more boxing until I joined the Guards.

Our cadets' force was very well organised and the training we did held us in good stead when eventually, we all volunteered for our favourite regiments. I always wanted to join the Guards, like Pa, but as you had to be 5 foot 10 inches, I thought perhaps I wouldn't make the height, so was undecided as to whether to join the Black Watch, Royal Marines, or Rifle Brigade, all first class regiments with a great military history. What sounds more exciting than 'The Black Watch'?

I remember going camping with our battalion. We went to Hurstpierpoint and were trained by a Canadian infantry battalion. One evening Father was Guard Commander. I was Sergeant of the Guard and Dan, Corporal of the Guard. According to Doug Williams, who was mess caterer, Father consumed large quantities of beer and whisky that Doug had held back especially for his favourite officer. Needless to say, Father was in no condition to visit the outposts he should have visited during his term of duty. I don't think I was much better as I slept most of the night - a prelude of things to come.

I kept a diary from the day I started work until I joined up. This has proved to be very useful as it refreshes my memory over certain points. I remember when the Huns unexpectedly invaded Russia. I entered in my diary on the 21st June 1941:

Germany invades Russia. We shall now win the war. I've always had a great admiration of the Russians, their courage, character, and great capacity to suffer.

In the First World War, they sustained many millions of casualties, crippling the German and Austrian armies. Without their help, I am sure the result of the 1914-18 conflict would have been quite different. As for the last war, World War II, without The Red Army we, today, would all be enslaved, that is, of course, if we hadn't been murdered one way or another. As Churchill said:

"They tore the guts out of the Germans."

Recently the German government disclosed their casualty figures of World War II, sustaining seven million dead on the Russian front. The USA, Great Britain, her empires, and the rest of the allies, killed less than a million.

Think of it. If the German army had not sustained those losses, where would we have been in Normandy? No chance. Thrown back into the sea. But of course Churchill and Roosevelt would not have deemed it possible to invade. In fact, if those 7,000,000 troops had invaded England, what would have happened? I'll tell you - defeat, and the start of world domination by Germany and their pals in Japan. However thankfully, because of Russia's fantastic effort in the Great Patriotic War, we survived. The USA claims it was their supplies that made the difference between victory and defeat. Nonsense. Our help, which was gratefully received, was but 4% of the total war effort and as Marshal Zhukov said:

"Our petrol driven tanks went up like torches."

The early years of the war were a very exciting time for us boys with so many things happening. Our thoughts mainly centred around the future course of the war.

Who would be Hitler's next victim of German aggression?

When would we be invaded?

Would Swedish and Turkish neutrality be violated?

Would the Yanks enter the war?

What are those little Japanese up to?

We all knew the Germans needed oil desperately, so where would they go to obtain this essential commodity?

All these and other questions were the subject of arguments, guesses, and forecasts. For myself, to end my nightly prayers, I said 'Please God, let Russia, the USA and Turkey come in on our side.' My prayers were answered, as the first two did join the allies and Turkey remained neutral. I put Russia first as the most important and reliable of the three.

One of the less exciting things was food rationing. We were allowed one egg a week, but if you forfeited your egg ration, you were allowed 1lb of 'balancer meal', which was a concoction of meal to be fed to poultry. I decided to enlarge my chicken population and my pocket by getting people to register with me. This enabled me to get several pounds of chicken food per week and I was thus able to maintain about 12 chickens that, in turn, laid about 50-60 eggs a week. Therefore, my customers got four times as many eggs as other people. I naturally charged over the odds and so my National Savings balance increased considerably. I have always had this great love of chickens since, at 12 years of age I sold my air pistol for 2/- and bought 6 day-old chicks which I reared by hand. The start of a lifelong association. In fact, when I was nearing demob from the army, I chose to go on a poultry husbandry course.

Come 1942 and without my parents' knowledge, I marched into the recruiting office in Queens Road, not 100 yards from where I worked. I had seen the recruiting sergeant passing my shop on his way to his office for the last couple of years. He sometimes acknowledged me.

"Well lad, what do you want?" he enquired.

"I want to join The Guards." I replied.

"Do you, by God?" was his reply. "Identity card" which I handed to him, "You're too young, come back when your nappies are dried."

I was crestfallen and returned to work. How did he know I was under age, I pondered. It must be my identity card. But there was no date of birth to be seen. I looked at brother Dan's card too and came to the conclusion that the last figures of my number revealed my birth to within 3 months, i.e. the 2nd December 1926 read: 1.4.26, the 4 covering October, November, and December. 'Oh!' Thought I, 'What to do now.'

A few months went by and I told my parents my intentions. Dad was proud. Mother was horrified and said I would be killed.

"Which is worse, joining Father's regiment or being a Bevan Boy?" I said.

Those who didn't want to fight had to go down the pit - coal mining if you please - considered a far more risky occupation than the infantry. This way I wore Mother down, who finally agreed that my idea was the best. Three of her sons were already in the services. Brother Jim was an RSM in the Royal Engineers and Elton a Sergeant in the RAMC. Flat feet John was in the Air Force and fought in the Battle of Britain as a fighter pilot. So now number 4 son was off to join the dreaded Guards.

During the war, one was called up at eighteen and a half but you could volunteer at seventeen and a half. I was still only 16 and was impatient to enlist. I made a few enquiries and laid my plans. I got my ration book from Mother and together with my identity card, I burnt them on the living room fire. Next I went to the food office and reported that they had fallen off the mantelpiece straight into the fire I produced the ashes and what was left of the aforementioned credentials.

"Well son" said the clerk, "You must supply three references as to who you are and then we can supply you with a new ration book and identity card. Hurry up or you will miss this week's rations."

I went first to my boss, Mr. Rose, who had no idea of my intentions. He was happy to give me a reference. Then to Mr. Harvey, manager of Dunn's at the clock tower, who was my company commander in the Army Cadets; then to the vicar of St. Nicholas Church, the Reverend Phillips, who was also commanding officer of all the Royal Sussex cadets. He had won the Military Cross in northern Italy during the First World War. The last two gentlemen knew of my intentions and gladly agreed to help. Together with my three references, I returned to the food office.

"You've been quick," said the clerk. "Let's fill in the forms. Name, address, date of birth?" - Just what I had been waiting for.

"2.12.25" I replied, not 2.12.26. Armed with my new card and six new laid eggs, I returned to the recruiting office.

"Hello son, how's business at the pawn shop?" enquired the sergeant.

"Okay" I replied. "Here are 6 eggs and I want to join the army."

"Didn't you come here some weeks ago and were too young?" He looked at my identity card "I see. You really are keen aren't you?"

He laughed, "I wish I had a few more lads like you. Since Singapore, nobody wants to join the army. Now which regiment do you want?"

"The Grenadiers please, Sir." I replied.

"You aren't big enough" he snorted.

"Yes I am, I'm just 5 foot 10 and 'n 'alf'. That was the minimum height necessary in the war years to join the Brigade of Guards.

"If you can't get in that mob, what next?"

"The Black Watch or The Rifle Brigade" I replied.

"Okay, you will be hearing from us."

Unknown to me at the time, another young man from Market Harborough, Leicestershire, had done the very same thing as I - put his age up to join the regiment.

In preparation to me joining up, I went running most days - and in boots - slowly increasing my distances up to 10 miles. This turned out to be good strategy for it came in very useful at Caterham.

After a while, I was told to report for my medical. So, armed with six new laid eggs (I was quite prepared to bribe the doctor), I hastened to the recruiting office in Queens Road. The sergeant was very pleasant and said that if I passed my medical I would be accepted in The Grenadiers. I was overjoyed. Over the first obstacle, now for the medical.

When I was about 10 years old I noticed that the bone of my left leg just below my kneecap was enlarged and very sore if I pressed it or knelt on it. I saw the doctor who sent me to the Royal Sussex County Hospital. I finished up with my leg in plaster of Paris for six weeks. The only good the plaster did was that I didn't have to wear a pad when playing cricket for the school team. Mr. Shepperd, our sports master thought I was very game indeed and praised me to the rest of the team. My leg had shrunk in captivity and the pain was the same. Gradually it became less painful and only hurt me when kneeling. The condition is caused by over-exercising and running long distances when your bones are not properly developed. This fits, as I was always running.

My leg worried me, as I knew you really had to be A1+ to join the Guards. I thought about this constantly before my medical. I hit on an idea. The night before I was due to report, I returned to my bedroom with an Ever-Ready razor blade. I had set my mind on cutting a lump of flesh off my enlarged bone. It's very difficult to do this I assure you and it must have taken me ages to pluck up enough courage to hack a piece off big enough to be noticed. I remember I bled a lot and wondered that if I died from loss of blood, people would say I had committed suicide rather than face Caterham Barracks. I sometimes wonder if I did the right thing but I also thought that if I didn't like the Guards I could always be downgraded by playing on my knee and finishing up in a more cushy job than the bloody infantry.

I was shown into the room where the medical officer examined me. When he got to my legs, he said

"What have you got that plaster on for?"

"Oh sir", I replied. "I got kicked at football last Saturday"

"So you play football do you? That will help you in the army" was all he said. "You're A1 - good luck to you."

I didn't give him the eggs but I gave them to my pal the sergeant. He asked me, as I had volunteered, if would I like to serve for 4 and 8 or 7 and 5. This means serving for 4 years and 8 years on reserve, when you may be called up immediately at any time after the 4 years with the Colours. I asked his advice.

"Well my lad" he said, "You have been good to me with these here eggs, so I'll give you a bit of advice. Just join for the duration then you won't be committed. And if you like the life you can always sign on when you are due to be demobbed."

"Thank you, Sir" I said. "I'll just join like you said for the duration of the war."

I signed some papers and he gave me the King's shilling.

"Don't spend it all at once and good luck son."

Then came the unpleasant task of telling my boss Mr. Rose, that I should be leaving his employment to join up. When I told him he was none too pleased.

"But you've no need to go for two years and the war will be over by then" I told him I had signed and would be told to report for duty fairly soon.

"You'll visit us when you get leave won't you?" asked Miss Nelson, who I think was rather proud at what I had done.

I received a letter that I must report to Caterham Barracks on the 21st February. It was a Monday and I laid my plans. I'll get my army boots polished to a high standard and I'll go in all my oldest cloths as I thought the rest would go into storage. Father gave me the brasses off his web belt.

Come the 21st, I bade farewell to my family. They were all in tears for one reason or another. Ma and Dan as they thought I might be an early casualty and Father with pride that his son was off to join his own regiment. He had also given me an address book with these instructions:

'You will meet many pals in the army. Any that you get on particularly well with, get their names and addresses in the book. In later years you will be glad you did this.'

How right he was.

I used my railway warrant to get to Purley. From there I caught a bus to Caterham. When I asked the conductor to drop me off as near as possible to the barracks, he merely replied:

"There are 3 stops up the hill to the barracks. The first is the lunatic asylum, then the barracks, and then the bone yard." (The cemetery, to the uninitiated!) "You had best get off at the first stop" he joked.

I had caught the slow train from Brighton to Victoria stopping at all the intervening stations. I think I got to the barracks at about 10 am.

Chapter 3

The Guards' Depot

It was an icy cold February morning when I entered the gates of that fearsome institute. The sergeant of the guard beckoned me into the guardroom where there were several very tall recruits busying themselves around the room. No one took the slightest bit of notice of me. At 12:30 a large tin of food arrived, presumably from the cookhouse, and the guard sat down and quickly devoured the contents. No one offered me anything to eat, although by this time I was quite hungry. By 4:30, I was wondering if I had come to the right place. Then, out of the blue, a chaplain arrived and asked if I was a new recruit. When I answered in the affirmative, he said:

"Come with me please." His tone was very unlike the abrupt utterances in the guardroom. "You're early," he said. "Most newcomers don't arrive till well after 8 pm."

"Oh" I said, "Dad said to arrive early so I could claim a good bed space"

"Oh no", he replied. "It doesn't work like that here. First, we will go to the reception room where you will await the remaining members of your squad. I'll see you get some tea. I'll bet your hungry."

"Yes I am" I replied.

He returned later with our normal evening meal of two slices of bread and jam and, I think, beans on fried bread. A large mug of funny-tasting tea was also served.

There were about 30 beds in the huts and neatly folded at the end of each were three blankets and a straw filled palliasse. There was also a pillow, the contents of which I cannot recall. And that was it. No sheets or pillowslips. The chaplain spoke to me for a while and said he was the Church of England Chaplain and hoped he would see me at church at 8 am on Sunday mornings.

"You'll get a bigger breakfast if you come to church, as when the rest of the recruits have gone back to duty you will be going with a few other church members to a late breakfast. The master cook always dishes up extra to these people, as he is a devout catholic. I'll be back later." he said and departed leaving me behind.

I could have spent another day at home, I grumbled. The day has been wasted. At about 7:00 pm other recruits began to arrive, mostly the ones who lived nearest to Caterham. I remember well Bill Watts and Doughty B. Howard and a big-nosed ugly guy from Gloucester by the name of Fisher. Later that evening a very large, smartly dressed young man arrived. He looked round the room and came straight over to the bed next to mine and threw his suitcase on the bed. He turned to me, eyed me up and down for a moment, and said:

"I'm Jack Gardner. Who are you?"

I told him and we sat and chatted for a while. He came from Market Harborough in Leicestershire and had put up his age, he whispered, so he could join up. As it turned out we were the only two volunteers in the squad, the other lads were all 18½ or more and had been called up. He gave me some cake his ma had made and we immediately started a friendship that was to last a lifetime. I made up my bed with no problems and noticed that he was having difficulties.

"Here" I said. "I'll do it for you, just this once."

Years later, he would introduce me to his friends as the little guy who made up his bed on his first day in the army.

Next morning in the washhouse, I noticed he was standing at the next basin. After I had shaved, I looked to my right as I was pencilling in my little bit of hair, an insult to a proper moustache, and I noticed that Jack was busy doing the same. We both laughed, especially when we both used liquid paraffin oil to smooth down our black hair. We couldn't afford Brylcreem in those days.

By midnight, everyone had arrived and we had lights out. The chaplain had spent the evening chatting to us all individually, putting our minds at rest that we would all survive and leave the depot as the world's most disciplined, well-trained soldiers. Next day, after breakfast, we had a very efficient medical exam. One lad failed because he was ¼" too short, so when it came to my turn to be measured, I stood on the balls of my feet. (If I could have stood on my own balls, I would have been well over 6 foot).

"Five foot ten and a half" recorded the medical officer. "You have just made it."

I had plastered up my knee once more and told the same story as in the recruiting office. The examining officer was also pleased I played football. From the medical, we went to draw our kit and, in my case, this presented a problem. They only had two sizes of underwear - large and very large - so my vests came down to my knees and my underpants were half way down to my ankles. When it came to battle dress, I was in luck as the store man bought out a size 14, which had the front buttons covered up and looked a lot smarter than the usual issue.

"I've been waiting to get rid of this for a long time," the store man said. "Fits you well" as indeed it did. So from the start I was a jump ahead of the rest of the squad.

We stuffed all our kit into our kitbags and were taken to the barrack room, York 4, as I remember, where we were to spend the next 20 weeks. We were greeted by Trained Soldier Glue -'Sticky' Glue, as he was known. In the Brigade of Guards, they have these old soldiers who supposedly look after a room full of new recruits. They rule with a rod of iron and are feared as much as we feared our squad instructor superintendent sergeants, drill sergeants, CSMs and RSMs. When we wanted to leave the barrack room for any reason, we had to stand to attention and shout out:

"Fall out Trained Soldier, please!"

"Yes" would be his reply.

Sticky Glue was an old man in our eyes and would be about 35 years. He was quite fair I suppose with the exception of treatment he gave to the recruit who slept next to him, a gentleman called Bryant. He had dodged being called up for a couple of years but finally the authorities caught up with him and, being 6 foot, they sent him to us. He was about 27 years and had a potbelly and because he was so old and unfit he must have suffered the most during our training. After some hard days, he really looked like death and we began to feel sorry for him and feared for his life. However, because his father owned one of the largest shoe factories in Northampton, he and the Trained Soldier got on very well. No doubt Bryant was paying the trained soldier for favours and I know for a fact that he helped clean Bryant's kit when he lay prostrate on his bed. I had very little to do with him, nor did the rest of the squad.

Later that day a corporal burst into our barrack room and announced himself.

"I'm Corporal Eastwood. I am your squad instructor."

We stood to attention at the head of our beds and he spoke to us all individually. When he came to me, I thought how much he looked like me and was a 'short-arse' too. Although he never showed me any favours during training, he never picked on me and he sometimes held me up as an example to the rest of the squad.

The training was very rigid and we would run every day between the different venues. Drill 8:30 to 9:30; 9:45 weapon training, which meant we had to return from the square, change, and get to the other side of the barracks in 15 minutes.

Everything was organised to the last minute. Even our meals. We had breakfast at 8 am, half an hour before our first parade and that was the only time we got to relieve our bowels. The toilets ran one side of a wall with no doors and very often, the orderly sergeant would rush along waving his stick and shouting to us to get a bloody move on. It was a bit embarrassing at first, but we got used to being spied on when sitting on the potty. We had tea at 4:30 and then it was sitting on our beds and polishing our kits. Each week we would concentrate on a new article of equipment.

"Gather round my bed" the trained soldier would shout, and he would then demonstrate what was to be done and how.

When it came to our brasses on our web belts, I didn't go to his bed when summoned.

"Hey you, big head, aren't you in this squad?" he howled.

"I think my brasses are okay" I replied.

"Bring 'em here" he shouted.

I did so, and when he saw them, he immediately checked his belt hanging under his locker.

"Thought you had pinched mine," he said. "When have you had time to do them so well?"

"I've done a bit each day," I lied. "I used sandpaper to start with."

"Did you?" he sneered.

The first thing we learned was barrack room swabbing. During our first week at the depot, the 'Trained Pig' gave us each a specific job to do. We were all responsible for our own bed space, which had to be spotless and highly polished at all times. The central floor space had to be polished, the large bath-size coal bin shone like silver, windows, washhouse taps and shit-houses were all immaculate. My job was to paint with a whitewash, a 6-inch border on the floor of the total perimeter of the landing in front of our barrack room door. It was an all-important operation, as it was the first thing the duty officer saw when inspecting our rooms.

The brahmer, Fisher from Gloucester, got the job of chopping firewood for our highly polished stove, which was situated in the centre of our barrack room. Instead of doing the job outside by the coal dump, the lazy bastard thought that he would chop his sticks on my landing. As splinters flew in all directions, it made a real mess. The first time he did it, I said:

"Don't chop your f---ing firewood on my landing or else!"

Next morning I finished my painting and returned to the room.

"Fall in Trained Soldier, please!"

"Yes"

A few minutes later, I could hear Fisher chopping his sticks outside the door. I wound a duster round my right fist and retorted:

"Fall out Trained Soldier, please!"

"Yes"

Fisher was kneeling down busily chopping away with his back to me. I quietly approached and with as much power as I could muster, I delivered a resounding blow on the right side of his head. He let out a

48

yell and sprawled across my landing, where he lay for some time. Sticky Glue hastened to see what all the noise was about.

"You'll be locked up for some time for that, Fear."

We were both put on a charge for fighting on parade and were marched first before CSM Betts who, when he heard what had happened, called me an 'orrible bully in spite of the fact that Fisher towered above me and was at least 2 stone heavier. We were remanded for memoranda. (Company Commander's orders) and were marched in front of the Fatherly Goodhart Randall. The Company Sergeant Major bawled out the charge:

"Contrary to regulations, these men were fighting while carrying out their daily barrack room fatigues."

"Fighting indeed," said our worthy commander. "This is a very serious offence in the army."

At this, I wondered if I had indeed joined the wrong army. Perhaps I'd have been better off in the SS. As a callow youth, and not having much brain for worldly affairs, I thought the whole idea of joining the guards was to fight.

"Have you anything to say, Fisher?"

"No, Sir."

"Fear?"

"I thank you, Sir, for leave to speak"

"Stop talking" bellowed the CSM.

"I thank you, Sir, for leave to speak" I repeated.

"Stop talking" bellowed the CSM a second time.

"Let him say his piece" said the captain.

"He was chopping wood on my landing after I had already cleaned and painted it. As he is so much bigger than me I thought I had better surprise him from behind, Sir."

A smile crept over Goodhart Randall's face.

"In future, Fear, restrict your tactics and fighting to the enemy. Have these men been in front of me before, Sergeant Major?"

"No, Sir"

"Under the circumstances, I'll give you both a warning. Don't let it happen again. Case dismissed."

We were both mightily relieved as we sped back to our squad drilling on the square. When Eastwood had halted the squad, I said:

"Permission to fall in Corporal, please"

"Certainly," he said. "I was not expecting to see you again for a long time. What did you get?"

"Case dismissed." I replied.

Later that evening our corporal approached me as I sat aside my bed ponging my kit.

"By the looks of Fisher's ear, you won" he said.

"Yes," I replied. "He never laid a finger on me."

I didn't explain my tactics to him or the rest of the squad, and I went up in the estimation of everybody except Fisher, who I always thought was a wanker. His very voice used to irritate everyone, but not as much as Nixon's. He had a high-pitched squeak, which sounded even worse with his constant whining. He moaned and grumbled about everything whenever the trained soldier had disappeared for a few pints at the NAFFI, compliments of Bryant, no doubt. Nixon came from Carlisle and this is where he should have stayed and joined ATS, or Women's Land Army. One day, Gardner had stood enough of Nixon's incessant whining.

"If you don't pipe down, I'll come up there and shut you up"

Nixon, foolishly ignored Jack and the next minute he strode up the barrack room and with one blow, flattened Nixon. It's a good job Sticky Glue was out of the room, otherwise Jack would have been 'put in the book'. All credit to Nixon, he didn't report the incident, but he certainly curtailed his moaning. Jack did us all a good turn. By and large we were a happy team and pulled together as best we could, to ensure we were not back-squadded and made to endure extra weeks in the penal colony.

Kit inspections were an ordeal to most of our squad and as large men, they were naturally ham-fisted and had great difficulty folding their vests and pants and other items of clothing. Not me, however, I had been folding up such articles daily for the past 2½ years. At our first inspection, which usually took place on our first parade at 8:30, our company commander, Captain Goodhart Randall did the inspection. He was a tall, slim, middle-aged man and wore the First World War puttees up to his knees. He carried a walking stick and wore a monocle. He was a regular toff and treated all of us as his children. When the captain, together with our superintendent, sergeant, and corporal entered the barrack room, the trained soldier would cry out:

"Stand by your beds"

We did this holding the shoulders of our spare shirt in each hand and a pair of clean socks over each arm. Our kits were laid out on our mattresses, and as the officer approached each of us in turn, we sprung smartly to attention extending our arms to full length, still holding the shirt with our regimental numbers printed on the front and on each arm, if you were very lucky, hung a pair of socks. If the socks fell to the floor on this difficult operation, the captain would comment and the sergeant would bellow out:

"Put him in the book, idle on parade."

If, however, you tried to raise your arms in front of you slowly so as not to drop the damned socks, you were also put in the book for being slovenly on parade. My crafty pawnbroker's mind hit on an idea and I secretly pinned my socks to the arms of my battle dress just before kit inspections. Hence, I often got credit for my kit.

Every fourth week we had a special inspection, which we all had to pass, or the whole squad would be back-squadded, which meant an extra week of training. On these big days, Sticky Glue would have us out of bed at 4 am to get our kits laid out properly. As I was the only one who could fold vests, pants, etc. properly, I had the mammoth task of laying out all the squad's underwear. In certain cases I laid out the whole kit for certain members of the squad, including 'Hairy Francis' who rewarded me with fruit cake - compliments of his Ma back in Billingborough near Sleaford, Lincolnshire. Every week he received a half size biscuit tin which contained a large fruit cake, a great chunk of cheddar cheese and a 10/- note. The money was equivalent to a week's wages for us poor recruits, who would soon be risking our lives for this miserable sum.

Francis and I stayed together for our entire army service. He was a strange fellow, covered from head to foot in hair. I suppose he looked a bit like a pre-historic man. He had the same stoop and when he walked normally he was about my height but on parade, and he had to draw himself up to his full height, he was over 6 foot 2 inches. If we happened to have one drill parade in the morning and one after dinner, he would have to hurriedly shave a second time. I remember one afternoon he had shaved ready for drill when, unfortunately, he left a little shaving soap behind his ear. At the normal inspection we always had before every parade, the poor chap was put in the book by the inspecting sergeant for 'Filthy flesh'. What a giggle. He got two extra parades for this offence and was told by the company commander:

"We won't tolerate a dirty guardsman here."

I clearly remember, at one of our kit inspections, a lad called Pearce. He somehow always managed to look dirty and had a permanent supercilious grin on his face, as if a hidden hand was tickling his balls. As our beds were opposite each other, I could always get a view of his performance at kit inspections. On this particular day, more through luck than judgment, Pearce managed to spring to attention and extend his arms without dropping his socks on the floor. I was a trifle disappointed at this as it usually caused a laugh. I think the fact that he had been so successful went to his head, for the grin on his face broadened and he started to blurt out his regimental number:

"2624... er... 2624... er... 2624... er..." His eyes were rolling round like a frightened black man and I mouthed his last three numbers, 916. He managed to lip read my advice and finally he got it right.

"2624916 Guardsman Pearce J. Washing at the wash, one pair of boots at the cobbler's shop, otherwise kit present, Sir."

Goodhart Randall studied his kit for a moment, adjusted his monocle, and said:

"Pearce where is your housewife?" (An army name for your holdall, which contained cotton wool, needles, thimble, and the like.)

"Thank you, Sir, for leave to speak"

This is a term particular in the Brigade of Guards where you always ask permission to speak to an officer. It doesn't always apply on active service, as this delay could result in one or other of you getting your head blown off. Imagine having to say:

"I thank you, sir, for leave to speak"

"Yes, Fear"

"Well Sir, there are three Germans aiming their machine gun on our position." instead of whispering: "Krauts! Get your head down!"

Back to Pearce who had asked for leave to speak.

"Yes Pearce"

"I thought I had it with me but I found it wasn't there" was his reply. We pissed ourselves laughing and an unpopular recruit ('cause he had crabs) called Walker, was put in the book for laughing on parade. Our good captain listened patiently then started to poke about Pearce's kit with his walking stick.

"There looks as if there has been a heavy struggle on your bed, Pearce. I am afraid you will have to show it again at six o'clock this evening."

When the hierarchy had left, everyone congratulated young Pearce on his performance and recommended he went on the stage. Feeling sorry for him I laid out his kit that evening and the superintendent sergeant said to Pearce, with a smile on his face:

"Well done, Fear."

I think Sergeant Shelton liked me, as he was always singing my praises for one thing or another.

"Why can't you be like this little chap? He can cope, why can't you? You long streaks of dehydrated pig-shit. It seems to me the bigger you are the more stupid you are."

He was quite gentlemanly compared to some of the NCOs we met later.

After the fourth week at the depot, the trained soldier had to nominate the four best members of the squad. Without even trying, I guessed I would be one. Wrong! He picked Jack Gardner, Bernard Doughty, Doug Smith and you will never believe it, Bryant. I thought the first two were a good choice, but as Smithy came from Stoke-on-Trent, I will reserve my opinion. The four had to sew a small stripe on their left-hand sleeve, a few inches above the cuff. I was surprised I hadn't been picked. On the first parade, when the squad instructor and superintendent sergeant saw that Bryant had been selected, they were obviously suspect.

"You're the worst member of the squad!" bellowed Sergeant Shelton. "Whoever picked you must be f---ing blind." Shelton turned to me.

"Did you refuse the stripe?"

"No Sergeant, I wasn't asked"

"Oh, we will see about that."

After the parade, we all returned to our barrack room where the Sergeant conferred with Glue. When the Sergeant mentioned my name, Glue said:

"I couldn't pick him. He's a chancer."

"Well," replied Shelton, "I wish I had a few more chancers in the squad."

Bill Watts took Bryant's place. We all were happy with this as Bill was a great guy. I can see him now with his blonde hair, baby face, and great big blue eyes. When we sat together, we appeared to be the same height, but when he stood up, he was 6 foot 4 inches and towered above me due to his great long legs. He was by far the best high jumper and long jumper in the depot.

After our initial training, we separated. He joined a rifle company somewhere. We exchanged Christmas cards for many years. One day, when my eldest daughter Jane was competing in a horse trial one-day-event near Loudwater, Buckinghamshire, I decided, without prior notice, to call on him. I parked my car outside his semi-detached. I knocked on the door and there was no reply. I enquired of his neighbour as to when he would be back.

"He won't be long, he's gone to the woods for some firewood."

A short time later I looked down the road and saw my dear old comrade trudging up towards me with a large bundle of branches roped together on his back. When he saw me, he stopped for a moment then flung the bundle down and we embraced each other like long lost brothers. We went inside his house for a cup of tea and relived our depot days with Sticky Glue and all the other bastards who had made our lives a misery. We talked about Jack Gardner and Jack Francis, and the unfortunate ones who were killed or wounded. He had a poorly paid job, but seemed happy that I had managed to get 'out of the rut'.

I said that as I was all tied up, I would not be able to return to see him that evening. I think I invited him to visit me at Foxdale but he never did, nor did I ever hear from him again. Not even at Christmas. I think, as with one or two of my old pals, he was a bit embarrassed at our different financial positions and the fact that I had left him a tenner hidden beneath the tea tray. There was no need for him to be embarrassed as I thought of him as a good man, a good laugh, and a friend for life. Dear old 2624918 Watts W., if ever we met again, and unless he has inherited a fortune, won the pools or the lottery, our financial position will be on equal terms now.

There is no place in the world like the Guards Depot. For the first few weeks, they strip you of all initiative. You do nothing unless you are ordered. You drill and polish, polish and drill and obey. There were even large sheds erected so you could drill when it was raining or snowing. However, they were never used to shelter you from the sweltering sun. You were completely crushed, but as the weeks went by, they slowly built up your confidence and by the time you left the depot you were told, and believed, that you were the finest, smartest, well-disciplined soldiers in the world.

We only learned the basic weapon training at the depot; firing the 303 Lea Enfield rifle and the ever-reliable Bren gun. We had also become quite efficient in physical training and had to do several tests, a couple of which remain vividly in my mind. One task was to run a mile, four times around the measured cinder track at the sports stadium in full battle order; boots, steel helmet, full pack water bottle, rifle, ammunition, etc. The time you were allowed was 9 minutes and the whole squad started together. I felt very comfortable and soon had a very healthy lead over everyone. Then I started overtaking the tailenders and finally lapped everybody. My time was 5.59. The PTI sergeant major came up to me,

"You'll stay here at the end of your training, boy, and go on a PT instructor's course. Well done. I remember you were the first recruit home on the 9 mile cross-country race"

"Sir" I replied feeling mighty proud of myself.

Back in the barrack room I was not so popular for showing up the rest of the squad.

"Did you have to run so fast?" I was asked. "Not necessary."

But Corporal Eastwood and Sergeant Shelton were pleased that a member of their squad had done so well. As for Gardner, for many years he always maintained I had only run three laps. He had come second and was none too pleased at being lapped.

Another incident involving Gardner came when we had to run 100 yards with an imaginary wounded man on our backs. At the end of the 100 yards, you put the man down and he ran back with you on his back. The officer offered 10 fags to the winner. It seems everyone in our squad was looking round for a little lightweight to carry and naturally, I was the target. However, Gardner got hold of me first and the 12 sets of competitors lined up. At the end of the first 100 yards, Gardner had gained about a 2-yard lead and he was thinking to himself, now this skinny little rat certainly won't be able to maintain this slender lead carrying his 14½ stone. Wrong, I bundled him onto my slender shoulders and not only did I maintain the lead, I increased it to 5 yards, and that is what we won by. Eight years later, when I met Jack's dad at the pub his son had bought him, he said when we were first introduced:

"I remember Jack writing home and telling us about you. 'This little chap from Brighton with tremendous strength' is how he put it."

He also told his dad he thought I was the best soldier in the squad. Mr. Gardner was horrified, however, at some of the escapades I got up to later in my army career.

There were two days in a year that were sacred to the entire inhabitants of the British Isles; Christmas Day and Good Friday. Not so in the brigade of guards. On Good Friday we drilled all the morning

56

and got 'put in the book' for all manner of trivialities, and they very sensibly had the Guards Depot - Cross Country Championship in the afternoon, half an hour after consuming as much stodge as we could stuff into our hungry bellies.

As it was a national holiday, the master cook thought it a good idea to have suet pudding for duff (pudding). It looked and tasted like a pile of constipated camel's dung. Being a clever bugger and knowing what was coming next, I ate very little dinner that day and certainly no camel dung. At 1:45 sharp, the whole depot turned out for the run, Colies, Jocks, Taffs, Micks and, of course, The Grenadiers or 'Bill Browns', as we were called. There were over 500 on the square dressed only in their brown plimsolls, socks rolled down as far as possible, blue PT shorts and white sleeveless PT vests.

We were all dressed the same with the exception of the PT instructors, who wore red and black rugby shirts. The PT chief sergeant major got us to attention and announced that the race would be started by the commanding officer firing his pistol. The winner would receive ten shillings, the second five shillings, and the third half a crown, which, in those days, wouldn't buy a pint of beer for the winner. He also said the last 20 home would be put in the book - idle on parade. At this point, I made up my mind not to be booked for being idle on parade.

At 2 o'clock sharp, the pistol went off and we all galloped through the gates and headed for the open country. The course had been well thought out by some ingenious bastard who had made up his mind to make it as unpleasant as possible. It seemed to be all hills and mud, just a long trail of endurance. As I left the barracks, there must have been 300 recruits in front of me and I jogged along with a couple of other lads from my squad. They seemed to be going very slowly and there was a lot of puffing and blowing and after 3 miles there were several unfortunate guys who, no doubt, had had two helpings of camel's dung, spewing their guts up on the side of the track. Watts said to me:

"Don't wait for us, get after the leaders."

"Okay" I said and got into top gear and started overtaking dozens of the forerunners.

As I got nearer the front it took more effort to overtake, but I battled on until I could see only 20 or so people in front of me, including the four red and black vests of the PTIs. At this point, the marker said 3 miles to go. 'No problem' I thought, and I got down to serious running. I was very fit at the time and I always enjoyed running.

We had all heard about Sergeant Tyler, who had won the race for the last 3 years and I didn't think I would catch him, but I thought if I could get second, it would be very nice to cop 5/-. I overtook a few more competitors until, with only about half a mile to go, I could see Sergeant Tyler about 100 yards in front. I made after him as fast as I could go and, as we entered the barracks and raced across the square to the finishing line, he was only some 10 yards in front of me. Another PT sergeant was third.

Corporal Eastwood was very excited that one of his squad was the first recruit home and he turned to Captain Goodhart Randall.

"He's in our company, Sir"

The captain came across to me and shook my hand.

"Well done boy, collect your prize from the company sergeant major in the morning and, corporal, give this man credit."

I remember that he didn't take off his glove when he shook my hand, which I thought was very ungentlemanly. A ginger haired lad from our squad named Dyer came in the first 15 and we would be included in the team to run in the London District Championship later that year. The guards' depot had won the race for many years running and they competed against the best of southern England's athletic clubs. Even our Trained Soldier grudgingly gave me a pat on the back. Poor old Bryant was near last and got two extra drills.

Before first parade next day, I hastened to the CSM's office. I knocked on the door and he bellowed out:

"Come in." He glared at me for a moment. "What d'ye want?"

I made the terrible, unforgivable, mistake of going up to his desk and, with both hands, leaned on it.

"I've come for my winnings, Sir"

"Get out you 'orrible little man. Get out of my office or I'll put you inside." He looked quite mad.

I had expected a more cordial greeting than this, especially as I had done so well for his company, but CSM Betts was a real peasant at heart and no doubt thought I was an intruder. 'Fancy beating the three other PT sergeants. I'll give him some stick'. And he did.

From that day on, I was a marked man and whenever he was patrolling the square watching the individual squads drilling, he would forever be bawling out:

"Hold your head up that little man in Corporal Eastwood's squad", "Swing your arms up", "Pick your feet up" or whatever came to mind, but it was always the same –'That little man in the front rank, Corporal Eastwood's squad.'

In an inter-company football match, we played the Welsh Guards. Their left back was a giant of a man who, mistaking me for the football, laid me out. Next day I reported sick as I could hardly walk. For my pains, the doctor said I was malingering and gave me 'M&D', which means Medicine (a laxative) and Duty as usual. Corporal Eastwood and Sticky Glue covered up for me for a couple of days and I remained in the barrack room doing menial tasks and polishing up to standard some of the less talented members of the squad's kit. My pals reported that the CSM had not missed me and continued to bawl out:

"Get a move on you, that little man in the front rank of Corporal Eastwood's squad" I wasn't even on parade and I made up my mind that many of these NCOs weren't all they were made out to be. Certainly, they were not up to the standard of my father.

I got my own back, however, for when Sergeant Tyler came to our room one evening and said that he was the captain of the cross-country team and that Fear and Dyer would report for training after tea next day, I thought a bit and said:

"I can't run, Sergeant"

"Why not?"

"My Father has a weak heart and I'm afraid I've inherited the complaint."

"Bullshit. Never heard so much crap in all my life." he stormed.

I was thinking to myself, I run around all day long for a pittance. I'm buggered if I am going to run all the evening as well, instead of sitting on my bed ponging my kit with the rest of the squad. I would fall behind with everything. Not likely, and besides, what was in it for me? Nothing! Unlike after the war when you would be struck off duty.

Whenever Sergeant Tyler and I met, he always asked if I had changed my mind. He never tried to persuade me to run. On the Saturday when the London district was due to be run, he came to the barrack room.

"Fear, I've decided that you can run in the team today as I am sure even without the training, you would do better than some of the 15 members."

"No thank you, Sergeant." I replied.

"What's your excuse this time?"

"You had better ask CSM Betts, he never paid me my winnings for coming second on Good Friday", I replied.

"Didn't he? The little bastard. Typical. I'll have a word with him. Okay Fear, I understand now. I think I would have acted the same." he said.

He was always friendly with me after that, and at the end of our 20 weeks training at the depot, he recommended me to stay and be a PTI, which would have meant automatic promotion. I declined the offer, however. The guard's depot team won the championship for the umpteenth time, even without my help.

I cannot complete my narrative of the Guards Depot without mentioning the regimental sergeant major 'Snapper' Robinson. He had joined the regiment as a drummer boy at the age of 14. Unfortunately, like another CSM, Amour by name, he had not grown to the required height of a guardsman, but if this happens, the regiment don't kick you out when you reach manhood. Many of these boys go on to become high ranking NCOs. Snapper was a very good nickname for the RSM. Like the company commander, he wore First World War putties. He was indeed very smart and had a wonderful word of command, and he really did snap at you at every opportunity.

During our first week, he had lectured the squad on what to do and what not to do to become a good guardsman. The only thing I can remember is his advice when confronted by queers!

"These despicable bastards prey on nice young guardsmen like you. Beware of them, they will buy you pints of ale and then snatch your arsehole. My orders to you are 'kick 'em in the bollocks as hard as you can, then in the head. If they die, you'll be doing us all a favour and we will protect you 'cause we all love guardsmen who kick queers in the balls."

In London a couple of years later, I only took half his advice. I am sure the RSM would have put quite a few guardsmen 'in the book' if he had seen the carryings-on between homosexuals and squaddies.

One of the funniest things I have ever heard, of anyone losing his name, was my pal, Sammy Small. He had failed to cross the water jump on the assault course and had got his boots wet. In an effort to get them dry for next morning's kit inspection, he put them close to the stove in his barrack room. Consequently, as they dried they curled up a bit. He polished them to a high standard that evening. Next morning, at kit inspection, his company commander noticed the boots and hooked one up in the air on the end of his walking stick.

"God, what size are these boots?" enquired the bewildered officer.

"A small 13" replied Sam.

"Ah, a small 13. I see" said the captain, recognising Sam's sarcasm. "Put him in the book, Sergeant."

'Curly boots'. That says it all. To escape from the depot without losing your name and being put in the book was impossible.

Peculiar to guards' regiments, is the daily breakfast parade. It was instrumented by none other than Queen Victoria.

At the Guards Depot, one didn't have time for these parades, but once you joined your battalion, you had them for the rest of your service, and what a pain it was. However, like everything else in life, one got used to it. God Save the Queen. It seems Queen Victoria, one summer's morning, thought that she would stroll across to Wellington Barracks to see what her chosen regiment was having for breakfast. It happened to be the morning after payday and, consequently, half of the men creeping across the square to the cookhouse were still in a form of stupor after their weekly 'piss-up' and, having consumed between 10 and 16 pints of beer, they were not a pretty sight. A Coldstream guardsman claimed, with the financial support of his homosexual friends, to have drunk 58 pints from 6 pm until closing time. Anyway, what the Queen saw annoyed her immensely.

"I won't have my personal bodyguards going to the messroom unshaven and improperly dressed. In future, they will have an inspection parade before breakfast every morning."

From that day on, and for over 100 years, all guards battalions have had this parade, and some bright spark added to our misery by suggesting the guardsmen should also produce an item of equipment in good order. So, every evening, the sergeant-in-waiting would write on the company notice board what that item would be. I remember one ignoramus of a sergeant who could not spell 'bayonet scabbard', so he hung one up on a nail on the notice board for all to see. Underneath was scribbled 'This will be seen on BP.'

Most of the wartime NCOs were good types who had earned their stripes the hard way. But after the war, when many of them were demobbed, their replacements, at least in our company, were not so hot. This is how the selection was made in our happy, friendly, company. First, the CSM would invite a few of the smartest, most intelligent men (including myself of course - the CSM's favourite). We, without exception, would decline the offer, which would entail going on a corporal's course.

Next he would put a notice on the company order board 'Anyone wanting to become an NCO please apply to the CSM'. No-one applied. Then, in desperation, he would pounce on any unsuspecting individual and say:

"You're on the next corporal's course."

Nine times out of ten, the poor bloke would agree. Few of them would ever become a Spratley, Muckett, Everit, or Amour.

On the last night of our twenty weeks training, the trained soldier said that he and Bryant had hired a room over a pub somewhere in Purley and that we were to have a 'passing out party'. Free beer and a nice buffet. Before leaving the barracks, we were all inspected by the sergeant of the guard, who happened to be Sergeant Shelton. As he knew us all and understood it was our last night, he didn't look at us too closely, and passed some friendly remark telling us all to be back by 10 o'clock or we wouldn't be going on leave next day. We found the pub in Purley and went upstairs to the reception room where they held dances sometimes. A bar had been set up and a table laid with lots of goodies on it that most of us had never seen before.

There awaiting us, were Sticky Glue, Bryant and his girlfriend, who I remember, as she was a stunner. Befitting a wealthy shoe manufacturer, she really was nice.

As everything was free, we soon got plastered. It didn't take much in those days to set me off. Two or three pints and I was ready for anything. I couldn't take my eyes off Bryant's girl and when I approached her and told her she was the most beautiful thing I had ever seen, she seemed quite pleased and we chatted away for a while. I could see her boyfriend watching us out of the corner of his eye. I must have said something very funny or rude, because she laughed her head off. In a few strides, Bryant was on me. He got me by the jacket and shook me like a rat. Next thing, Gardner had hold of Bryant and was shaking him likewise. Sticky Glue and the girlfriend quietened things and we settled down to getting wonderfully pissed.

It's a good job Sergeant Shelton was on the gate when we arrived back at barracks at 9:55 or we would have all been stuck in the cells for the night or marched in front of the company commander the next day for being drunk and disorderly - a condition I frequently got into, until I grew up at about 40 years of age.

When we got to our room, York 4, we thought we would do nasty things to Trained Soldier Glue who had made our lives so unbearable for so long, so we threw his mattress and bedding out of the window and tipped all his gear out of his kitbag into the coal bin and whilst the bin shone like a new pin, the coal didn't. We then lay on our beds and saw the ceiling going round and round. Several of us rushed to the washhouses to be sick as dogs.

All this was going on in darkness, as it was lights out at 10 pm. The permanent staff were allowed out of barracks until midnight and it's then that our very pissed up trained soldier returned. When he could see what had happened to his kit, he went frantic. He switched on the lights and called us all the names he could think of. The one that has stuck in my mind was when he called us ungrateful bastards. Ungrateful – that's rich, that's a laugh if you like.

Anyway, he finally told us that we must all lay out our kits and he would inspect us all that night. This meant we had to unpack our kitbags. Can you imagine us 23 (one of our squad of 24 who couldn't stand the pace, had committed suicide after about 5 weeks. Jack and I can always remember him, as he was always singing 'Paper Doll', a happy little song that was popular in those days. I know it was tough going, but not worth committing hara-kiri for), the 23 that were left of the squad, all under the influence trying in vain to lay out our kits?

The trained soldier soon got his act together and was laid out on his remade bed fast asleep. As soon as this was announced, we all followed suit. Some of the lads actually fell asleep on top of their hastily laid out belongings.

Reveille next morning was at 6:30 and all of us were out of our beds like a shot in spite of the inevitable hangover. The trained soldier was normal and didn't mention the night before. It seems it always happened on the recruits' last night and from his point of view, to have his bed thrown out of the window was an occupational hazard. After a hasty breakfast, we returned to the barrack room to collect our kit. Superintendent Sergeant Shelton, Corporal Eastwood, and the trained soldier were there to shake each of our hands. I always remember Sticky Glue's last words to me.

"You're a chancer. You'll win the VC or finish up in the digger."

I must admit, I had to fight back my tears at our parting from the three men who had changed all our lives forever. Now we were fully-fledged guardsmen, off home for our seven days in heaven.

It seemed strange on arrival at Brighton station, marching down Queens Road in full battle order, carrying my rifle and kitbag. I felt proud and thought everyone must be looking at me when, in fact, no one took any notice. I must have looked a right twerp on reflection. The family were pleased to see me. Dad was proud as punch and we went out for a drink on several occasions. He told everyone that I would soon be promoted and had already been asked to be a PTI. He had high hopes for me and my failure to attain his wishes soured our relationship in the future.

As it happened, after three days brother Jim, now an RSM in the Royal Engineers came to visit us mainly to see how I was going on. He had 14 days leave and spent most of it with his wife and children in Mitcham. From what I gather, all was not well with his marriage as Madge was acting rather strangely due to his absence from home. He said she used to send open postcards to him, on which was written in large letters:

"If you don't come home now I'll cut my throat."

This wasn't very nice for the RSM to receive and caused a few strange looks from his fellow NCOs. Nevertheless, we had a few good days together and drank in many of the pubs surrounding the clock tower in Brighton. It's not often that a private drinks and enjoys himself with two regimental sergeant majors.

I remember calling on Mr. Rose, my old boss. He and Miss Nelson were very pleasant and asked me for a photo of myself in uniform to display in the shop, together with his sons and other assistants who had worked for him and had been called up. He told me my job was waiting for me when the war was over. He didn't give me a pound or two as a sweetener, which I had hoped for, and as I left the shop I thought to myself 'If he thinks I'm going back there, he's mistaken'. I had served my apprenticeship and worked for peanuts. After the war, there would be no Canadian soldiers to subsidise my frugal wages. No way would I return to being 'Pawn Shop Dick'. I suppose that is how the rich stay rich, by being tight-fisted.

From T.D. Rose I called on Mr. and Mrs. Burley, in Duke Street. They also offered me a job when I was demobbed. He gave me £1 for a few drinks and I thought maybe I would work for him one day as a watchmaker-come-jeweller's assistant. On parting, he said:

"Keep an eye open for any German watches; they are very good I understand." I assured him I'd bring him home a sack full. We both laughed and I thought what a nice guy he was.

As always, my leave was soon up and I returned to Victoria Barracks, Windsor, to complete my training as an infantryman. There were not so many drill parades there, as the main object was to turn us into proficient assassins, and as we did our weapon training, we all had to shout out 'I will kill all the enemy'. If you didn't shout loud enough for the instructors pleasure, you were put in the book; 'Idle on parade'.

We were formed into platoons, each containing three sections of 10 or 12 men. Both Frances and Gardner were in my platoon, but the rest of the squad were dispersed into other platoons. In each section was a Bren gunner and as I had done well at the depot with this weapon, I was given the job. Okay at times, but on route marches and forced marches it got heavier as the miles went by.

Half way through our training, we had to do a 30-mile forced march. On this occasion, I only had to take a rifle, the same as everyone else. To get an even pace, the platoon commander, a second lieutenant, thought it best if we ran and marched in pairs instead of the normal columns of three. He said that Gardner - tall man - and Fear - short-arse - would set an even pace for the rest of the platoon. We had a time limit to get the whole platoon home, so it was a team effort. Some of us fitter runners finished up carrying the kit and rifles of the lesser men who, in some cases, were in a terrible state. The officer was great and kept up with us with no problem, and the PT sergeant kept a careful watch over us all on his bicycle. It seems doing 30 miles every day would be a bit too much, even for a guard PTI.

We finished our 30-mile ordeal at the rifle ranges, where we had to, without a minute's rest, fire 10 shots with our 303 rifles, at a target the size of a German's head at 50 yards. The idea being it's no good racing 30 miles to fight the enemy and then not able to hit the bastards. I still have my target, which our platoon officer took to the

66

officers' mess that night and returned to me at a later date. All of my 10 shots were in the bull. Tearing out an inch hole bang in the centre of the Hun's swede. The Chico said I would be a sniper at the end of my training.

After the march, we returned to the barrack room for foot inspection. My feet were in good order, but some of the lads had bad blisters and had to report sick. As I had stopped wearing socks half way through my depot training (to ensure I always had clean socks for kit inspection), my pals were amazed that my feet were in such a healthy state. None of them copied me however. As for me, I have never worn socks winter or summer ever since, not even at my weddings, important occasions or my three visits to Buckingham Palace. Apart from anything else, it must have saved a fortune these 50 years and saved my poor wives no end of washing and darning. Yes, I suppose I am a strange fellow.

On one of the visits to Buckingham Palace, guardsmen and NCOs were instructed to wear dark suits or blazers, white shirts and regimental tie. The officers, in morning suits and top hats. I was searching unsuccessfully to recognise some of my old pals when I saw a face I knew well. It was Captain David German. He approached me and greeted me.

"Hello Fear. I've had a five pound bet with my wife that you haven't any socks on. Her reply was that I shouldn't be so silly as no one would dare to come to Buckingham Palace improperly dressed. Do you mind?" and with that he reached down to lift my trouser leg, revealing my naked ankle. "Pay up. Pay up you" he declared to his lady wife.

We exchanged pleasantries and went our separate ways. Incidentally, David's father was Senior British Officer at Colditz, the famous castle, where the Germans kept their most desperate prisoners. He had been captured in Norway (another of Churchill's follies) and had spent 5 years locked up.

We also learned to fire the Piat, an anti-tank rocket launcher, two-inch mortars and the Thompson machine gun. However, because of the cost of this fine gun, the 'powers that be' decided on a new invention, the Sten gun. It was a laugh. I think it cost about 7/6 and hundreds of lives through malfunction and jamming. At the most fatal moment in a poor Squaddy's life, when he came face to face with the enemy in house to house fighting, the f---ing thing would misfire, jam or fall apart. Disgusting! The Germans had the Schmeiser and the Russians, a great machine gun similar to our Thompson, but we were issued with this pile of tripe. But, of course, the people who decided to issue this disgusting weapon were safe at home scoffing their ill-gotten steaks and smoked salmon - obtained, no doubt, on the black market.

We had all had practice throwing hand grenades, undetonated. Then came the test - when we had to throw a live grenade. We did this from a specially constructed trench, some 5-foot deep and 4-foot wide, zigzagging for 50 yards for safety reasons. We went in pairs with the weapons training instructor, to the firing point. The grenade was primed, and then we had to throw it at an imaginary target some 25 metres away. We withdrew the safety pin and, after it left your grasp, it exploded in 6 seconds. My partner was Francis. I went first and my grenade exploded near the target. I was surprised at the din it created. Then came Francis' turn. Out came the pin and he hunched himself up in the most remarkable position and hurled it with all his might, not at the target, but straight up in the air. It hovered directly over our trench and started to descend, straight on top of us. The Sergeant screamed out:

"For God's sake" and took off round the corner of our trench.

Both Francis and I quickly followed suit. We did two corners before the explosion and even though we were twenty yards from where the grenade landed, there was a tremendous blast, which nearly knocked us over. There was no shrapnel, thankfully. The lads in our section were none-too-happy with poor old Francis and naturally, the Sergeant 'put him in the book' - idle whilst throwing hand grenades. Old Jack should have stayed at home. He was a much better poacher than a soldier.

After duty one day, a guardsman came into our barrack room and shouted out:

"Which one of you is Fear?" I stood up and said
"I am Fear"
"Major Beard wants to see you."

There was a deadly hush in our barrack room. 'What's Fear been up to?' wondered my room mates. Tabby Beard, as he was called, was the quartermaster at Victoria Barracks. An old soldier who had returned to his regiment to be of some use in our fight for freedom. He must have been about 60 years old and spent most of his time in short sleeves working in the gardens of the barracks. He never put anyone 'in the book'. I was led to his office by his servant.

"That will be all," he said to his lackey. "Come in and sit down" said Major Beard.

What an honour, I thought, to actually sit down in an officer's sanctum.

"I saw your name on one of my lists and wondered if perhaps, Dan Fear was your grandfather. He was an old friend of mine"

"Dan Fear is my father," I replied. "And he served in The Grenadiers from 1892"

"The same man, so he must have had you when he was in his fifties?" the major said.

"That is correct, Sir"

"Well, well, well, the old bugger. We were recruits together and were in the Sudan and South Africa. I was standing next to him when he was wounded. At Omduman. Got a dervish spear in his chest. Touch and go, you know, but takes more than a spear to kill the likes of your dad. By God, he could down a pint" To think that Major Beard could remember Dad's drinking habits after nearly forty years.

We talked for some time and he asked for our address in Brighton. He wished me luck and said if he could be of any help to me in the future, to come along to his office where I would always be welcome.

Being very young, I didn't take advantage of his kind offer, mainly because I didn't want my squad mates to think I was a 'creeper', a label I feared more than anything else. It's true, I always got on well with the officers and senior NCOs, but no doubt, it was as

I was an asset and a volunteer, and during the war because 'I was only a young lad' and they sought my company, not I theirs.

One day our platoon was marched to the library. When we entered, there before us was a huge table. On it were some 30 white foolscap sheets of paper on which there was a door lock, bicycle pump and bicycle bell and one or two other mechanical devices, all mixed up and in pieces. We were ordered to stand in front of these puzzles. We all looked at each other and wondered if indeed the commanding officer had gone mad. For God's sake, what next? No explanation was given by our platoon commander.

"When I blow my whistle so," (he blew a short blast), "you will put together all the things you see in front of you and when I blow my whistle so", (another blast on the only instrument he could play) "you will stop."

We gazed at our pile in amazement.

He blew his whistle and we started to endeavour to put together all the puzzles. I glanced round the table and could see everyone else was struggling to achieve what I had completed. I looked at poor old Francis, standing next to me, and saw he was trying to fit part of the bicycle bell into the lock. I said:

"This will cost you a large lump of your Ma's fruit cake" and slid his foolscap into my place and gave him my completed set. When the Chico blew his whistle for us to stop, he walked round the table checking the results and noting how many each guardsman had got correct. On the final analysis, only two men had 100% and that was Francis and myself, and I had done both.

The outcome of this exercise was that 'the powers that be' considered us two bright sparks mechanically minded and said we would be dispatched to the Royal Armoured Corp. Training Wing at Catterick Camp, Yorkshire. 'F---ing hell', I thought. I don't want to go in the tanks. Sitting ducks and we all knew a German 88mm could knock the turret off most allied tanks and certainly penetrate the armour of all American and British tanks. The Russian T34 tank, however, was so designed that unless the gunners were very lucky, the

88 would ricochet off these first class tanks, which the experts say were the best battle worthy tanks of Word War II.

What to do, what to do? I know I'll apply to see the company commander, a Captain McLean. I wrote out my application and handed it to the company sergeant major.

"You're wasting your time." was his only comment.

Next morning, Francis, who also didn't fancy being burned to a cinder inside a Churchill Tank, had also asked to see the C.O. and so we paraded in front of the company commander. I marched in first and after being told to stop talking a couple of times from the CSM, I said my piece,

"Sir, my father was a grenadier and served in the 1st Battalion. I should like to do the same, Sir!"

"Well Fear," began Captain McLean. "I've been looking at your records. They're remarkable and you should be very proud. You could have gone on a corporals' course and become a PTI Bren gunner sniper. In fact, I am sure you could do my job. However, we need men like you in the tanks. I understand your reasons for staying in the infantry, but I am afraid I must decline your request. I am very sorry, as I am sure whichever course you took you would be a success. Good luck, Fear. I am sure you will become a very good tank man. Case dismissed."

I was marched out and the CSM said:

"I told you so." I don't know how McLean summed up old Francis, but he finished up like me. In Churchills!

One more comical incident that happened at Windsor that I would like to report, was that of Ray Bray. He was a lovely lad who wouldn't harm a fly. He lived in Windsor and finished up his working life as Transport Manager at Mars Bars. From the moment we joined up, we got on well. A couple of weeks before our infantry training finished, we were out doing funny things to pass the time of day. On this occasion we were learning to jump coils of barbed wire and when there was more than one fence erected, one poor guardsman had to fling himself on top of the wire so the rest of his buddies could run over him and the wire. A very frightening experience. I was lucky and was never ordered to do this painful task.

Bray was not so lucky and after the platoon had run over him, came the difficult task of disengaging his battered body from the barbed wire. Tempers were running high and some of the platoon started pulling frantically at poor old Ray. He was in great pain and when he was checked over, it was to find that one of his balls was still hanging on a strand of barbed wire. They actually sent him to hospital. I would have thought from past experience in the guards, they would have got the company tailor along to sew up the jagged wound with the MO giving him M&D for so trivial a wound. After he returned to duty, he was known as 'One Ball', to which he would reply:

"I may have only one ball, but it's better than f—k all, so 'F'k 'em all!'"

After we finished our infantry training at Victoria Barracks, we went on seven days leave. On this occasion we took all our equipment including our rifles with us. Getting all our worldly possessions into our kitbag and small pack was no small task, but we managed it. I think four of our platoon, including Jack Gardner, were to go on a corporals' course at Barnard Castle in Yorkshire and Doughty B. was to become a sniper. The rest of the platoon were to go into the PBI (Poor Bloody Infantry). I would exchange my posting with any one of the platoons. It was very pleasant to be on leave again and sleep between clean sheets instead of the threadbare blankets. In fact, the Daily Mirror got hold of the story that the army-issued blankets at Windsor had never been washed since they were first issued in 1900. Shaken violently every Saturday morning, but never washed.

Flight Lieutenant Daniel Fear
Royal Flying Corp. 1917

Mother Fear 1920

Brother Jim

Brother John before joining the R.A.F.
1938

Brother Elton (Richard)

Brother Daniel Aged 17
Too young for the war

Private Ray Fear Aged 14
Royal Sussex Cadets

The author Aged 19 years

Jack 'Hairy' Francis

Hazel – Wife 1

Rita – Wife 2

Linda – Wife 3

Sylvia – Wife 4

Chapter 4

Catterick Camp

My leave, like all leaves, went by all too quickly and with my railway warrant, I headed for Catterick Camp in Yorkshire. What a dump - a huge clutter of huts where thousands of troops were doing one type of training or another. Francis and I finished up in a large hut which housed about 40 troops. Besides us two grenadiers, there were four Scots Guards and one Coldstream Guardsman, who were also training in Churchill's and were to become part of the 6th Guards Independent Tank Brigade - supposedly the only tank men in the World who took their rifles and bayonets into action in their tanks. The idea being that if your tank was knocked out, you were (if you had not been burned alive) able to leap out with your gun and continue the fight as infantrymen. Whoever thought that one up must have been under the influence of drink or had some inborn grudge against the Brigade of Guards.

Our Brigade consisted of the 4th Battalion Grenadiers, 3rd Battalion Scots and 4th Battalion Coldstream. I still wonder why the powers at the war ministry, and no doubt Mr. Churchill, decided to put the cream of the British infantry - all tall men to say the least - into the small compounds of a tank. Five guardsmen inside a tank didn't leave much room to manoeuvre I can assure you.

In our room were 30 or so Royal Armoured Corp. wallers. They didn't like us much because of our bull-shitting ways and we didn't like them much as a bunch of undisciplined short-arsed know-alls. Francis and I were to become gunner mechanics, which meant we not only had to learn to drive the tank, but also fire the 75mm gun. Also, the Besa 7.92mm machine gun, of which there were two in a Churchill, one by the co-driver and one in the turret next to the 75mm. There was also a 2-inch mortar in the turret. The 75mm was certainly an improvement on the 2 pounder that was first installed in the original Churchill tank. The two pounder was a laugh, not much bigger than your rifle. They first went into action at Dieppe and in the western desert, but were a complete failure. They were soon rejected and a 6 pounder was introduced, followed by the 75mm.

The German 88mm, the most feared gun by all the allies, was originally an anti-aircraft gun. It could pierce with ease any tank the allies had. We also had anti-aircraft guns, the 17 pounders that were just as effective. Our tank bosses wanted these guns in our tanks to match the 88mm, but Churchill in his wisdom said no.

"I won't have our cities stripped of our anti-aircraft defences. No. The tanks must manage, our civilians come first."

Not that the AA guns did much shooting down of enemy aircraft, but at least they did keep the Luftwaffe at a height which made their jobs of bombing strategic targets more difficult. The answer, of course, was to produce 17 pounders instead of 6 pound or 75mm. Simple deductions I would have thought. During the last 3 months of the War, 17 pounders were installed on some Churchill tanks, all too late I am afraid. Another of Churchill's blunders.

Our course was to last several months. The first job was to learn to drive a 15cwt. truck. The two FF's were always stuck together and Francis and I shared one instructor – a very small lance corporal of the Royal Armoured Corp. It soon became apparent that Francis would never learn to drive. On one occasion, while manoeuvring a steep hill, the instructor kept shouting out:

"Stop, start, stop, start"

I, in the back, was enjoying the fun. It was like being at the fairground in a bumper car. In the end, the truck came to a sudden halt and Francis leapt out, ran round to where the instructor was sitting, dragged him out of his seat, and bellowed:

"Why don't you make up your frigging mind? Stop, start, stop, start – you're driving me mad!"

I intervened and saved the corporal. No action was taken against Francis but he was cautioned. I drove back to camp where a report was made on Francis' behaviour and he was transferred to another course, that of a wireless operator. He finished up as a very good wireless man, much to my surprise.

Quite a few things happened at Catterick that stuck in my memory. We finished our training at 12:30 on Saturday afternoons and were then free until first parade on Monday. I bet the German and Russian soldiers didn't enjoy such privileges and I am sure working a six-and-a-half day week would have shortened our courses considerably, which would have suited us no end. One Saturday, after our midday meal, Francis and I were about to take to our wanking pits for a couple of hours before tea, and our weekly visit to Darlington to have a few beers. As I was about to get into my bed, Francis flung me his boots.

"They are wet through. Dry them by the stove for me there's a good chap."

I obliged and put the boots near enough to dry but not burn. At 4:30 the bugle sounded for tea and I obliged Francis by passing him his size 11 boots. The trouble now was that they looked like a pair of 6's, with the sole nearly hanging off the uppers.

"You little Jewish bastard" as he always called me when I upset him. "What have you done to my frigging boots? You had better get me another pair my size by the time the passion wagon is ready, or else."

Knowing what 'or else' meant, I awaited everyone to make his way to the mess room. I then hastened to one of the other huts, made sure no one else was about, and hunted round for a size 11 boot. Impossible in a hut of RAC Wallers, with their average size of 6, 7, or 8. Me thinks, 'Ah, I know where other guardsmen are housed', and made my way to where several Coldstreamers were billeted. No one was about, so it was easy, and I was soon having my tea with my old pal. He moaned a bit when he saw my replacement boots, as the shine wasn't up to his standard, but I think that underneath he was grateful as it was hardly my fault that some trooper had stoked up the stove while we slept.

Another incident that involved Francis happened when I was short of cash. Poor old Jack Francis had a tail. Yes, a tail! Well, it was like an extension to the base of his spine and quite hairy. As he resembled an ape in many ways, this was not surprising. I know apes don't have tails, but Jack was an exception. He agreed with my plan as long as we shared the proceeds.

"Gather round lads," I shouted out, "and for one fag apiece, I will show you my friend's tail."

"Tail, what tail?" was the quick response.

"For one fag from each of you, I'll take off his trousers and show you this freak of nature."

I soon collected a good few cigarettes. Francis lay face down on his bed and I slowly removed his trousers and then his underpants. There were gasps of amazement at what I had revealed and the entire room gathered round to get a better view of 'The Tail'. After some time I announced that for one more cigarette each, my friend there would wag his tail. More gasps of disbelief and I soon had my hat full of fags: One seemingly wealthy non-smoker said: "I'll give you 10/- if he can do this trick.

In the meantime, Francis had lain quiet as a mouse and I think a trifle embarrassed. I whispered to him what he was expected to do and he said:

"F--k you, but I'll try!"

"Now then, everybody watch carefully he's not a Dalmatian and he cannot perform for any lengthy period. So keep you eyes on the spot." There was a deadly silence and I cried out in a confident manner:

"Come along Francis now. Wag your ta-ta, wag your ta-ta."

Low and behold, Francis took a deep breath and the veins stuck out on his neck like whip cords. He grunted a few times and then let out a mighty fart. This eased the tension and everyone laughed. Francis continued to perform and finally, with my encouragement and to everyone's delight, he managed to get his stump to move sideways several times. Bravo, bravo, and then to everyone's glee, someone started to sing 'For he's a jolly good fellow; for he's a jolly good fellow, and so say all of us.' We shared the fags but Francis let me have the 10/- note. After this, our relations with the RAC improved and Jack was always very popular.

One day soon after this incident, I noticed that Jack's bum seemed to be getting larger. I pointed this out to him and he snorted:

"So would yours if you hadn't had a crap for 10 days."

He had always had problems with his bowels. No doubt because of the rich extras Ma Francis sent her beloved son in her weekly food parcel. On this occasion, things seemed more serious, so he went sick and was admitted to the local army hospital. To keep him sweet, I thought I had better visit him and so one Sunday afternoon I made my way to the hospital. It was a large Nissen hut with about 25 beds on each side of the room. I spotted Jack half way down the room. He looked quite gaunt and the first thing he asked me was if I had brought him anything to eat. When I said no, he seemed quite put out and demanded why I hadn't brought his Ma's weekly parcel. I had thought of this and the post corporal had refused to let me have it.

"Only Francis can collect it." he declared.

"How are you getting on?" I enquired.

"They are trying to starve me to death. I haven't had any real food for 10 days and they stuck a pipe up my arse, the bastards."

He stuck a 10/- note in my hand and I made my way to the NAFFI, where I bought 10 Eccles cakes. This should keep him going, I thought. As I walked along the patch back to the Ward, Francis was hanging out of the window next to his bed.

"Watcha got? Givvus them here", he cried.

He snatched them out of my hand and immediately took a bite out of the first cake. 'Greedy pig' I thought and made my way down the side of the hut and into reception. I passed the time of day with a male nurse and asked him how my pal was behaving.

"Him?" he cried. "He ain't normal, he's got a bloody tail."

I smiled to myself and continued to Francis' bed where he seemed to be in a better mood.

"Can I have one of the Eccles cakes?" I asked.

"Sorry," was his reply. "I've eaten 'em all." And so he had. All 10 in the time it took me to walk about 100 metres.

"If you get me another twenty and pass them through the window like before, you can have a couple."

I stayed with him a while and brought him up to date with what was going on at the camp. When I left, I retraced my steps to the NAFFI and got him another 20 Eccles cakes. I took my two cakes out and quietly went back to where he was reaching out of the window.

"Thanks pal," he said and "Keep the change."

It was strictly forbidden to take patients any sort of food. All I know was Francis was returned to duty within the week.

After our class had finished its driving instruction, we went straight onto tanks. Driving a tank came easy after the 15cwt. truck and we all soon mastered the technique. There are two ways of viewing the outside world. One is through a visor, which is a hinged door about 12 x 8 inches and 6 inches thick. When in action, this is closed and you operate with your periscope and the verbal instructions through the intercom from your tank commander in the turret.

During my training, I had a couple of mishaps. One was when we were crossing over the bridge in Richmond. I must have been dozing off for the next moment there was much screaming from the tank commander and a few shudders from the tank.

"Driver halt. Driver halt."

We came to a standstill and I clambered out to take stock of the damage. The tank had knocked about six foot of stonewall into the river. We were but three tanks and no officer on parade, so our worldly tank sergeant said:

"Come on, let's get the hell out of here"

We drove off as fast as a Churchill will carry us - and that's about 12 miles an hour - but as you peer through the open visor you feel you are doing at least 40 miles an hour, a very funny sensation. It's the same when you're driving using the periscope. There was not a scratch on my tank and nothing more was heard of the incident, but when I was travelling that way some 25 years later, I could still see where the bridge had been repaired.

The second incident was of a much more serious nature. I was merrily bowling along one day in the driver's seat. As I approached a sharp bend in the road, my visor, which I hadn't fixed properly, swung shut so I was driving completely blind. Very exciting! Next moment I heard the tank instructor bellowing over the intercom like a mad man:

"Stop for Christ's sake, HALT!"

All too late. The next second the tank started to lurch from side to side and climb up in an alarming manner that you wouldn't expect on the well tarmacced open road. We came to a stop and I thought that as the front of the tank was a couple of feet higher than the rear, I must have run over something or other. Correct! I clambered out, or I attempted to, which was very difficult because my tank commander was reigning blows on my head and calling me all the names he could lay his mind to:

"You stupid gormless imbecile, see what you've done. You'll be in the army for the rest of your f---ing life paying for the damage"

Ah, the damage! It seems that a very large corporation wagon had parked on the bend while the driver had disappeared into the café opposite to take some refreshment. The first thing that struck me when I had forced myself from the incensed sergeant, was to see the driver of the truck dancing like the 'Wild Man of Borneo' and screaming abuse at yours truly from across the road. His once very large truck was now a very small one with its prop shaft sticking through the radiator. It resembled an anti-tank gun with water and petrol everywhere. My tank had clambered up the back of the truck and slowly crushed half the truck into the road. I saw the funny side of the situation and started to laugh. This outraged the sergeant and driver even more.

"As I am going to have to pay for the damage, I may as well enjoy the scene" I said.

The rest of the crew thought it amusing and thereafter I, like Francis, was quite popular amongst the RAC wallers who, no doubt like us, wondered why they had brought this bunch of oversized infantrymen to try to turn them into tank men.

I mentioned earlier that there were four Scots Guardsmen in our Hut, Messrs. Davison, Dunken, Scobie, and Jimmy Patterson. All good Scotsmen and true. Scobie, however, came from the slums of

Glasgow and when he had drunk a few pints, became very aggressive. He picked a quarrel with me one night and challenged me to a fight. So outside we went and on our own, in the dark, we had a big punch up. I very quickly realised I was no match for the tough Scotsman, who had an inborn hatred of the English.

"Enough Jock" I cried, but he took no notice and continued to knock me about. I defended myself as best I could. In the end he said, much to my surprise:

"You're too good for me." I was very relieved and thought he must be drunk, for there is no doubt he was the winner.

I didn't socialise with Francis in those early days and my best pal at Catterick was Jimmy Patterson. He was built like a God, same height as me but twice as broad. He was nearly bald, but in his hat and uniform, looked a perfect specimen of guardsman. He was over 30, so quite a fatherly figure. He loved wrestling and would teach me a few tricks when we had a go. He came from Ayr and before the war had a string of donkeys on the Ayr Sands. We corresponded at Christmastime for many years, but for some reason or other, I heard no more from him.

Our course at Catterick Camp finished and we were granted more leave. From home we had to report to Bovingdon Camp in Hampshire for more active tank training. This was great fun, for on the ranges we would fire our guns with live ammunition. You can imagine firing your 75mm gun at moving targets from 1,000 yards. Great fun for a 17 year old lad. We fired anti-personnel shells and armoured piercing shells according to the targets. I was amazed at their accuracy and wondered what would be our fate if the German gunners were as proficient, which indeed they were. The Besa machine guns were also very formidable.

One day on the ranges, we had to fire the 2-inch mortar housed in the turret of the tank. Come my turn and the instructor said:

"Be careful. You're going to demonstrate the phosphorus anti-personnel bomb."

I was inside the turret, the instructor, and the rest of the crew standing around the turret. I unscrewed the head and primed whatever

I had to prime. I adjusted the mortar so it was pointing up the range, and then on the order 'Fire', I fumbled with the bomb and it clattered on to the floor of the turret. I was paralysed with terror and thought it would explode any second. I stared at the bomb for a moment or two and thought the best place for it was up the spout of the mortar. So I reached down, grabbed the bloody thing, and popped it safely in its rightful place.

When I finally looked out of the turret, it was to see that the nearest of my crew was over 100 yards away. It seems when I had this mishap they all took off like jack rabbits, expecting an explosion at any moment. Unlike the tank corp. instructors, the Guards instructor was very sympathetic but said he was afraid he would have to 'put me in the book'. Next morning, on memoranda, I was marched in before our squadron commander and the charge read out.

"Dropped a bomb? Dropped a bomb? Good God, the man's in the Guards, not the Royal Air force. Never heard anything so ridiculous in all my life. Don't come here wasting my time in future, Sergeant. Case dismissed."

We were stationed quite near an airborne division and it was arranged for 3 or 4 of our tank crews to go for a day with the famous division. They, in turn, sent a platoon of paratroopers. After we had a tour, they asked us if we fancied a drop.

"What do you mean by a drop?" we asked.

"You know, up in a Dakota issued with a parachute and jump into the training area. It's a lovely day, you will all enjoy it."

"We have had no training" we explained.

"No matter, you're guardsmen and fit as fiddles. You'll be okay. You have as much chance with your first jump as your last and you won't have to carry any equipment. Piece of cake." the officer said.

So we all agreed to have a go. Not one of us wanted to be branded a coward. Rather stupid when you look back. Anyway we took off and that was the first time any of us had flown. It was a great thrill. We circled the training area, lined up, and adjusted our parachutes. Then the sergeant opened the door and within a very short time, we were sailing down to earth. My word it was a wonderful experience for us young soldiers. There were no mishaps and I think the airborne Chico was very relieved, as no doubt he would have been in deep trouble for such a hair-brain scheme.

That evening we were entertained in the sergeants' mess and the 20 airborne lads who had been riding around in Churchill tanks all day returned to join us. They too had experienced a very exciting day, but thought their job was safer than being a sitting target in a tank.

Chapter 5

France – Germany

Next thing we knew was that we were soon bound for France and action. An officer got us together.

"Anybody here under 18½?" he asked.

"No Sir" was the unanimous answer, although I was still under 18. One had to be over 18½ before you were actually allowed to fight for your country.

We landed in France and were immediately sent to the 6th Guards Brigade Forward Delivery Squadron. There you stayed until there was a vacancy in our 4th Battalion due to casualties. We had just settled in under canvass when we were detailed to take German prisoners from the front to one of the major ports in our possession, from where they would be shipped to Great Britain. It turned out to be a trainload; 20 or 30 cattle trucks and 50 prisoners herded into each.

Our instructions were to allow each truck two 14-man packs of rations a day and to let the prisoners out to do their business once a day. We were given no instructions on how to deal with 30 trucks, or as to how many to release at a time. As there were only a dozen guardsmen and, I think, an NCO of the military police, two of the carriages were sort of guardrooms for us - six in each, one half way down the train and one at the tail end.

Because of bomb damage and other causes, the journey was to last several days. I'll bet the longest trip without a break was less than 2 miles. As soon as we left the forward area, and whenever the train stopped, the local population would surround the train clamouring for food and cigarettes. We, in turn, were supposed to get out of our carriage and patrol along the trucks and, of course, take it in turns to let the occupants of each prison truck out to stretch their legs and go to the toilet. We had a wood-burning stove in our truck, which was very comfortable and none of us had the desire to feed and water 1,500 Huns, and certainly not allow them freedom. 'Leave them where they are', was our unanimous decision.

Looking along to the end of the train, we observed that the other six sentries were also inactive. From the start it was clear that the sergeant was dealing with the locals as he was seen handing over the 14-man packs and receiving something in return. Good idea we thought, and at each stop, we did our business deals. Mind you, most of the food we gave away free to the poor starving civilians, and in particular the children. The Germans had stolen the food from the occupied countries for 4 years and on their retreat had ransacked most towns and villages, so we felt no pity for our prisoners and, in fact, we never fed them and certainly didn't undo or inspect their wagons. We in turn, made ourselves as comfortable as possible and cooked our corned beef and spam, and on several occasions we were offered fresh eggs from the farms we passed. One egg, one fag was the going rate. So we didn't fare too badly and, of course, there was plenty of local wine. We played cards too, pontoon and brag mostly and I remember losing quite heavily during the days on the train.

Finally, we reached our destination, a station near the embarkation port. It was crawling with Redcaps (military policemen) who were to take over the prisoners and furnish us with a meal and transport back to the Forward Delivery Squadron. Suddenly there was uproar all about us.

"Where are the prisoners?" was the cry.

Some of the wagons were completely empty and some only had half the correct numbers. We hurriedly inspected the trucks and found that floorboards had been removed and seemingly, during the numerous stops, the prisoners had escaped. One thing that sticks in my mind was the stench in those wagons. It was horrible, the poor buggers had nowhere to poop except on the floor. Every army has its own smell. I suppose we smell to other armies, but the German army had a wretched stench that lingers with me still. Wherever we took over buildings or barracks that they had vacated, there was always this smell, caused, no doubt, by their diet of black bread, sausage, beans and sauerkraut - and the tobacco they smoked which was the dried leaves of mangel-wurzels and cabbage.

The MP Sergeant in charge of the Guard was whipped away and we never heard his fate. We returned to our unit and never gave the incident another thought. We were never detailed to do another trainload of prisoners.

Back at FDS it was very uncomfortable and no one seemed to know what was going on. Confusion reigned. Now and again one of our numbers would be dispatched to the battalion as casualties mounted. One day an officer called out my name and I was told I was to be a gunner in No.2 squadron. That's 'Stiffy' Clifford's squadron I thought. He's a good egg. No problems with him. Takes care of his men, we had heard. He had been a motor racing driver before the war and had won the Belgium Grand Prix. He always carried a picture of himself, all garlanded receiving the winner's trophy as he sat in the driving seat of his racing car. He even had this picture in his tank. He got the name 'Stiffy' as he had been severely injured whilst racing and one of his arms was shorter and stiffer than the other.

My first impressions of our squadron were that all the tanks had spare tank tracks welded on the front and on the turrets for extra protection. The men seemed several years older than me but very kind and friendly.

Next day we were ordered to advance. Then it was a case of stopping and starting and not seeing very much at all. We stopped at one point, turret down, which means we were half-hidden, and there I was told to fire some shells on the fringe of a wood as the infantry, the 15th Scottish Division as I remember, were going to clear out the enemy. I think I fired half a dozen shots, which landed on the right spot, much to my relief, as this was dead serious business at last and no more room for larking about. The tank commander seemed pleased with my aiming and said:

"You'll do. You will get a chance to drive this thing soon"

After our action and towards nightfall, we were pulled out of the line and took up a safer position in the rear of the infantry, whose job it was to protect us, as we were all sitting ducks at night. We also posted sentries around our vehicles. After a bit more excitement, my tank commander said:

"How old are you, Fear? Come on now, the truth. You look like a school boy, no more than 16"

"Come off it Sergeant, I'm nearly 18", I replied.

"I thought so." Next day, 'Stiffy' Clifford sent for me.

"Stand easy" was his first remark. "Your sergeant tells me you aren't old enough to be out here. It is a court-martial offence to tell lies about your age. Did you know that, Fear?"

"No Sir, I didn't, but I've done my training like everyone else and I am a good soldier"

"There's no doubt about that" he replied, "But I don't want your blood on my hands if anything was to happen to you. How do I explain things in my letter to your parents? I'm always having to write these sad letters when one of our lads gets killed. I've just finished one now. I'll tell you what I am going to do. I won't send you back to Blighty as I should, but I'm going to return you to FDS for a while and when things have quietened down a bit you will be called back. Your sergeant said you're a good gunner and that's good enough for me. Oh, Fear - I hear you're a good miler; we will need you after the war. The battalion champion is a Guardsman Barge from HQ Squadron. He has been champion for years. It would be nice for our squadron if you could beat him."

"Thank you, Sir. I'll do my best when the time comes."

And so I reluctantly returned to the FDS. Who knows, this might have saved my life or serious injury. Someone must have forgotten my age for soon after I rejoined No.2 Squadron for the final advance to the Baltic. Our squadron finished up at Plon, very near Lubeck, and it was there we celebrated the end of the war.

It is sad to relate that we lost Lieutenant Minnette Lucas just before the end. He had been with us at the Guards Depot and had always been a regular gentleman.

On the eve of V.E. Day, I accompanied my old pal Francis into the woods looking for something to eat for a celebration dinner. Suddenly, several Germans leapt out of a ditch only a few yards in front of us. I quickly threw up my arms in surrender and noticed my comrade had very sensibly done likewise. We then beheld that the six Huns were also standing with their arms up in surrender. What a relief! We did look a comical lot, but this called for action. Feeling very brave, we quickly disarmed the Germans who readily gave us their weapons. We understood they had deserted from the Russian front not far away, hoping to get better treatment from the Tommies. However, I wonder if they made the right decision for we finished up with four rifles, two machine guns, three pistols, six watches, four fountain pens, and a pair of Zeiss binoculars. We also refused to take them prisoners as we were too busy hunting.

Francis did bag some game and we celebrated victory the next day with an excellent table and plenty of hooch from displaced persons who seemingly all had their own stills. I often wonder what happened to the six Jerries and still laugh when my children ask 'What did you do in the war, Daddy?'

A couple of days later I happened to be in our guardroom when these six same Germans were brought in. One of them sidled over to me and, grasping my arm, begged for the return of his wedding ring I had ''alf-inched' when we first met. He went on to say that his wife had been killed in an RAF raid on Hamburg. The ring was the only memory he had of her as all else had been destroyed in the raid. Being a right old softy at heart, I hastened to my billet and collected the ring. I returned to the guardroom and returned it to its rightful owner. I shall never forget the look of gratitude in his eyes and he clung to my outstretched hand and kissed it murmuring something in German. I had hoped my comrades had not seen my actions, as I didn't want to be labelled soft-hearted.

Our first duties after the end of hostilities were to do guard duty at Kiel. We had to guard a large warehouse that contained the personal effects of the German U-Boat crews; kitbags and suitcases galore. It didn't take us guardsmen long to discover that these personal belongings contained loot that the Germany crews had nicked from the unfortunate sailors of the ships they had sunk or captured during the Battle of the Atlantic. We were warned by the guard commander not to tamper with these kitbags. But, of course, these orders fell on deaf ears and we plundered whatever we could smuggle inside our greatcoats. Coming off guard, I sometimes looked like Humpty Dumpty. The sergeant of the guard, in most cases, overlooked our thieving ways as long as we gave him a cut; a watch or a pair of binoculars. With my pawnbroking experience, I could see a lot of money could be made with our ill-gotten gains.

Unfortunately, our stay in Kiel was not to last and we drove our tanks from northern Germany down to the Köln area. Our squadron was stationed at Blankenheimerdorf, a small country village. Our quartermaster took over the main street's houses to billet us. God knows where the householders went, but there was no complaint from the civilians.

We had been warned that the Nazis would form legions called Werewolves and give us a rough time. Not so. In all my experience during the time after the war, we never encountered any unrest or anti-allies. They were truly beaten and as we arrived, the inhabitants all hung white sheets from their windows in total surrender. I could hardly believe that such a warlike nation as Germany could be tamed so quickly. In fact, it was quite nauseating to see how some of the men cringed and begged for favours. At first, Montgomery issued orders that we were not allowed to fraternise with the enemy. This was totally unacceptable to us, as our older soldiers were keen to sample the local girls who, in turn, were keen - for a few fags, a bar of chocolate or soap - to grant them these favours. Coffee was at a premium at the time and it didn't take us long to get cart loads of it sent to us from Great Britain. But more about our 'Black Market' deals later.

While we were in the Rhine area we held our Battalion's Athletics Championships in an ex SS Barracks called Vogelsang. It had a magnificent sports arena with the then up-to-date cinder track. Our squadron's team captain was Sergeant Coward, a lean, hungry looking man from Liverpool. We started training about 2 weeks before the event and trials were held in the different events. It soon became quite clear that we had a very strong team in all the track events and also some good field eventers.

Come the big day, Sergeant Coward took me aside to discuss how to beat the Mile Champion, GDSM Barge.

"He will take the lead from the start, if I know him," said Coward. "This is what I want you to do. We will stay with him if possible and then on the last bend I want you to race to the front and go hell for leather for the finishing line. He will be taken by surprise by you, the dark horse in the race. Let's face it, nobody has ever heard of you yet. Then I will overtake you both and win. You will be second and you will have sacrificed winning with our tactics, but I'll let it be known all round what we have planned."

"Okay Sergeant,", I said. "I'll be very pleased if I can come second and I've still got a chance in the 5,000 metres."

To this day, I think I could have won the race by not attacking until the last 50 metres, but I did what I was told and on the home turn, Coward yelled out: "Now" and off I went and took GDSM Barge by surprise. He raced after me and blew his chances of winning. There was only 5 yards between us at the end and the roar that went up from the large crowd could be heard at HQ five miles away. The company commander rushed over to us and congratulated us most profusely.

"You'll go on the next corporal's course." he said to me. "And you can have a couple of weeks at the rest camp."

"Thank you, Sir." I replied and I thought to myself, 'Rest camp, yes, but corporal courses, not on your Nellie.'

The squadron won the competition with Sergeant Astal winning the 100 and 200 metres and I did win the 5,000 metres. However, the Mile was the blue ribbon of the event. The Rest Camp, as it was called, turned out to be a large shooting lodge belonging to Herman Goering, the head of the Luftwaffe, who was safely tucked up in jail.

It was a splendid house that was run by a sergeant and a couple of guardsmen from HQ squadron. It was run like a country hotel and there was a maximum of ten guests at a time. I acquired a beautiful shotgun inlaid with mother of pearl and I would go out alone in the forest, which was stocked with deer and boars. I have a photo of myself with a young deer - my first kill - and I must admit I felt very uneasy to have killed such a beautiful animal. I made up my mind not to shoot deer again and, although I saw plenty of boars, I was unable to bring one down. They were very crafty and I am sure their thick hides protected them from the pellets of a shotgun. To hit them with a 303 was also very difficult because of the speed they ran.

Whilst I was there, I purloined a beautiful banqueting tablecloth, handmade in linen and sewn together in patches of red and white. We still use it at home on special occasions. The shotgun I lost in a game of cards. What would Goring's shotgun fetch today?

At about this time we had to take our tanks back up to Kiel and revert back to Infantry. So now we were No.2 Company 4th Battalion Grenadier Guards. We held a special parade to mark this occasion; a large field was quickly turned into a parade ground where all our tanks were lined up. We drove them in review order over some nearby hills and disappeared from sight of the general assembly on the parade ground. We got out of our tanks and formed up with our rifles, clad in our normal infantry uniforms. To the music of the Regiment's pipes and drums, we marched back to the parade ground to the tune of Auld Lang Syne. All very original. Many were sad at the loss of their tanks. Not me. Less work and only yourself to look after.

On September 7th 1945, a victory parade was held in Berlin with all the allied forces taking part. It was a great occasion with thousands of Berliners lining the route. In his book 'Reminiscences and Reflections', Marshall G. Zhukov, the Russian commander of the parade remarked 'The British Guards were the best drilled on parade.'.

We, at a later date, held a Brigade of Guards' Drill Competition. To find a squad to represent each Battalion we held an inter-company drill competition. Company Sergeant Major Burden had gone and we now had 'Titch' Amour as CSM. He, like RSM Spratley, had joined as a drummer boy, but unlike Spratley, had never made the full height of a guardsman, hence his nickname 'Titch'. Because of my running activity, he loved me, never found fault and certainly never ever gave me unpleasant tasks or put me in the book. He also 'saved my bacon' on several occasions. Under his word of command, we won the

Battalion Drill Competition, so now we had to compete against the other four companies of the brigade. In the end, it was between a company of the First Irish Guards and us.

Unfortunately, to the total dismay of all the officers in the 4th Battalion, poor old Amour gave the command halt on the wrong foot, which caused a slight check in the proceedings and didn't go unnoticed with the judges. So we came second and Amour was 'sent to Coventry' which, for the benefit of the younger reader means that he was boycotted by everyone. At the first occasion I had a moment with the CSM, I told him it wasn't his fault and anyone could have made such a slight error (creep, creep!)

"Thank you, Fear, I won't forget what you have said."

His brother NCOs were not so kind as I, and one evening when they were having their nightly piss-up in the sergeants' mess, which happened to be on the first floor of a convent, four sergeants got hold of poor old Amour and one, two, three, flung him off the veranda into the rose bed below. Being paralytic drunk, the fall didn't hurt him physically and I understand he was left there to sleep it off all night. He was a tough old soldier and was on first parade next day as if nothing unusual had happened.

The fraternising ban had been lifted and we were allowed to mix with the Germans. We had an official interpreter named Herr Brunes. He was a skinny old man of 70 years and could speak very good English. He gave our company German lessons, which I attended. I can hear him now.

"Not isht Mr. Fear, Issssssht!"

He was an ex-Nazi all right and hated the Poles and other displaced persons. He asked me about my love life and when I told him I was going with Yadska, a beautiful Polish blonde, he was very upset.

"Why go with a Polski when there are so many lovely German girls who would love to have such a handsome Englander. Vot vil your Mutte say if she knew?" he enquired.

Yadska had been a maid, forced labour, for a rich German family. They had treated her well and she lived with her equally beautiful sister in a small lodge. I had my first sexual experiences with her and although she said she loved me, I could never get her drawers off. Try as I may, she had a grip of steel in both her arms and thighs. At this time, I, with Ginger Smith, had met a couple of Belgium girls who had also been torn from their homes and forced to work for little pay in a German factory. They were a laugh when we first met them in a café and it wasn't until we made love that I discovered my girlfriend had a club foot. I first caught sight of it when I was on top and she threw up her legs in ecstasy. I assure you that when I spied this out of the corner of my eye, my dongleberry fell out of the Promised Land. Her disability didn't interfere with her love making. In fact, I fancy that because of her deformity she was over-eager to please. For a laugh, one evening, I put a couple of marbles in the end of my 'French Letter' (condom) and after the act was over, I withdrew and held it up for her to see.

"Feel this," I said. "I am a Superman"

She laughed for a long time and shouted out to her friend busily entertaining Smithy. They weren't far away in a different part of this bombed out house we had taken over for our love making.

One evening the sergeant of the guard came to me and said:

"There's a girl at the gate wants to see you."

I followed him back to the guards' room and from a distance, I could see a very finely dressed lady. Magda, I thought. How did she know I was at Euskirchen? I had a date that night with 'Club Foot', so I didn't want my plans upset by Magda who had travelled from Bensburg near Köln just to see me. The Sergeant must have told her he had delivered her message for she stood there a long time.

Then came zero hour when I was supposed to meet my Belgium girl. How to get past Magda standing opposite the guardroom? We all had to report to the guardroom before leaving barracks, a procedure carried out to this day. What to do? What to do? I asked for Smithy's help and when we got close to the guardroom, waited for a batch of guardsmen who were also hell-bent to meet their women.

About 50 yards from the gate, I turned round and walked backwards, guarded by Ginger Smith. The ploy worked for I got out undiscovered by Magda. Ginger and I made our way to the café where our girls were waiting. We had a few drinks and a laugh when, some two hours later, the cafe door opened and there was the lovely Magda. She looked quite angry and beckoned me to come outside. I made some excuse and hastened to the door. In the street outside, she flew at me.

"How could you treat me like this? I have travelled many kilometres to be with you and have booked us into a hotel in the town. There you are with those scum. Slaves! How could you?"

I murmured some excuse, took a packet of cigarettes from my pocket, and offered them to her as a peace offering. She snatched them from my grasp, threw them on the pavement, and jumped on them smashing them into the ground.

"Keep your f--king cigarettes" she shouted and disappeared into the darkness.

I often wonder what might have been as she was a bit of class and came from a wealthy family. But like all other Germans, she had been brought down to one level. I had met her only a couple of times in Köln. It was she who had said to me:

"You have never been with a woman have you? I will teach you, but not tonight. Ich bin krank."

I never saw her again, as with no notice we moved on. It seems she was rather keen to 'teach me', for to come so many kilometres in those days was some ordeal.

One day we had to pass through a small town, or rather, what was left of a town called Durn. It was one big pile of rubble covering the whole area of the town. Seemingly, just before the end of the war, it sustained a 1,000 bomber raid by the Yanks. The Germans had been putting up some fierce resistance in the area so in went the bombers. What stuck in my mind was the number of wreaths and floral contributions covering the rubble. Many old men and women were everywhere rooting in the bombed out buildings looking for what was left of their homes and, no doubt, in most cases, for loved ones buried in the rubble.

One day Amour sent for me.

"You ain't doing much duty Fear. I've a job for you. We have a new subaltern coming to our company and I am detailing you as his servant."

In the brigade of guards, the man who looks after an officer is referred to as a servant, unlike all other regiments where they are called 'batmen'.

"He will be a young officer, whose nappies are hardly dry. You can 'break him in'."

"I don't want to be a bloody servant!" I replied.

"He will pay you" he said.

"What do you mean?" I asked.

"Officers always pay their servants a wage on top of their guardsman's pay"

"That's different" I replied. "How much?"

"That's for you and him to discuss."

From the moment I met The Honourable Peter Hayes Fisher, he treated me as his superior, which was, of course, the case. We got on fine from the start. I cleaned his kit like my own and I set up his peak cap like an SS officer. I enjoyed turning him out as the smartest officer on parade and he appreciated this by paying me over the odds. On one occasion, he said there was a big officers' dance to be held in the best hotel in Euskirchen and asked if I would like to go in his place.

"You can borrow my uniform"

"I'll go if Ginger Smith can borrow Lieutenant Rolls' uniform and come with me"

"I'll do what I can." he said.

A bit later that day, Smithy and I got dressed in our bosses' uniforms. I stuck up my medal ribbons as Hayes Fisher had none, and I must say I looked the part. On the other hand, Smithy looked like a sack of potatoes tied in the middle and wouldn't have passed as a Chico, no how. So I decided to go alone. After fortifying myself with a couple of glasses of Schnapps, Hayes Fisher organised a jeep to take me to the hotel. Privates of some Scottish regiment were acting as waiters and one relieved me of my cap and cane on arrival. I didn't recognise anyone, so I drank as much as I could in a very short time and then decided to mix with members of a Scottish regiment.

I got on well with these officers and I am sure they were amazed that a guards' officer would lower himself to even talk to a member of the line. As I was a little apprehensive regarding my accent, or lack of it, I let it be known that I had risen in the ranks because of my athletic prowess. We all got plastered and later on, I spied some of our battalion officers eyeing me from a distance. Feeling very brave, I thought the best policy was attack. So I went over to them, stood to attention, and said:

"How do I look?" They all laughed and agreed not to report me to HQ.

"You'll only be getting your old friend into trouble." I said.

"You will set our caps up for us won't you, Fear?" A couple of them said. I got the message.

The do was okay, but not in the same class as our own Guardsmen's company do's, which we held in the 'Café in de Veldt', a large cafe with a dance floor situated in the middle. We were billeted in a convent in a village called Rheinbach. It had its own train station and we would get into the centre of Hamburg in about half an hour.

Our Battalion's duties there were to guard a former death camp called Neuengamme, where we could see for ourselves the atrocities that had been committed by the Nazis. The gas chambers bore obvious signs of where the terrified inmates had tried to claw their way out through the concrete walls. The small holes in the roof of these tombs were where the cyanide capsules were dispensed. Neuengamme was one of the original death camps where the ovens could only dispose of one body at a time. The pile of worn out shoes and boots was at least twenty metres high. The German officers now interned there were forced to view their leader's abominable handiwork. It housed several thousand German officers of the Navy, Army, and Air Force. They had all been imprisoned and awaited to be interviewed in the Denazification Courts to see if they had carried out any war crimes. Our routine was to do a 24-hour guard, one day free of all duties and one day escort duty.

The guard duty was the worst as you did 2 hours on, 4 hours off, which meant you did 4 turns on-guard up in a watchtower making sure the prisoners didn't try to escape. There was a 3-metre electric fence, then a pathway and then a canal, which ran all around the camp. In daylight, sentries patrolled between each watchtower. At night, there were searchlights but no patrolling, only sentries in the watchtowers. Our days off followed the guard duty, but even so you had to be careful as the sergeant in waiting (duty sergeant for one week), might descend upon your room and send you off on some menial task; cookhouse fatigue, scrubbing this or that, sweeping up leaves, etc. I always had my answer when I was approached, 'I am training today, Sergeant. You can check with Lieutenant Naylor Leyland'. Training meant a short run and an early train to Hamburg.

The escort duty consisted of two guardsmen taking a batch of about 24 prisoners out to the fields for weeding, potato picking, and other simple agricultural tasks.

The camp was run by the Educational Corp. and it was they that handed the prisoners over to us at about 9 am. As many of the corp. were Jews they gave the prisoners a rough time, unlike us who just wanted a quiet life. The squad would line up and the senior officer amongst them would then salute us and order his squad 'Quick march'. They were very smart and reacted to their leader's orders promptly. One of us guardsmen would march in line with the right-hand officer and the other would bring up the rear. We would march a couple of miles or so to our appointed field where we would decide which was the best spot for us to be out of sight of any unfriendly eyes. There the prisoners would go to work. We would say to them that we wanted to sunbathe and so let us know if anyone approached.

I remember once an officer coming to us as we were sunbathing. He saluted and apologised for disturbing us, but he asked if one of his men could go to the village to the local café to fetch a bucket of beer. We readily agreed - if we could have a drink ourselves. Later, when he returned with the bucket full of beer, we called a halt for lunch. We had our haversack rations and they had some black bread and sausage. They didn't take any notice of us and seemed quite happy, No doubt they all had clear consciences and were just waiting their turn to be interrogated and cleared. Before we returned in the evening, they asked if they could smuggle some potatoes back to camp. We had no objections and they put small ones down their trousers. Their leggings stopped the fruit from dropping out.

When we got to within about ¼ mile from camp, and out of sight of the guardroom, the squad leader would always order 'Halt'. He would then turn to us and say:

"We would like to thank you two soldiers for your kindness and hope to get you again in three days time."

As we approached the guardroom, we two guardsmen changed our attitude and started bawling orders to our squad. This pleased the camp commanders, they counted our contingent, we signed something, the prisoners went to their huts and we awaited the truck that would take us back to Rheinbach.

When I was on night guard, I always felt very weary and thought 'Up half the night for 21/- a week don't seem right somehow'. When all was clear, I would lie down flat on my back and have 40 winks. After a few times I trained myself to sleep for just half an hour. I would awake spot on time, have a look round, and then back on the floor for another nap. I would take a small piece of material to fold up and make myself a small pillow. The floor was of wood and always dry and when I totally relaxed it didn't seem too hard, and anything was better than standing up gazing on the empty compound. This went on for several months and I told my secret to no-one.

I was on 2 am to 4 am guard one night and awoke a few minutes before the sergeant would bring my relief round to take over from me. Fortunately, I looked down in front of the tower and, to my horror, I saw in the half-light a pile of earth had been heaped up on both sides of the electric fence, which was about 4 foot wide. At the bottom a tunnel was quite visible from where I stood. 'Good God, some of the prisoners have been busy and dug their way out', I thought.

As the relief approached, I clambered down the ladder as quickly as I could and placed myself in front of the pile of earth. The sergeant gave me a bollocking for leaving my post before he arrived and I made some feeble excuse that I didn't want to keep him waiting. Jack Furness, a giant of a man, took over from me and climbed up to the watchtower as we made our way back to the guardroom, relieving two other sentries on the way. I had a mug of tea and threw myself on my bunk and quickly fell asleep. I was awoken by an uproar sometime later when the sergeant came into the guardroom accompanied by Jack Furness, who seemingly was taken to HQ Company under close arrest.

Next morning, when the usual roll was called on the prisoners, it was reported that thirty prisoners were missing. A search of the camp was made and the commander came up with the same answer - thirty prisoners missing. This is what had apparently happened. Some of the Germans who had nothing better to do, must have observed the sentries and their habits and came up with the following observation: 'Watch that little fellow with the black moustache. He goes up to his box, looks around for a few minutes, and then disappears. I'll bet he goes to sleep'. As indeed I did. Perhaps they tried me out on occasions and approached the wire to see what my reaction would be. It must have been after a few rehearsals that they decided to make a break, as I never reprimanded them for approaching the wire, being fast asleep.

No doubt, the thirty prisoners who escaped were wanted criminals with bad records who were desperate to be free before their turn came for interrogation. As for Jack Furness, we heard no more about him or the outcome of the break out. HQ was miles away and we guardsmen had no contact with them, nor did we hear what happened to Jack. I was never questioned about the incident. It never occurred to me to own up and say the tunnel was dug when I was on duty and not when Furness was on. Nothing was said and at the time, I knew nothing of his fate. I quickly forgot the incident but was more careful with the length of time I spent sleeping on guard.

We were not allowed to talk to the prisoners but some would approach the wire and collect dandelion leaves to subsidise their miserable diet. I had no objections to this, although some of the guards were stricter. One day a Kreig marine officer asked me if I would like a watch. He handed me a very nice waterproof 17-jewel Swiss watch. At this point, I could have told him to piss off and kept his watch without payment and there was nothing he could have done about it. Instead, I asked him the same old question.

"How about 4 oz. of tobacco?" he said

"I've only got 2 oz. with me but I'll give you 100 cigs. when I come on duty in 3 days."

"Okay" he said and took the packet of tobacco. I was about to hand him back his watch when he said "No, you keep it. I'll see you in 3 days."

It's quite remarkable that we former enemies trusted each other implicitly. I had no need to take him the 100 fags next time I was on guard, but I didn't hesitate and as arranged he came over to me 3 days later and I handed him the fags.

"Danke schön" he smiled and said. "I knew you were honest and I'll bring you some of my comrades' watches in the future. Same price if that's okay with you?"

"The tobacco is hard to come by but I can give you 200 fags for a good watch." I replied. And so became a profitable sideline as I made a small profit from the Germans and always told my comrades 300 for a watch. So, for every three watches I gained one for me. Some of the lads tried to muscle in on my contact but the German officer said:

"I will only deal with Guardsman Fear"

At about this time we heard stories about a Guardsman Siddall from No.1 Company. He was a Brahma and lead the NCOs a merry dance. Once, while on Neuengamme guard, he threw one of the sentry boxes into the canal, clambered in, took off his jacket, and using his rifle as a paddle, manoeuvred his canoe through the water. The German prisoners gathered around in their hundreds to view this very unusual happening by a member of Britain's foremost regiment.

The sergeant of the guard, knowing he wouldn't be able to handle the situation, telephoned HQ and very soon Drill Sergeant Harry Muckett appeared. He hurried to where Siddall was performing and before he could say anything, Jimmy bawled out:

"Hi Harry, come to join me have you? Just like Blackpool. It's lovely!"

Poor old Harry finally got the sentry box and its occupant back on dry land. Jim was placed in close arrest and finally received 14 day CB, a punishment he was quite familiar with.

Some time later on a very hot day, Siddall was up in the tower and getting hotter by the minute. Now, in our regiment you always had to wear a jacket whilst on duty. The exception is when the CO announces 'Short sleeve order', which means no jacket, but you have to roll your shirt-sleeves up very smartly and both the same length of course, and his order applies to everyone in the battalion.

Half way through his term of duty, Siddall decided enough is enough and telephoned the guardroom and asked to be put through to the commanding officer, Peggy Brownlow. Finally, he got through to HQ.

"I want to speak to the commanding officer." Jim said.

"This is the adjutant speaking, what do you want?"

"Are you deaf Sir? I want to speak to the commanding officer." was Jim's reply.

"Who's speaking?" asked the Major.

"Never you mind." said Jim.

"This is the commanding officer speaking, what is it?"

"I am Guardsman Siddall, Sir. I am stuck up here in one of those stupid watchtowers and I am f--king hot. When are you going to pull your finger out and order shirt-sleeve order, Sir?"

"Oh, I am sorry Siddall, quite forgot. I'll give the order straight away. You won't be put in the book, it's my fault."

"Thank you, Sir. Oh yes, if you fancy a little boating, I can fix you up"

"Another time." replied the bemused officer.

These happenings spread round the battalion and Siddall was treated with great awe. He had a pal called Cardwell and the pair gave their company a hell of a time. Thinking it better if they were split up, Jim was transferred to our company where some of us welcomed him with open arms. On his first drill parade, in his new company, he went on parade with one highly polished boot and the other covered in dry clay. The inspecting officer and CSM were flabbergasted.

"What's the meaning of this behaviour?" they enquired.

"I thank you, Sir, for leave to speak"

"Yes, carry on"

"One's to show you I can do it and one's to show you I f--king-well won't." We all laughed aloud and Jim was rushed to the guardroom. Next day he got his usual 14 days CB.

Once a week on a Saturday morning, when the whole battalion would parade together, we had commanding officer's inspection. On one occasion, the night before, Jim was busy spitting a ping-pong ball out of his mouth - he got quite expert and could launch it several yards.

"What are you up to Jim?" I enquired.

"You'll see tomorrow." he said. And this is what happened:

We were all formed up on the square and the inspection by the CO and his entourage began. When the CO came in front of Siddall and while his eyes were fixed on Jim's boots, he spat the ping-pong ball straight at the CO. I was standing two places from Jim and saw exactly what happened. The ball struck the CO on the chest and bounced on to the square. He looked down then up then down again, quite bewildered.

"What's going on?" he demanded from RSM Spratley.

"Don't know Sir," was his reply. "But I will find out" and the inspection continued. We heard no more about it and it's my belief that Spratley had an idea where the ping pong ball came from but knew he would be wasting his time if he questioned his suspect.

In the summer of 1946, our battalion went to Krefelt, the Germans' biggest army camp, comparable to our Aldershot. We were encamped under canvass on a large airfield. I cannot remember much about our duties, but I remember some of our pastimes. One evening our little gang of Small, Murphy, Webster, Stevenson, Vanbruggan, Grey, Arnold and Fear, sat and played a game called 'Shitty-Shankers'. It would take too long to explain the rules, but all I remember was we consumed large quantities of ale and after our game decided to play cowboys and Indians. The four smallest guardsmen got on the backs of the big boys. Sam Small was my horse.

The rest of the company came out of their tents to see what the uproar was about. Someone suggested we attack the company sergeant major's tent where poor old Amour resided. So we went to our tents and got 3 rifles and a Bren-gun, which I had, and loaded up and remounted our gallant steeds. We sent off in the direction of Amour. At this point he appeared, probably pissed as well, but he shouted at us to go to bed as lights out had been blown a couple of hours earlier. Someone suggested we gave him a few shots and we didn't need any second bidding. In near darkness I let off a burst with the Bren gun in his direction.

When you think about it, it was a very stupid, dangerous thing to do, but under the influence, one does stupid things. Seemingly, Amour took off somewhere and we returned to our tents. Next morning on breakfast parade, Amour was there, smart as paint. After his normal inspection, he remarked that last night certain guardsmen had tried to kill him and with a wry smile said:

"It will take more than you lot to get rid of me." He took no action against us and seemed to have enjoyed the incident as much as we had. A day or so later he took me to one side.

"I've heard you had the Bren-gun. You didn't really try to hit me did you?"

"Course not, Sir. It was all in good fun"

"You're getting into bad company Fear, watch yourself" And that was that.

Before our return to Rheinbach, we held a brigade sports meeting on our airfield. The day before the meeting was due to be held, the sergeant-in-waiting said:

"You're on guard tonight, Fear." I protested that I would be running in the sports next day and shouldn't have to go on guard. To which he replied:

"I'm afraid as your fairy Godmother is on leave, you are on guard." He was referring, of course, to CSM Amour who was indeed on leave. So I reluctantly had to do guard. Next morning I took to my bed, as was permitted after guard duty. At midday, our team captain called at my tent and said:

"Come on Fear, get your things together for the sports"

"I am not running." I replied.

"What was that?"

"I am not running. I've just come off guard"

"That's no excuse," he said.

"I told the sergeant in waiting, I would not run if I were put on guard." I said. He took no notice and disappeared, and I continued to sleep. Next thing I know, our company commander was standing beside my bed.

"What's all this I hear about you not running, Fear?" I told him the facts and he said: "Come along now, the battalion is relying on you in the 1,500 metres" (Both Barge and Coward had been demobbed). Then I hit on an idea.

"I'll run, Sir, if you get four guardsmen to carry me to the start on my bed."

"You are bloody mad Fear. Granted."

And so I warmed up a bit then I got changed and wore a turban made out of my towel and I must admit, brown as a berry, thin as a lath and with the turban set squarely on my head, I looked for all the world like Sabu the elephant boy. There were plenty of volunteers to carry my bed and as zero hour approached, they lifted me up and carried me from my tent across the airfield to the start line of the 1,500 metres.

As this was an open meeting, there were competitors from every branch of the BAOR (British Army of the Rhine). I was told by the team captain that an MP Sergeant was my biggest threat, and so he was. In the last 100 metres, we ran neck and neck and it was declared a dead heat. I thought I had just won and so did our company commander, who lodged a complaint. We all went into the judge's tent and to everyone's surprise the MP Sergeant said:

"Fear won by a whisker!" I could hardly believe my ears - and from our archenemies the Military Police. I won a small silver cup for my efforts and was very popular with the lads.

The members of our team were invited to the sergeants' mess, a large tent set up in our company lines. We soon got stuck into the free drink and I spied the sergeant in waiting, who had just finished his spell of duty. We hit on a plan. I got a pint of beer, emptied some on the grass, and topped it up again with pee. A couple of lads spit into the froth and a little cigarette ash was added for flavour. I then approached the sergeant and said:

"Here Sergeant, have a pint on me." He put down his pint, took the one I held and drank a third of it in one go.

"You see Fear, me putting you on guard made you run faster." 'Ha-ha', I thought to myself, 'you lousy bastard, I'll have a word with Amour about you when he returns from leave.

I went back to my friends and we had a good laugh. The cocktail didn't affect the sergeant, but I always thought he was a piss head. Eventually, CSM Amour said to me:

"You did well beating that MP. I've heard all about your antics" I told him about having been put on guard the night before.

"Don't worry," he said. "Won't happen again and I'll fix his duff." Which means 'I'll get even with him, extra duties and such.'

I would visit Hamburg as often as possible with Siddall or Stevenson. Steve was a Sherman tank driver in our 2nd Battalion. He had been a coal miner from Bolsover Derbyshire. He was an excellent swimmer and had a well-developed body. Although in his early twenties, he had a complete set of false teeth, which came in very handy, as you will hear later.

Hamburg had been one of bomber command's main targets during the war and in the course of two days, it sustained three 1,000 bomber raids. In the early raid, many of the bombs were incendiary, which, with the help of the hot dry weather, set the place ablaze. In fact, it caused a firestorm that swept through the city like a hurricane. Many of the residents made for the Alster River, but at points, the water boiled. Thousands of civilians died from asphyxiation. Consequently, as you approached Hamburg, it appeared intact, but when you got inside the city, many of the houses were still standing but burned out. So now, in 1946 nearly everyone lived in cellars.

Our first port of call was to Black Market Alley, where the local inhabitants and spivs gathered ready and willing to sell all manner of

108

merchandise for coffee, cigarettes, tobacco, soap, and chocolate. Money was of no value and one could get a good watch for 200 fags. The British Army were given a ration of cigs. a week and for the non-smokers, this was very fortunate. Many of the non-smokers in our company didn't bother to do black market deals so I soon sorted them out and bought their ration of cigs. for English money, which I had sent from home. I also got Mother to send an endless supply of coffee as it became available to her. I did some good deals in Black Market Alley and my Post Office savings account grew substantially.

I was about to catch the tram to the station one evening, when it started to rain. At the tram stop were two girls sheltering under a large umbrella, Steve and I muscled underneath with them and at that moment started my first real love story. Two lovely faces confronted me. I introduced us as Steve and Raymond Charles Sebastian Gigor. They could speak English very well and said their names were Erica and Sonja. I only had eyes for Sonja and as she related later, she fell for me there and then. We told them we were waiting for a tram to the station and they were awaiting a tram to a different part of town.

"Can we see you again in 3 days?" I asked, and they agreed. "At the station, we will be on the train from Rheinbach which gets in about 7.30 pm."

"We will be there." they said. Our tram arrived and we bid them goodnight. I could think of nothing else for the next 3 days. Would she turn up? Why didn't I miss my tram and stay with her a few more hours and get to know her more. Her face haunted me for 3 days and I kept wondering. Will she, won't she. I didn't have the sense to ask her for her address. What a fool I am. Steve was no help and said that she probably had a boyfriend and certainly wouldn't bother to keep our date.

Come the evening I asked Steve if he would be coming to Hamburg.

"What for?" he asked, "There's a dance at the Café in the Wood, I'm going there."

"I'll go on my own." I replied.

The train seemed to take hours to reach Hamburg, but when it did all my fears were gone, for there standing waiting alone was Sonja. I hastened to her and we shook hands. I remember the handshake to this day, for I was unable to release her hand. I explained that Steve had to do extra duty and was very sorry he couldn't keep the appointment. Sonja was more honest and said Erica had said 'Don't bother, they won't turn up.'

"What shall we do? ", I asked.

"I know a nice cafe where they have a small orchestra playing" she replied, and that's where we spent the evening. We were both 19 years old and I fell in love with her that very evening.

She was tall with lovely chestnut hair and blue eyes. She dressed very smartly and wore knee length jackboots. Very fashionable in Germany in those days. She worked in a government office somewhere. She lived with her mother and father in a cellar of their bombed-out house. She had a brother who had served in the SS. He was a tall, very smart, good-looking chap who had been wounded twice on the Russian front. He had been an infantryman, not a member of the infamous Internment Camp Guards. We only met a couple of times, but I think we liked each other.

Sonja's dad had been in the fire service and was 2nd in command of Hamburg's fire brigade during the bombing. I would have thought he had good reason to hate me and forbid his daughter from associating with the people who had destroyed his city. On the contrary, he was very polite and he quoted something from Shakespeare.

"Sir Walter Raleigh had bought tobacco to Europe." This was the extent of his English. Her mother was very kind and somehow always managed to knock up a few cakes when I visited them.

We used to frequent the café a lot and go to the theatre, which had miraculously been undamaged during the raids. ENSA put on shows nightly for the British servicemen who could take their partners without any problems. We would find a doorway after the show where we could kiss and say goodnight. We said we loved each other and would marry one day. Then, like all servicemen, we were on the move again, this time into barracks at Neumunster, which was some way from Hamburg. At the time, it was very difficult to get from Hamburg to Neumunster. We were very sad when I told her the news.

"I'll come over at weekends," she said "and I'll write to you every day." she added. So, the first weekend, the sergeant of the guard called in my room.

"There's a girl at the gate asking for you. You haven't wasted much time getting fixed up," he said. "We have only been here 3 days."

"No, she's come from Hamburg." I said. I rushed to the guardroom and there she was, as radiant as ever.

"I've booked us into the little hotel in the centre of the town." She explained where I must meet her when I was allowed out after our tea at 5 pm.

Now we were back in barracks, the whole battalion ate in one large mess-room. After our dinner that day, I collected leftovers from the meat dishes and at tea I managed to get a few slices of bread and butter. I packed this carefully in my mess tin and hastened to the little hotel she had outlined to me. I waited outside for a few moments, being too nervous to enter. She came out and led me to reception where a very understanding landlady shook my hand. Sonja said she had ordered some soup and a couple of glasses.

We made our way to the small bedroom she had booked for the night. It was comfortable, with table and chairs. I set out the bits and pieces I had collared from the mess room, plus a bottle of Mosel wine. A little later, the hotelier brought us an urn of boiling hot soup with soup plates and spoons. After seeing the meat and bread, she asked if we would like knives and forks.

"Yes please" I replied. She apologised that the soup was the only food she could offer.

"It's cabbage and potatoes, a bit thin as we have nothing to thicken it with" she explained. We enjoyed our simple fare and Sonja said she had never tasted such lovely bread.

After dinner, we lay on the bed. I was most apprehensive and had been on tenterhooks since I learned she had booked the hotel for the night. I had never been to bed with a woman before and I must admit I felt very uneasy. To cut a long story short, I didn't get a perk on and jokingly said I had been wounded in the war in my private parts. I told her, as I had to be back in Barracks by midnight, I had better be going. She seemed a bit crest fallen and begged me to stay.

"Next week I'll sort things out," I said "And I'll be able to meet you here at noon. I'll miss dinner and tea, but I'll bring as much food for us as I can scrounge." We kissed and parted.

I had a couple of wanks during the week to confirm that my dongle was in working order and by Sunday had accumulated a load of scoff. I asked a new lad who had joined the company, and who I took a liking to, if he would book me in at the guardroom at about 11.55.

"You betcha, Charlie" replied Jimmy Fanning from Bethnal Green. He was my height with jet-black hair and a faced chiselled out of granite. He was quite fearless and I noticed the NCOs treated him with great respect.

I met Sonja at midday. I had received a couple of letters from her during the week. Neither had mentioned my inability to get the horn. Over dinner she asked me straight out if I had been wounded during the war.

"It's all I have thought about all the week. I haven't been able to think straight."

I laughed and told her I had been joking. She was delighted and said all you have to do is relax and stop thinking about it. After lunch, she said:

"Take your clothes off and get into bed and have a sleep. I'll wash up and you just relax." I was glad of this suggestion as I had run 10 miles with the cross-country team that morning. As was my habit, I was soon asleep. The next thing I knew I was being caressed by Sonja who had joined me naked in bed. Needless to say, there were no more problems with my dongle and we made love from after nap time till 5.30 am next morning. I got back to barracks just before reveille and climbed the wall at a well camouflaged spot where no doubt the German army had scaled before me. At breakfast I sat next to Fanning who said he had no problem booking me in as he had never seen the sergeant of the guard before.

Sonja and I had several more of these glorious Sundays before it was announced that the Battalion was to return to England and be stationed at Chelsea Barracks. I was devastated at the news and when I told my beloved, she broke down and cried. Come our last Sunday together, it was heart breaking to say the least. I remember Sonja's Ma sending over a birthday cake for me, which we devoured during our last hours together. We lay awake all night swearing our undying love together. I would be demobbed, get a job and then send for her, and I really meant it at the time. We parted at 5.30 am and it was 50 years before I met and married a comparable woman.

As we parted at her bedroom door, another grenadier was bidding farewell to his frauline. We descended the stairs together and in the street took different paths back to the barracks. I never ever saw him again. I didn't see Sonja either for another 10 years, but more about that in a later chapter.

When the battalion gathered to embark for England, we were due to sail from Cuxhaven. As I have mentioned earlier, our 4th Battalion had disbanded and half of our company was now in the 1st and unknown in many respects. On the last 4th Battalion parade, we were inspected by some general or other. Before the parade, we had a company inspection. When the company commander and CSM Amour got to me, they agreed my hair was too long. And my cap?

"God help you!" they said. "You'll probably finish up inside." On the inspection, as the general approached, one had to bawl out:

"GDSM Brown, Sir." or "GDSM Small, Sir."

When I was confronted by the general and commanding officer, company commanders and RSM, I squealed out in the most ridiculous manner imaginable,

"GDSM Fear." and then I paused for several seconds before shrieking out: "Sir."

The general stopped in front of me, thinking this lad isn't going to say 'Sir'. But after I had finished screaming, he was still standing eyeing me up and down.

"A very well turned out soldier. Smartest on parade. Take his name." said the RSM and the duty sergeant put me in the book. 'Credit on General's inspection'.

Next day I was marched before the company commander and later the commanding officer, who both agreed I must take the tapes (be promoted to corporal), and I was excused guard duty for some time. My company commander, Major Wedderburn said:

"You seem to have set up all my officers' caps except mine. Get it organised with my servant and tell him how much, but keep it as cheap as possible. From what I hear, I am not as wealthy as you."

The next thing we knew, we were ordered to pack for our disembarkment from Cuxhaven. We arrived at the port but as the North Sea was very rough, our sailing was put back for several hours. Very unwisely, the commanding officer ordered that we could stack our kit and go into town for a few hours. I opened my kitbag and took out several packets of fags. We made our way to the centre of the town, which had had its share of bombing, but we found a large café with music playing. A waiter appeared and fags were put on the table.

"I've something special" he said as he pocketed the packs.

Special! It was some sort of Schnapps with a generous helping of gunpowder. It nearly blew our heads off. In those days, drinking was no problem. Everything went down my throat, no matter what. I was never legless, but I acted funnily, never aggressive, and always sick, which always helped next day, when I seldom got a headache. Wine followed the Schnapps and finally an NCO came into the café saying we were sailing in 2 hours, everyone back to the port.

Several NCOs had been sent out on this mission to round up the battalion. Accompanied by Sam Small, Steve and Fanning, we decided to break all the windows the RAF had missed. We also went into a club where they were playing snooker. Snatching the cues from the bewildered owners, we commenced playing baseball and Sam took a pot shot on the table, which he managed to rip wide open. At this point, we beat a hasty retreat, as the owners were getting a bit irate. We sang as we approached the docks and were approached by a couple of military policemen who seemingly wanted to put us under arrest. Knowing we would have the full support of our regimental officers, we told them to 'F--k off' and, in fact, I kicked one.

We caused an uproar when we got back to our company as we were late and very disorganised. Several NCOs came to view these drunks. Finally, I made my way up the gangplank and as everyone knows it can only take one person abreast at a time, half way up I decided to sit on my kitbag and sing 'Knees up Mother Brown'. Suddenly, Drill Sergeant Harry Muckett appeared at the bottom of the gangplank.

"What's your name?" He shouted up.

"Fear, and I ain't a-feared of you, Harry."

By this time, the whole battalion was viewing these goings-on with much amusement and finally I took up the kitbag and slowly ascended to the deck. After a few paces I spied an open door. It looked rather dark so I threw my rifle down and descended the steps. Next thing, Harry was peering down at me.

"You're under close arrest" he bellowed. "Come back up here."

"Put him in irons." he bellowed to the sergeant. But as there was no guardroom or jail aboard, I remained in open arrest until we reached England.

I can't remember where we landed, but we finished up in Chelsea Barracks where I was quickly put inside. I was surprised to learn that I was the only guardsman who had been locked up. As far as I was concerned everyone was pissed that night.

Chapter 6

Chelsea

As it happened, our old company commander had been transferred as company commander to my new company at Chelsea. Therefore, when I was marched before him he admitted he had enjoyed the show but that the commanding officer was expecting me, as it was a serious charge I faced.

"But I'll speak up for you, Fear, never fear" and he tittered at his own joke.

Later that morning I was up before the commanding officer of the 1st Battalion Grenadier Guards, Lieutenant Colonel Lort Phillips, who was then in command. When one is under close arrest, you are marched before the CO under escort, one guardsman in front, one behind. As you are ordered to march in by the drill sergeant, and before you enter the office, an orderly GDSM snatches off your headgear. Before I was marched in, old Harry Muckett came up to me and leered at me for a while then said:

"You'll be inside for a very long time."

The order 'Quick march' was given and we marched in single file. When the orderly snatched off my cap, I stopped in my tracks, took out my comb, and did my ruffled hair. In the meantime, the escort in front of me was making time in front of the CO and the five company commanders who stood in line behind his seat.

"Prisoner and escort halt" should have been the order given, but because of my grooming this was impossible. However, we were told to right turn and thereby I faced my judge. Harry read out the charge as follows:

"This guardsman was drunk and disorderly at the docks at Cuxhaven. He insulted every NCO who approached him. He kicked an MP and delayed the sailing by an hour. He was insubordinate to me." He took a deep breath and added "He lead half the Battalion down the coal 'ole, Sir."

At this point, all the company commanders were laughing into their handkerchiefs and even the CO had a smile on his face. I was gaining in confidence and poor Harry was getting more confused by the minute.

"What have you to say for yourself, Fear?"

"I thank you, Sir, for leave to speak"

"Stop talking" bellowed out Harry.

"I thank you, Sir, for leave to speak" I repeated.

"Stop talking" bellowed Harry a second time.

"Let him say his piece" announced the CO.

"It was my 21st birthday, Sir, and I went out and celebrated, Sir!"

"Very understandable," said he, "But your celebrations went a bit too far. I ask you, leading the battalion down the coal hole. We would have the miners on strike in no time."

He turned to my company commander and asked:

"How does this man do?"

"Fear was in my company in the 4th Battalion. I can't speak too highly of him and he received credit from the inspecting general only recently."

The CO sat quietly for some time, then announced:

"This is a very difficult case for me to judge. Bearing in mind what Major Wedderburn has said about you, you'll be fined 10/- and this means you won't ever get the Long Service Good Conduct medal."

At this point the drill sergeant asked:

"Fined 10/-, Sir. What do you mean?"

"Read your manual" said the CO.

"Prisoner and escort, right turn. Quick march and outside the office, halt."

Muckett came straight over to me, dismissed the escort, and stood alone with the prisoner.

"You think you're bloody funny don't you? You wait, I'll have you before long."

But he never did. It seems the CO had looked up rules and regulations before hearing my case and the fine was some law that had been passed in Field Marshall Lord Roberts day, instead of the usual flogging. It was a get-off for which I must thank my commanding officer.

At this time the dockers' were on strike and troops were called in to unload and carry out the normal dockers' duty. Early one morning the battalion was being allocated their jobs. I was detailed to work in the large walk-in refrigerator at Smithfield Market. We were all mustered on the square and our names called out for our appointed jobs. On this occasion Harry Muckett was senior NCO on parade, and when he called out my detail and shouted my name, he added:

"If you don't move faster in the freezers than you do on commanding officers' orders, you'll f--king well freeze to death."

I smiled and he smiled, and I thought 'You ain't a bad old sod after all' and I fancy, like all the senior NCOs, he had heard that Pa had been an RSM too and treated me with a certain amount of respect.

We travelled to Smithfield Market by tube each morning. We took our small packs, which contained our haversack rations and water bottle. Our detail soon learned the ropes and the most important one on how to steal the cheese, butter and bacon that was available by the ton. We learned to take a sharp knife to cut the goods into sizes to fit our small packs - usually about 4-5 lbs. Not having much experience of travelling on the London Underground with a block of butter, it never occurred to me that in the heat of the train the butter would melt, and that's exactly what it did on my first assignment. It was a mess when I got back to barracks, all runny and impossible to transfer it to my girlfriend's home. The cheese and bacon was fine to travel and eventually I transmitted the butter in old cocoa tins and jam jars.

You may wonder why we went to such trouble for a few dairy products, but Britain was still rationed and to think the ration of butter, cheese, and bacon was but two ounces per person, per week. Mum, Dad and brother Dan were overjoyed with the extra supplies, as indeed was my girlfriend, Eileen. I had met her in a Saturday night singsong in one of the London pubs. She had been keeping company with a Sergeant in HQ Company. When I first spied her, I nipped over to her and suggested we meet at the 'Bag of Nails' in Buckingham Palace Road the following night. These quick arrangements were made while her sergeant was relieving his bladder. Next evening I ponged up ready for the date, only half expecting her to turn up. But turn up she did and there began a very nice, friendly relationship which lasted until I was demobbed.

She was ten years my senior, married, with a son still in grammar school. She lived on the Mill Bank Estate near Victoria Station. Her husband was a chauffeur for the owner of a very famous flour producing company. He drove a Rolls Royce. Eileen was a charlady who cleaned offices in the West End. She could please herself when she did the job, either in the evening or first thing in the morning. This enabled her to have such freedom with our dates.

I always think of Eileen as the most glamorous of London chars, as invariably she was clad in a mink coat when we met. She knew how little pay we guardsmen received and always gave me a 10/- or one pound note on our evening excursions. We went to the London Palladium and Victoria Palace together and many of the lively pubs. She was a good sort and I still think of our happy times together, a couple of which I may relate.

Sometimes when I was on CB or jankers of some sort, I would ask her to come to the barracks and ask for me, the time to tally with my appointed punishment parade. The sergeant of the guard would send an orderly to fetch me, saying:

"There's a very nice lady in a fur coat wanting to see you. I've sent her to the library."

I would head there and have a nice couple of hours in her company. Much more satisfying than peeling potatoes, scrubbing floors or other such menial tasks the powers that be had in store. The brigade of guards knows exactly how to treat a lady of fashion and the guardsmen who accompanies her, even if he is on jankers. Jimmy Siddall, hearing of my good fortune asked me if Eileen had a friend.

"I'll enquire" I promised.

One evening over a quiet drink, Eileen and I hit on a plan to curtail Jimmy's ever boastful plans on how he could always get his way with any woman. I forget the name of the lady who was to become part of our scheme. She and Eileen worked together, but unlike Eileen could only get out alone on the odd occasion as her husband was very watchful. We three met up one morning in her friend's flat in the same block as Eileen.

"I'll fix a piece of raw liver in my knickers after we have had a few drinks, then we will go over to nearby Hyde Park and see what happens." She said. We did laugh at the thought of what was to be.

I told Siddall that I had fixed him up with Eileen's pal and we were to meet in a couple of days' time.

"She's a cracker and she's sex mad" I warned him. As planned, we met up and had a few drinks.

"We had better get to the park," Eileen suggested, "Before it's too late. You know you have to be in barracks by midnight."

We made our way across to Hyde Park and sat down on the grass a respectful distance apart. Eileen and I lay down and listened for the storm to break. All of a sudden, the shadowy figure of Jim reared up from where they were laying.

"God almighty, Christ!" was all I heard and away he galloped into the darkness.

We joined his girl and as forecast, after a few kisses he had put his hand up her skirt and into her knickers. We returned to the pub full of merriment. When I got back to Chelsea that night, Siddall was awaiting me.

"Bloody hell, Charlie, that woman was deformed. She had a fanny like a lump of liver." I nearly wet myself and went to sleep happy. I always referred to Eileen's friend as 'Hanging Liver'.

One day Eileen said her husband had to take the boss down to Cornwall and he would have to stay the night, so I could spend Saturday night with her. Great! We went to the Victoria Palace then on to a pub and finally finished up at her flat. Her son was fast asleep in his bedroom. After supper, we went into her bedroom into which she brought a bucket and said:

120

"That's in case you're sick"

"I'm alright, don't worry"

In the middle of the night I was roused by Eileen frantically shaking me.

"He's here," she cried. "He's sounded his horn"

She looked out of the window and confirmed the Rolls Royce was parked below.

"He will be here any second. Get your clothes and stand behind the front door. When I let him in, the door will hide you"

There was a knock on the door and I hastened to get my clothes together. He knocked again and Eileen opened the door. He greeted her with complaints at being kept waiting.

"I was fast asleep," she said "and anyway, what are you doing coming home? I didn't expect you till tomorrow"

By this time, he was along the passage and into the living room. I was outside like a shot, completely naked, clothes in one hand and shoes in the other. I ran down four or five flights of stairs to the ground floor. Thankfully, at 4 o'clock in the morning, no one was about and I was able to dress on someone's front door mat.

It was impossible to return to barracks until after 8 am when the civilian employees and the permanent staff, who, if married, could sleep out of barracks, started to arrive. I made my way to Victoria Station and was surprised to find the waiting room closed. However, there were several trains stationed at the platforms, so I climbed into a first class carriage and quickly fell asleep. I was awakened by a friendly porter who said:

"Unless you want to finish up in Dover, you had better scarper"

"Thanks pal."

I hadn't booked out at the guardroom the night before and there were no problems when I returned in time for Sunday breakfast which was, of course, the best of the week.

Our duties at Chelsea included Buckingham Palace Guard, St. James, and the Bank of England. I only did one palace guard for the following reason:

A statement on the company order board stated that the under-mentioned would not do public duties. The reason for this was as follows. Stevenson had seemingly had a brainstorm whilst on guard at the Palace. He put his rifle in the corner of the sentry box - which in those days was outside the Palace gates. He then sat down in the sentry box and lit up a fag. A patrolling policeman, on seeing this unbelievable sight, rushed over to Steve and asked if he was ill.

"No I'm alright, just fancied a cigarette." was his reply.

With this, the policeman hastened over to Wellington Barracks to report this incident. In no time at all the sergeant of the guard appeared with a relief sentry.

"Are you ill?" were his first words.

"I don't know what all the fuss is about, all I wanted was a quiet smoke" replied our hero.

The new sentry took over and Steve was marched back to the guardroom. No action was taken against Steve and we never found out how the sergeant of the guard handled this. All we knew was the lettering on the company notice board, 'The under-mentioned will not do public duties: Guardsmen Fear R., Small J., and Stevenson C.'

A couple of weeks earlier, Wales were playing England at Twickenham and London was full of Welsh supporters. Some paid a visit to the Palace, where Sam Small was on guard. A couple of Taffies started poking fun at our Sam and one said:

"He's not allowed to move" and with that stuck his face right up close to Sam's and made a rude gesture.

"No, I can't move" whispered Sam, "but there's nothing in regulations to say I can't spit at you" and with that he spat in the poor Welshman's face.

These goings on had been witnessed by the other sentry near by and he must have told the rest of the guard, including the guard commander. It seems that in the company office, it was decided by the NCOs that as Steve and Small had misbehaved, not to be outdone, Guardsman Fear may be thinking up some prank or other, so it's best if the three of them don't go on Palace guard again.

I would like to relate what happened on Bank of England guard before I was banned. Normally, we would mount guard in the afternoon and then march all of six miles to the Bank. On this occasion, we had a real brammer officer in charge of us. (Yes, there were some brammers amongst the officer corp.). When we were clear of the barracks, he marched us to Sloane Square tube station where he halted us.

"Look here chaps, I don't fancy marching all the way to the Bank, do you?"

"No Sir" was the instant reply. The sergeant was a bit cautious but as he was due for demob very soon, reluctantly agreed.

"Right, off we go."

At the other end we were over an hour early so the officer took us into the snack bar and treated us to whatever we wanted to eat and drink. A real card, was Lieutenant Naylor Leyland. It was said that he arrived late for dinner one evening, dressed in a very bright unmilitary shirt. The commanding officer, Peggy Brownlow, was enraged and said:

"Don't come down here in my mess looking like a gipsy. Go to your quarters and change."

Naylor Leyland did just that and returned to the mess in his pyjamas. He didn't last long in the 1st Battalion and was shipped off somewhere or other. I remember him coming into my room once while we were in Germany, and saying:

"I just fancy a game of soccer, Fear. Get some of your pals together and we'll have a game"

I did what I was bid and we finished up having an enjoyable game of soccer. Afterwards he stayed chatting with us for some time.

"That's the first time I've ever played football," he admitted. "We only play rugger at Eton."

I met him again many years later when my daughter Jane was competing at his stately home somewhere down south. He remembered me instantly. We had a good laugh and he took great pleasure in introducing me to all his aristocratic friends, as the man that saved his life on a couple of occasions. Quite untrue of course, as

I had never served with him during the war, but who was I, a humble guardsman, to argue with the cream of the aristocracy and a guards' officer to boot!

Writing about guards' officers reminds me of the time in Germany that CSM Amour sent for me and said:

"You aren't doing much around here. You can look after the company commander while his servant is on leave. He'll pay you well." he added.

I took over the duties next day and had an hour's schooling by his regular servant, GDSM Parsons. As I've mentioned before, 'Stiffy' Clifford was a real gent and as far as I can remember, never put anybody 'in the book'.

The first morning I took him his tea at around 8 o'clock. He was laid out on his bed fully dressed in his mess uniform and at first sight, I thought he was dead. I shook him and he sat up with a startled look on his face.

"Who are you?" he demanded.

"I'm looking after you while your servant is on leave"

"Oh yes, it's Fear isn't it? God, Fear, I am a sick man. For God's sake, go to the MO and get me something."

I could see he was still under the influence and suggested he took off his clothes so I could clean them, and for him to get into his bed.

On my return from the MO, he eyed me up and down and wailed:

"Oh Fear, I am a sick man. A sick man. Never again. Please light the fire, I am very cold"

I quickly laid the fire and thought that, to help things along, I'd add a little petrol. There was a jerry can full at hand and I must have been too generous, for when I threw the match into the fireplace, there was a resounding explosion, which blew everything from the grate into the bedroom. I was nearly blown over and got my hair singed. After poor old 'Stiffy' had disentangled himself from the bedclothes under which he had taken shelter, he said:

"Are you trying to finish me off completely? Never do that again, there's a good fellow. My nerves won't stand it."

124

Like us guardsmen, the officers were taking advantage of all the wine the Germans had purloined from the rest of Europe and was readily available to the British Forces for a few fags. Unlike us, most of the officers' drinking was done in their mess. At the end of the two weeks, the CO thanked me for looking after him so well.

"You can take care of me when Parsons goes on leave again."

"It was a pleasure." I assured him.

Most mornings he looked a mess, but never as bad as the first day. As Amour had predicted, he paid me well. He also entrusted me on a special mission. There had been a couple of nasty accidents in our company, where guardsmen had been killed while playing about with the pistols we had looted from the enemy, and so he had issued an order that all pistols were to be handed into the company office. Anyone not obeying the order would be severely dealt with. About 200 were handed in and Amour had suggested that Fear would be the best businessman to take them down to the American zone and sell them or exchange them for whatever I could get.

Leslie Dance, the company driver, took me a long way down to the American zone in a 15 cwt. truck and was told by the CSM not to return until I had got rid of all the merchandise. Me thinks that sounds good advice. I could visualise myself established in the American Army.

At the border of our two zones, we had a lot of trouble explaining our mission to the British military police, but none from the Yanks who greeted us with open arms. We gave a couple of pistols to the two Americans on duty and proceeded to the town where we'd been told there was a large military establishment with thousands of troops. As soon as we had parked our 15 cwt., we were surrounded by dozens of Yanks who came to view us two Limies.

I had in my holster a long barrelled Lugar pistol which could hit a duck at 100 metres. It was a lovely weapon which I had confiscated in Kiel from the kitbag of a U-Boat officer. They passed it around with much wonderment and everyone wanted to possess it.

"Not for sale," I told them, "but we have two kitbags full of every sort of pistol"

I explained why we had come and they took us to a very large messroom that must have seated over 1,000 men. We set out our stall at one of the tables, but only had a couple of pistols on show at a time, as I didn't want the mob stealing them. They might have felt that as we had stolen them they were entitled to do the same. Fortunately, these Yanks were greenhorns and had arrived in Germany after hostilities. We could get a decent watch; Bulover, Westfield, Omega or Rolex, in a straight deal for just one pistol. We also got two packs (400) cigarettes, a pair of binoculars or the odd camera for the same price.

Half way through our transactions, it was chow time and we were invited to dine with them. What followed was unbelievable. We collected knives, forks, and plates and joined the queue. When we got to the food, we were amazed to see the variety of scoff you could choose from; steaks, chickens, stews, curries and umpteen vegetables. There was nothing to stop one from having portions of everything. Les Dance and I went for steak, not having seen any for years. It was beautiful. Although there was no wine on the menu, one of the soldiers flourishing his newly acquired Lugar, bought us a bottle of Mosel.

The most amazing thing was not the food, but the way the Battalion was eating it. All the way round this huge mess-hall they lay on the floor with their legs straight up the walls, and their dinner plates on their chests, and that's how they ate. Ice cream was plentiful in a variety of flavours.

We two British soldiers wondered why we had such simple fare and only a third of the pay the Yanks got, but we settled with the knowledge that a hungry underpaid soldier is a good soldier, while the spoilt Yanks were, by and large, poor soldiers lacking in discipline.

We stayed for a couple of days and were well looked after. On leaving, we were taken to see the battalion commander. He treated us as equals and asked us a lot of questions about our regiment, which he had heard so much about in his initial training. He was obviously very impressed with our regimental history and discipline. I compared this CO with ours and I came to this conclusion; Give me 'Stiffy' Clifford anytime and our tradition that holds us together as one man in times of trouble.

Dance and I sorted out a nice little haul for ourselves before we drove back to our company and then it was the quartermaster sergeant's job to sort out who got what for what. I had selected out a nice Rolex for 'Stiffy'. He seemed quite touched when I gave him the watch and added:

"I'll be returning home in a couple of weeks. If I can ever be of help to you in 'Civvy-street', don't hesitate to ask me. You can always get my address from Regiment HQ." I never took advantage of his kind offer.

Back to Chelsea Barracks and to continue my story.

London was a wonderful adventure to us young soldiers. With so much going on nightly we would be off as soon as we had tea. I was rather luckier, having Eileen, than most of the other squaddies, as I need never be short of dosh. Many of my pals, having run out of cash, would head for the pubs that catered for the 'Queers'. A guardsman could always have an evening's free drinking by attending these places of ill-repute. They didn't have to fall for the sordid invitations of these sick men, just listen to their tales of woe.

One of our most popular sergeants, who was welterweight champion of the brigade, fell in with an officer of a Highland regiment. All 'Robbo' had to do was wear his army boots when he visited the officer's flat. It seems he got his kicks by licking the soles of the sergeant's boots complete with the 13 studs. For this service, 'Robbo' was paid well.

I had a few encounters with queers. I was returning from Sloane Square tube station and heading for the barracks, when out of a doorway stepped a smartly dressed gentleman, complete with bowler hat and briefcase.

"Good evening, guardsman. May I have a word with you?" As I was familiar with this approach, I said:

"Yes, Sir, what do you want?"

He beckoned me into a doorway and asked what I had been up to that evening. I told him I had been out for a drink and was unlucky as I hadn't found a bit of crumpet, to which he enquired:

"What do you do if you don't have a woman?"

"I have a good wank." was my reply.

"Wonderful. Will you give me one?" he said.

"How much?"

"You guardsmen are all the same. All you think about is money. Think of the pleasure"

He undid his fly and got out his penis. He grasped my hand and guided it towards his dick. At this point, I did what I had planned. I grabbed his dick with all my might and demanded his wallet.

"If you don't cough up, I'll rip your bloody cock off"

He fumbled for his wallet and handed it to me. I let go of his cock and made my way to the barracks as quick as I could. As I made off, he called me all the names he could bring to mind, including 'a thieving bastard'. In the guardroom, I had a quick look in the wallet. He had come fully prepared for such an assault, for the cheap imitation leather wallet contained nothing. Nothing! He had obviously been tackled like this before and had come fully prepared.

Another time, Jimmy and I met a couple of guys in the 'Queer Pier', a renowned pub for homosexuals. After a few pints, they invited us into Hyde Park. I separated from Jimmy and sat on the grass with my fellah. I had been eyeing his expensive shoes all the evening and guessing he would not be carrying much dosh, I set my sights on his shoes, which appeared to be my size.

I agreed with all the rubbish he was saying and bided my time for the attack. When I struck, I managed to prise off one of his shoes but before I could relieve him of his second shoe, he was up and away with me in hot pursuit. I hurled his shoe at him and chased him with all my training. Halfway across Hyde Park I lost him in the darkness and tried to retrace my tracks to where I had left my cap. I found his shoe but after a long search was unable to find my cap. All I had got out of my escapade was a left footed shoe, minus my cap, which would set me back a week's wages. Not very funny.

Whilst I was happy to accept free drinks from these unhappy specimens, I never again attempted to rob them.

During the summer of 1947, it was announced one breakfast time that our colonel, Princess Elizabeth, would visit Chelsea Barracks. The Princess had become colonel in chief of The Grenadier Guards on the death of the Duke of Connaught, who had recently died at the age of 92. He had been a colonel for many years.

Before taking lunch in the officers' mess, the Princess would visit our mess. At breakfast, we had to practice what to do. When the Princess called out;

"Any complaints?" We had to reply in a loud voice:

"No Marm"

Our half-hearted response infuriated the RSM, who threatened to keep us there all the morning if we were not more co-operative. Eventually he was satisfied and we returned to our barrack room to plan our own reception for our beloved colonel in chief.

Our barrack room was on the second floor and from one side of the room we could view Chelsea Bridge Road and from the other side, the square. The entourage was to travel along the road, turn into the barracks and cross the square to the officers' mess. This is what we did:

The bathhouse was across the square from our building, so we got twenty guardsmen to get into their underpants and droop a towel round their middle. As the procession entered the barracks, the twenty half-naked guardsmen were to cross the square in single file just in front of the leading car (no rule to say guardsmen must not take showers!). We, in our barrack room, had inflated a couple of dozen 'French Letters' (condoms) to float down on to the square on the approach of H.R.H.

These old-fashioned condoms had a large nipple on them and they blew up to quite a size. As zero hour approached and we saw the cars approach, we raced across the room and threw the condoms down onto the square. What followed was very amusing. As we had foreseen, the balloons landed all over the square and poor old Spratley, with aid from Everett and Muckett, rushed around trying to pierce these offending French Letters with their pace sticks. As everyone knows, this is a very difficult task as the rubber was designed to withstand prods from irate sergeant majors' pace sticks. We danced about in glee from the safe distance of our barrack room. The Princess and Prince Philip passed this remarkable scene though unfortunately, we couldn't see their reaction.

Soon after their arrival, cookhouse was blown and we made our way to the mess-room. On entering we were amazed to see nice little bread rolls laid out on our tables for twelve men. In our entire army career, no one had ever seen this delicacy, no doubt for the Princess's benefit compliments of the master cook. This enraged us no end and we decided on what action to take. The procedure was as follows: The commanding officer would enter the mess-room with H.R.H., the adjutant, duty officer, and RSM. The RSM would bawl out:

"Battalion, Schunme" and we would sit bolt upright with knife and fork in each hand. H.R.H. would ask, in a most lady-like manner:

"Are there any complaints?" to which we should have replied:

"No Marm"

Instead, when we were asked if there were 'any complaints', all hell was let loose. Bread rolls were hurled from table to table and in all directions. We on our table aimed the missiles in the direction of the Princess, as indeed did many other tables. The CO and his entourage all endeavoured to protect their colonel from this unprovoked attack, and she was quickly ushered out of the mess-room.

We had a very nice dinner served with all the trimmings, reminiscent of Christmas Day. After dinner we returned to our barrack rooms to await the storm to break, and break it did! At about four o'clock the bugle sounded for us all to get on parade and we were told by our room sergeants to get into drill order with rifles.

The Battalion formed up and we were addressed by RSM Spratley. No officers were on parade, only the two drill sergeants, Everett and Muckett. He gave us all a really good dressing down saying how disgusted he was with our behaviour. We were drilled continuously for two hours and the battalion was confined to barracks

130

for two weeks. In respect, the RSM never sort out the ringleaders of these escapades, but I am sure the whole battalion enjoyed what went on and never was a finger pointed at us brammers.

Years later when the then Colonel Spratley stayed at my home during the North Staff annual dinner, I reminded him of this incident. He looked at me for a long time in deep thought and then he said: "We guessed who the ringleaders were but everyone was throwing the bread about and how can you put 800 men in the book for chucking rolls at the colonel?" We both laughed and he added: "Our biggest worry was if the press got hold of the story." Which they did not.

In 1947, the brigade resumed the 'Trooping the Colour' ceremony on horse guards' parade. It is to celebrate the Sovereign's official birthday and used to be on the first Thursday in June. Now it is always held on a Saturday. Our company was to form one of the guards. It takes a good deal of thought and practice to get this fantastic military ceremony organised. We would do short programmes daily on the square at Chelsea and once or twice we did a rehearsal on horse guards parade early in the morning, 6am or so. We then had a proper dress rehearsal in preparation for the big day.

On one of the training stints, Harry Muckett carried out the duty of handing the standard to the officer, who was to carry it during the actual troop. This meant he had to relinquish his pace stick, which he very unwisely stood against one of the pillars that were erected on one side of the square. As it happened, Master Siddall spied Harry's stick and decided to shorten it a bit. He carefully sneaked the stick away and while Harry was carrying out his duty, Jimmy broke the pace stick into several pieces and carefully, without being seen, returned Harry's pride and joy to its original place, only now it resembled a pile of firewood. We never heard what happened when the misdeed was discovered. All I know is that Siddall gave me one end, the piece old Harry was so fond of sticking up young guardsmen's nostrils.

While at Chelsea I had the good fortune to meet Reginald Lawrance, a South African gentleman who had come all the way to England to join the world's most famous regiment, as he put it. Like me, he had decided very early to remain a guardsman. He was a good all round sportsman and resembled Orson Wells, the film star. Much better looking than Wells however, with large green eyes which he would roll round his head when confronted by any officer or NCO. I can hear him now answering an NCO who had demanded his name for some misdeed or other.

"Lawrance, with an 'a'", with much emphasis on the 'a'.

Very often, on his return from a night out, he walked to the middle of the square and gave a very good rendering of Santa Lucia at the top of his voice. As it was always near midnight, he was not very popular with the sergeant of the guard and when asked his name, it was always the same reply:

"Lawrance, with an 'a'."

Like me, he had grown a little pencil moustache. I never had any problems with mine but it seems RSM Spratley took not only a dislike to Lawrance, but to his moustache, and on one parade said:

"Show yourself clean shaven without that bit of hair under your nose at six o'clock in the guardroom."

Reginald slipped out long before six o'clock, but on his return from town, Spratley was waiting for him.

"Stick him inside now" he shouted.

He visited Reg a bit later and said:

"You'll be let out of here when you have properly shaved."

Lawrance stayed inside for a week. He was visited daily by the duty sergeant, who must have reported things to the RSM. After seven days, Spratley called on Lawrance.

"Are you or are you not going to shave off that moustache?"

To which Lawrance replied.

"Sir, when you shave off your ridiculous looking moustache, I'll shave off mine."

Nothing more was said and Lawrance was released next day complete with his nicely pencilled moustache.

Reg and I got on very well together and he always addressed me as Charles. If any of the other lads ever called me Charlie, he was very cross, rolled round his large green eyes, and said:

"His name is Charles. Never, ever, let me hear you address him as Charlie again. And I am Lawrance, with an 'a'."

He had been dating a married woman for some weeks and then found another girl whom he liked better. The married lady was very cross indeed and one day the police arrived accompanied by this woman. Reg's kitbag was searched by the police and the woman claimed a pair of socks in his kitbag were indeed her husbands, and that Reg had stolen them. He was arrested there and then. Next day he was up before the beak at Bow Street.

Now, in the brigade of guards, the officers look after their men at every opportunity and they do everything in their power to assist any 'would-be' transgressor. So an officer was sent by the battalion to defend our Reg. He felt sure that when he explained what happened, the case would be dismissed. Wrong! When the charge had been read out and explanations given, the judge turned to the grenadier officer and said:

"How does this man do?" and to everyone's surprise, the defending officer replied:

"He is the worst man in the Battalion. The longer he is in prison the better."

With this, the Judge announced sentence. 28 days in jail. So off poor Reg went to Pentonville Prison. It seems the RSM got his revenge.

When Reg was released after his sentence was completed, he told me what had happened, and this is what he had already told the court.

"I got out of bed and reached under for my socks. I must have got hold of the wrong pair for when I got back to the barracks I discovered the mistake. I did not give it a second thought as I had left my socks behind and exchange is no robbery."

After the trooping ceremony in June, our company was sent to South Wales on manoeuvres. We found it hard to believe that although most of us were due to be demobbed before the year's end, we had to waste our time running up and down the Welsh mountains playing soldiers. We were stationed in Nissen Huts in a wood. My section of 12 men was commanded by a Sergeant Pickford, commonly known as 'Pitchfork'. He was a comparatively young soldier whom we mistrusted and considered an upstart. At breakfast, our section all sat at the same table and it was there that we decided to have a day or two at Barry Island instead of farting about on manoeuvres.

We all dressed in our walking out uniforms and just before 'get on parade' was blown, we quickly disappeared into the surrounding woods taking up a vantage point from which we could get a good view of the parade ground and the forthcoming comedy.

"Section commanders get on parade" was bawled out by the CSM. The four sergeants got on parade quickly followed by their sections, with one exception - poor old Pitchfork. He stood awhile thinking no doubt that his section was late on parade. But when the CSM demanded to know where his section was, Pitchfork's immediate response was:

"Don't know, Sir"

"You had better go and dig them out." was the CSM's reply.

Our unhappy Sgt galloped off in search of his wayward section to return some time later with the news that it was his opinion that they had all deserted. As one knows, desertion is a very serious offence, punishable in wartime with death. We all found it hilarious to view the scene. Everyone on parade with the exception of No.2 Section, one sergeant and one corporal.

We hastened to the bus stop, which took us to Barry Island. We agreed to meet at 8 pm in time to catch the last bus back to camp. Reg Lawrance and I decided to stay together and let the other lads do their own thing. We walked around this popular holiday resort, not knowing exactly what we were looking for. We were examining the counter hands in Woolworths, when we spied three very pretty well dressed females. We approached them in our usual confident manner. Reg did the introductions.

"I am Reginald Lawrance with an 'a' and this is my very good friend, Charles."

They turned out to be young ladies from Denmark on holiday with an aunt who lived in Barry. This sounded as if they were girls of some means, which added to their attraction. Linda Rassmussen was the girl I was attracted to from the first. Her older sister and their friend made up the trio. Reg was undecided as to which one he liked best. We had some tea at a nearby cafe and succeeded in keeping the girls laughing. They all spoke perfect English so there were no problems in that direction.

Near 8 o'clock we went to the bus station where there were only two other guardsmen. Both had girls on their arms. They advised us that the other eight of our section, fearing severe punishment, had returned to camp by an earlier bus. Our two comrades said they were going to stay for a couple more days until their money ran out. We bid them bon-voyage and then accepted an invitation to 'come and meet Auntie' by our three Danish beauties. She was a very nice lady indeed and questioned us on several points.

"How is it you are on leave on Barry Island? You're not Welsh!"

In the end, we told her the truth - that we were 'absent without leave'. This worried her a great deal and she feared the military police would be knocking on her door at any moment. We tried to inform her that this was not possible as the guards would be the last people who would ask assistance of the military police.

She gave us a very nice dinner in full party spirit. When she learned we had no place to lay down our heads, she invited us to stay the night as long as we returned to our camp next day. To which we readily agreed. After breakfast, Linda and I, Reg and the friend, decided to have a day at the large fairground. We had an enjoyable day and I fancy Linda and I were falling in love. She was a lovely girl with naturally blonde hair and blue eyes. Her father owned a large bacon factory in Copenhagen. I told her I was to be demobbed in a few months time and she said:

"You must come to Copenhagen and meet my parents, then you can pretend to return to England and I'll book us into a hotel for a few days. It will be great fun and they will think I have returned to England to meet your parents. They have told both my sister and I that it's time we were getting married and settled down."

She was a bit older than me, but not much. Unlike the German girls, she hadn't had many sexual encounters, which added to her charm. Come that evening she begged me not to return to camp so we found a place to sleep behind one of the counters at the fairground. Next day she got a real telling off from Auntie, who made her stay at home all that day, but she managed to get out in the evening. I drew out some money from my National Savings account and she always had a wallet full, so we were able to eat very well at the local restaurants. Towards the end of our absence, her aunt invited Reg and I to sleep at her home again, which was a Godsend after roughing it under the counters at the fair ground.

I must mention that while we were at Barry, I decided to visit brother Jim, who lived at Bridgend, quite near to Barry. I thought it unlikely that he would be on leave, but at least Joan would be able to give us a meal and a bob or two. I knocked on the door and was confronted by my brother Jim, RSM Royal Engineers.

"Goodness me, what are you doing here? ", he demanded.

"I am on the trot." I replied "Can you lend me £3 please?"

"It's my bound duty to arrest you and have you sent back to your regiment, but come in and have a cup of tea and I'll see if I have enough money to give you some." He kept to his word and this enabled Reginald and I to stay a day or two longer. I promised my brother we would return to camp next day.

At the end of the holiday, Reg and I decided to return to camp and face the music. We went by train to Cardiff and then back to a station near our camp. It was easier to travel free on the railway than it was on a bus.

When we eventually returned to our company, we were placed in close arrest and next morning appeared before Major Britten who, much to our relief, gave us 14 days CB. We had been expecting a much more severe sentence as we had learned that the lads that had returned on the same day as they went absent also got 14 days CB. Major Britten seemed to sympathise with our 'cakey-bars' excuses, and I fancy he didn't want to have two of his best runners locked up with the Battalion Sports taking place on our return to Chelsea.

Linda wrote to me weekly from Copenhagen and after I was demobbed she visited me at Brighton. I remember her visit well and as

I grew older, wondered why I made such a cock-up of our relationship. We arranged to meet at Brighton station and when the train arrived from Victoria, I saw her approach the barrier.

"My God," I thought, "Who is this, a film star?"

She was dressed in a pony-skin fur coat and an extraordinary hat. It might have been Ascot. She looked magnificent and yet I was embarrassed and overwhelmed with her appearance. I hid behind a pillar, but she had seen me and laughed at my antics.

"Still the same old Charles, trying to play games with me" she said. "Before we go to your home, let's have a walk on your famous seafront."

So we left her suitcase at the luggage department and made our way down Queens Road and past the pawn shop where I had spent nearly three years of my life. We walked to the front and along to the Palace Pier. I was certain everyone was looking at us. I was most embarrassed and, when possible, pretended she wasn't with me. Why did I do this? Why was I ashamed to be seen with such a beautiful girl? I suppose it was the same inborn shyness that prevented me from accepting promotion in the army, and to this day I feel terror if I am asked to make a short speech in public. I can handle man to man, woman to women talk, but ask me to make a short speech and I am frightened to death. Lack of education, no doubt. I suppose I must count myself lucky to have made my way in life without having to make any speeches, not even as a best man at a wedding. I always made excuses and got someone else to do the job.

We collected her luggage and got a taxi to my home. Mum and Dad were very surprised when they first met Linda. They hadn't reckoned on me collecting a film star, and brother Dan was 'gob-smacked', as they say today. She returned to Copenhagen and I played it cool. She wrote regularly and I answered irregularly. Finally, we stopped corresponding. She got married and I got married, but some years later, out of the blue, she wrote to me to say that her husband was a pig and could she visit me. I wrote sympathetically but said a visit was impossible. A couple of years passed and I received another letter to say she was divorced and had contracted tuberculosis, brought on, as she said, by her love for me. Could I please come to Copenhagen and renew our friendship.

"It may save my life." she pleaded.

At that time I was deeply involved with my bookmaking business. I was making plenty of money but as is always the case, I had to stick to the job and not take one-off holidays. TB frightened me a great deal and I am a little ashamed now to admit that I didn't want to get involved as it was thought to be contagious.

'From hardness of heart may the good Lord deliver us.'

I did write, promising to visit if I could only find the time. I never heard from her again.

We returned to Chelsea from Wales, but only stayed for a few weeks, and from there to Windsor to await our demob. The night before demob was spent in the local pubs in Windsor, where we all endeavoured to get as pissed as possible. As most of the old gang had been demobbed, I was pretty well on my own. Being seen by our regimental police hurling geraniums (complete with pots) through peace-loving civilians' windows meant I was quickly dispatched both to barracks and the guardroom, where the sergeant of the guard refused to give me a blanket which, in the depths of winter, isn't very funny. My pleadings were in vain so I decided to sing at the top of my voice some vulgar ditty. I soon got my blanket.

Next morning, the 3-tonner trucks were lined up outside the guardroom waiting to leave for the demobilisation centre where we would collect our demob suits and other odds and ends. One man was missing after roll call.

"Ah, Fear! You will have to face the CO and no doubt, after punishment is dished out, you won't be getting your release today."

Those were Harry Muckett's words. He seemed very gleeful and ordered the sergeant of the guard to march me, under escort, to the company office. A Corporal had been sent post haste to the officers' mess to ask Major Wedderburn to get across to the company office to 'see Fear off'. As we marched passed the officers mess, a window opened, and Major Wedderburn peered out.

"Prisoner and escort halt" yelled the sergeant.

138

"Can you come to your office straight away, Sir?"

"Good morning Fear. What has he been up to now?" he enquired.

"Drunk and disorderly in Windsor last evening, Sir", replied the sergeant.

"Oh dear me, getting quite a habit isn't it? Case dismissed and good luck in 'Civvy-street' Fear. You'll need it."

I walked to my barrack room to collect my kit, which luckily I had packed the night before, and then back to the guardroom. The inmates of the 3-tonners were getting very restless and shouted to me to get a move on. Harry came up to me and made his usual speech.

"You think you're bloody funny, don't you? One of these days I'll pick up the News of the World and see they have hung you and I'll be f--king glad."

I clambered into the back of the truck and said:

"Good morning, Harry" and stuck up two fingers in salute. So ended my career in the Brigade of Guards. I had been a good soldier, particularly until the end of the war, but then boredom had taken over and I had mixed with the wrong company. Upon demob they enter your character in your pay book: Exemplary, Excellent, Very Good, Good and that's all, but in my case Major Wedderburn made an exception and he wrote in his own hand:

'He has done his work well and has been a keen and active member of the athletics team'. Not that his comments did me any good, but I did appreciate the thought of this very fine and understanding officer.

We lined up at the Demob Centre and I observed with horror some of the suits they were dishing out to the unsuspecting soldiers, resembling the suits made up in the prisoner of war camps in Germany prior to attempted escapes. Come my turn I shook hands with my attendant and left a £1 note in his hand.

"Size, Sir?" he enquired. I told him

"42 chest, 32 waist and 31 leg."

"I've the very suit for you, Sir" and disappeared. He returned with a very smart, chocolate brown, doubled breasted suit.

"Try on the jacket." It fitted perfectly. "I've held this suit back for someone like you." he declared.

I think he fancied me but whether he was 'one of them' I'll never know. When I wore the suit, no one would believe it was a demob suit. 'Lucky old Fear', and as I have already mentioned, I sold it to Harold Benzie for £3 some years later.

Jack Gardner
British and European Heavyweight Boxing Champion 1950-1952

CSM 'Titch' Amour
Major 'Stiffy' Clifford - 1946

Duke of Connaught
Our landlord in the early 'Thirties

Guardsman George Lee, Scots Guards with Guardsman Fear

Guardsman James Siddal in
'Bollock Order One' pouch
Company Office - 1946

Lawrance with an 'a'

Sam 'Curly Boots' Small

Steve 'I Like a Smoke on Palace
Guard' Stevenson

Lieutenant Colonel Arthur Spratley M.M. visiting Foxdale 1970

South African Veteran Bill Maddocks at his 90th birthday
celebration at Foxdale with A.E.H. Heber Percy

144

923 Gardner J. and 924 Fear R. attending the 300th anniversary dinner of the formation of the guards

The author, fined ten Shillings for drunkenness at the docks at Cuxhaven and leading half the battalion 'down the coal 'ole'

Churchill Tank ready for action

Foxdale, Wetley Rocks. - Winter 1965

146

Chapter 7

Demobilisation

I arrived home and spent Christmas with the family at Mother's new house at 70 Southdown Avenue, Brighton. Where Mother got the money from, I will never know. Then for the next couple of years life seemed strange. It was difficult to switch from army life to civilian life and I am afraid I became anti-social.

I did not work for some time and was finally called up with the 'spivs and drones' as we ex-servicemen who had not sought employment were called. I reported to the labour exchange as instructed and a clerk asked me if I had done any pressing. Thinking he meant ironing, I told him I was a good presser.

"Good, you can go to the Errol works at Portslade. They may be able to employ you."

I went for an interview and the manager agreed to take me on as an under-presser.

"Won't take you long to learn", he assured me.

How wrong he was. I must have ruined thousands of garments while carrying out this boring task. The only attraction at the factory was the fact that it employed several hundred girls but only a few men, and they were mostly middle aged Jews doing the more important jobs in the manufacture of ladies garments. Me, I was just a low paid unskilled slave, but starting there was to change my life. One or two tales that took place while I was employed at the Errol works are worth mentioning. Firstly, I met and courted my first wife, Hazel.

The first year I was there I took time off to see 'Trooping the Colour' in London. The boss heard about this and said it must never happen again. If it did, I would be sacked. Next year, as the big day approached, I got dear brother Jim to send me a telegram from South Wales to the effect that he had fallen off some scaffolding and was hovering between life and death and I must visit the hospital immediately. I took the telegram to the boss who unhesitatingly said:

"Get off now and I hope your brother fully recovers." As it happened, the telegram arrived the day before 'The Troop' so I was able to view this magnificent spectacle with Lawrance and Siddall who lived together at Shepherds Bush. Unfortunately, it was a very hot summer's day and I went to work next day with a very healthy tan. Mid-morning I was summoned to the boss's office where he asked if I had indeed enjoyed 'Trooping the Colour'. Before I could answer, he said:

"Collect your cards from the office, you're sacked."

Helen Webb was a supervisor working at the far end of the factory. I only ever saw her from a distance. One lunch time she called me down to her department and said:

"Hi Ray. I am Helen Webb. Would you like to come for supper tomorrow night?"

My heart missed a beat as I perceived this very attractive Scottish lady. I had never been invited out so briskly before and was a bit stunned. However, I quickly thought that as it was Hazel's 'hair washing' night, I would be free to go. So I agreed wholeheartedly. Her next sentence came as an even bigger surprise.

"My husband would like to meet you." My heart sank and all the exciting intimate thoughts that had first flashed through my mind quickly evaporated. "Yes," she continued. "I've told him all about your antics and he is keen to meet you. Be warned however, he's a bit difficult and doesn't make friends easily. Oh, yes, and bring Hazel along too."

And so Hazel forgot her hair washing evening and accompanied me to the flat in Hove of the redoubtable Kenneth Webb. He was a most remarkable man of moods. He could be as mean as scrooge and yet capable of great generosity. He was happy and carefree one moment, and the next down in the dumps. We were the same build, but that's where the resemblance ended. His father was a bookmaker whose main interest was running a fixed odds football coupon. Ken was slowly being introduced into the business, but from all accounts, he wasn't too keen. He had been educated at Oxford and had joined the Fleet Air Arm when he was called up just before the war ended.

We had a good laugh that first evening together and it was to start what was to become the one big chance in my life. He asked if it were true that I had a fight on the way to work and threw a guy (who had called me fancy-pants) in front of an oncoming bus. Was it true I had eaten a large hairy spider that had suddenly appeared on a thread suspended from the ceiling in the middle of the factory? Was it true I had taken out the best-looking girl at the factory who happened to be the boss's 'bit of stuff'? Was it true about 'Trooping the Colour'? And so on. I started to tell him some of my army exploits as well as Siddall's, whom he wanted to meet as soon as possible.

I had kept in touch with several of my old comrades including Siddall and Lawrance, who shared a flat in Coverdale Road, Shepherds Bush. Most weekends we would meet either in Brighton or London. Either way only cost us a platform ticket and a ticket from Clapham Junction, Victoria or Preston Park, Brighton, depending on which way we were travelling.

At this time, 923 Jack Gardner had developed his talents as a boxer. He was favourite to win the heavyweight gold medal in the 1948 Olympics in London, but was beaten on points by some Swiss gentleman. Jack was banking on his big knockout punch and left it too late. The opportunity didn't occur and he was narrowly beaten on points by this wily Swiss competitor. However, after the games he turned professional and won a Jack Soloman's competition to find a 'New White Hope'. This set him on the road to an early encounter with another very good heavyweight, Johnny Williams of Wales.

Williams was the fastest heavyweight around in those days and the fight was a sell out. In one of the most bloodthirsty fights on record, Gardner narrowly won on points. Both fighters needed a sewing machine to patch up their faces and poor Williams was detained in hospital suffering from severe concussion. As Jack said after the fight:

"Had I lost, I would be the one in hospital with concussion."

This fight was an eliminator, the winner to earn the right to fight Bruce Woodcock for the British Empire and European Heavyweight title, to be held at Earls Court in November 1950. As it happened, Jack's training quarters were to be at the Crown and Anchor, Preston Park, Brighton, not a mile from where I used to live and 2 miles from 21 Dorset Gardens where I now resided with my new bride, Hazel.

Jack and I had always corresponded since we had taken our different paths back in 1944 and we were delighted that we would be able to see each other when he started his training at The Crown and Anchor. We had had a week together back in the summer while he was preparing for the Williams fight. It was there I met and took an instant dislike to his manager, John Simpson. When he had learned that Jack, after a hard day's training, had gone swimming in the sea with that 'ne'er-do-good' Ray Fear, he went mad.

"Swimming's no good for boxing," he declared. "You keep away from that man Fear."

To this day I am sure, and Jack's sentiments are the same, that had he had a modern-day trainer with all the know-how on training, e.g. what to eat, etc., he would have been a world beater. Simpson was a pre-historic, who fed Jack on heavy meals and suet puddings and a yard of steak just before a fight 'to build up his strength'. What a laugh. No wonder Jack was always described as a 'slow starter'. He spent the first five rounds digesting the steak his manager had so unwisely prescribed.

The Jaeger factory at Burgess Hill, where I now worked, laid on a bus for the big fight at Earls Court. The ringside seats were £3.3s. each and I sold a busload to my factory friends. I saw Jack daily in his build up to the championship fight. He really was fit and confident. He confided in me that he had difficulty getting off to sleep at night. So I gave him a few tips on how to overcome this difficulty and to finish up by saying his prayers. He admitted to me that the exercise had worked and he slept well right up to the eve of the fight. It was I who couldn't sleep the last couple of nights before the big encounter.

150

I travelled to Earls Court with Ken Webb in his 1939 Riley. We joined the other Gardner supporters inside the arena. After the preliminary bouts, came the announcement from the ring:

'This is a heavyweight contest for the British Empire and European titles between the champion, Bruce Woodcock of Doncaster and the challenger Jack Gardner of Market Harborough."

From round one I though Jack's superior physique and ability to take a good punch would see him through, and that's what happened. After an exciting fight, Woodcock failed to come up for the twelfth round and Gardner was declared the new champion. Webby and I had lost our voices through our continuous shouting during the fight and we could hardly communicate with each other on the way home. I remember we got lost in Streatham and spent half an hour getting back on the A23. We were so elated it didn't matter how long it would take us to get home. At work next day, one would have thought I had won the title. Everyone wanted to shake my hand, including the boss, Mr. Kaye.

Jack returned home to Market Harborough a hero, and the newspapers gave him a very good write-up, declaring him a new Jack Dempsey, the Marauder. They did resemble each other incidentally. With his purse, Jack fixed up his dad, Len, with a nice country pub at Oxenden, just north of Harborough and he bought himself a 60 acre farm at East Langton where, for the next 25 years I was to be a constant visitor and where I spent many of my Christmases with our families. We had some great times there including our annual Boxing Day East Langton Steeple Chase, in which we both took part, and our 5-day test matches.

After the excitement of November, it was back to the boring slog at the Jaeger factory at Burgess Hill. During the summer there happened to be a quiet spell on the production line. I asked the boss if I could go into the gardens surrounding the factory and clear things up a bit. This he willing agreed to, as it must have grieved him to have to pay his employees for standing about doing nothing. I was able to strip off and enjoy the sunshine. I made a good job of the garden and whenever we were quiet inside, I was able to nip out into the fresh air to keep things looking respectable in the gardens.

One day Mr. Kaye asked me to go to his home and tidy up his plot. He lived in a detached house not far from the factory and his red haired wife, still in her dressing gown in mid-morning, greeted me. She was a highly-strung lady who always had a fag stuck in the corner of her mouth. She asked me in and told me she had lots of mice in her kitchen and could I do something about them. I bunged up some holes and laid some traps and told her I would bring some poison with me on my next visit. She was always most pleasant to me and I remember feeling a bit sorry for her, as being married to Mr. Kaye must have been some ordeal.

There was an old chicken house in the garden which I told Mrs. Kaye was an eye sore.

"Get rid of it." she answered. So I sold the hut to a rag and bone man and charged Mr. Kaye for taking it away. Double profit! He asked me to plant some bulbs in his front garden, like his neighbours.

"No problem" I replied.

I bought a pound of chestnuts and one Saturday morning, as I was busily planting them, he came out and asked me what they were.

"Oh, daffodils and tulips"

"Great. How much do I owe you?"

Many years later when I visited Brighton and Burgess Hill, an old acquaintance told me that Mr. Kaye's garden was like a forest and his house had a distinct tilt - no doubt the result of the large roots put out by the chestnut trees.

Another happening worth mentioning, was at Christmas time. Walking from the station to the factory, I had spied two 20 foot Christmas trees growing in the garden of a large detached house. Me thinks: 'Ah one of those would look very nice in our lounge.' The top 6 feet, of course.

A couple of days before we broke up for the holidays, I took a small handsaw with me and after work I delayed a while not wanting to catch the normal train to Brighton as the other workers would have seen my misdeed. It was dark at 4 pm, which enabled me to climb the selected tree undetected and saw off the top 6ft. I had misjudged the length and it was nearer 8ft than 6ft. 'Never mind,' I thought, 'I can trim it when I get home.'

It was snowing slightly and by the time I reached the station my tree had a light covering of snow. The later train arrived and I hastened to a first class compartment. I struggled in and endeavoured to place the tree on the luggage rack above the seat where several severe looking businessmen, complete with bowler hats, were sitting. There were murmurs of discontent, especially when the snow on the tree melted and dripped on to the other unfortunate occupants of the carriage. The only comment made directly to me was:

"It's a good job Christmas only comes once a year."

Hazel was delighted with our find and we spent most of our Christmas bonus on decorations and many a happy hour decorating it. The landlord, who also lived in the basement of our flat, thought we must be very rich to have obtained such a tree. When Webb saw it, his comment was:

"Where did you pinch that from?" I went even higher in his estimation when I told him the truth. He called on Christmas morning and said:

"Let's go for a drink while Hazel is preparing lunch."

We went straight to the Grand Hotel on the front. After a couple of drinks, we decided to paddle in the fishpond in the reception area of this five star hotel. One thing led to another and we finished up dancing naked, much to the amusement of the guests, but not to the management who summoned a large commissionaire to throw us out. At the revolving doors, we asked the angry gentleman if we could have our clothes.

"Tomorrow if you're lucky. Bugger off!"

So there we were, on a cold and frosty morning, barefooted and naked. I had seen some large geranium plants growing just inside the front doors, so I nipped back in and grabbed a couple. I gave one to Ken and we covered up our private parts, which had shrunk to minimum size in the cold air. I didn't want any of the neighbours seeing my dongleberry in such a reduced state.

It was only about half a mile from the Grand to Dorset Gardens and we did it in record time. I gave him some clothes to see him home and after a hot toddy, he roared off in his Riley. He telephoned me next day and asked if I could go to the Grand and collect our clothes. Not a very pleasant task under the circumstances. However, on confronting the large commissionaire, I noticed he wore an association badge and I asked him if he had served in the Guards.

"Yes, the Coldstreams!" I told him that I was in The Grenadiers.

"Ah, that explains your behaviour yesterday. I might have guessed." he smiled, and we exchanged a few regimental incidents.

He added that he was sorry for being so harsh yesterday, but he wanted to impress the boss and guests alike.

"Your clothes are a bit crumpled up. I'll get one of the porters to have them pressed and I'll get you a drink while you are waiting."

He had worked there since he was demobbed and relied on tips to make up his frugal wages. Ken's and my clothes were finally delivered and I bid farewell to my newly made friend, promising to visit the Grand Hotel soon. It was ten years before I returned, but this time as a paying guest staying for a week's holiday.

Later in the New Year, Gardner was to fight Ceasar Brion of Argentina, the winner hopefully to earn a crack at the world title. Unlike today, there was only one version of the world title. It was held by Rocky Marciano who eventually retired undefeated.

While Jack was in Brighton training, we decided to hold our own pentathlon competition. Ken Webb was to make up the trio competing. Two events were to be compulsory and we could each choose an event. The 1,500 metres and discus were compulsory. Jack chose the 100 metres, I the 800 metres and Ken chose, above all things, 'lamp-post hanging'. This involved hanging from the bar which was used to support the ladder for the old time lamp lighters. Points awarded were 3.2.1. Gardner won the 100 metres and, surprisingly, the 800 metres. I won the 1,500 metres and discus and Webb, the lamp-post hanging fiasco. But as I got three seconds to Gardner's two, I won the trophy. I bought a new chest of drawers with the prize money.

A letter written to the Brighton Evening Argus by some wise wag suggested that Gardner should spend more time in serious training for his world title eliminator, rather than wasting his time hanging from lamp-posts on Sunday afternoons. We disagreed with this guy as Jack pointed out he always felt carefree and relaxed in our company, rather than sitting in some dreary boarding house wondering how much suet pudding he must consume.

Everywhere he went he was recognised and feted, and everyone wanted his autograph. He sometimes introduced me as Sugar Ray Robinson, so people wanted my autograph too. A tailor in North Street made Jack two suits free of charge and I asked the shop owner if he could make me a camel haired overcoat.

"No problem, you bring me the material and I'll do the job."

Every few months Jaegers would have a remnant sale for their employees. Master Kaye would announce from his rostrum that there would be a remnant sale after work that evening and at lunchtime I galloped to the cutting room, selected several lengths of very nice material, including enough camel hair for an overcoat. Come 5 pm we queued outside His Lordship's office and one by one entered where he would price the remnants. Come my turn I dropped all but one of my selections outside the office and entered with my one length. He looked at me a bit hard and said:

"Is that all? Ten shillings, please." I paid up, left the office, picked up my large armful of merchandise, and made my way to the station as usual. Nothing was said next day or thereafter, in spite of dozens of my work-mates seeing my tactics.

I took my material to the tailor who gave me two fittings and told me to call on the third Saturday when the coat will be finished. On the appointed Saturday, I went to the shop in North Street and was surprised to see my coat adorning a dummy in the window. The boss suggested that I should not get excited as he was prepared not to charge me a penny for making the coat, if he could leave it in his window for a month. To this, I readily agreed. So now, I have a cashmere camel haired overcoat 48 years old, looks new, fits perfectly and I look like a millionaire. God knows how much such a garment would cost in Harrods today.

Mother liked my coat and said it didn't suit a factory worker.

"Why don't you get a better job?" she asked. She had seen an advert in the Evening Argus 'Young man wanted as trainee Masseur'.

"Go along and see what it entails" she insisted, "Anything is better than the job you're doing at the moment."

To please Ma I called at the address in First Avenue, Hove. Dr. Gordon Marsden answered the door, a very healthy, tanned, gentleman in his seventies. He only looked about fifty and had a very firm grip. I told him I was applying for the position he had to offer. His first words struck me as strange.

"Ah, the man I've been looking for, come in." I must have suited him for I got the job, part time to start with until he opened his health clinic.

The evening work suited me as I could continue with my full-time job. I had quite a lot of homework to do which I did very early each morning before going to the sweatshop. Dr. Marsden was an Australian well into the keep-fit business. In his book, he spelt out how to attain 'good health and longevity'. How right he was. Today he would have made a fortune, but he was fifty years before his time.

"Do you eat white bread and white sugar?" was one of his first questions to me.

"Yes" I replied.

"Throw it in the dustbin and never eat white bread again." My mother agreed and we as a family never ate white death.

In two weeks, I learned how to massage for weight reduction. He had converted part of his home into a massage parlour and it was there I first laid my hands on the overweight ladies that frequented the place. I found out that after half-a-dozen treatments, the ladies bodies became much firmer and certainly they lost weight, mainly because they had been instructed to eat less.

My problems started when the not-so-fat ladies became very nice fit ladies and I found I was feeling very fruity most of the time. I well remember one such damsel murmuring aloud

156

"Oh Mr. Fear, that's lovely, please don't stop. Oh please don't stop." After the treatment she gave me a handsome tip and her telephone number. "You should start business on your own" was her advice.

Lucky for Mrs. X, I received the letter to report to the Poultry Farm. By-the-way, I later understood Dr. Marsden's opening remark to me. It seems I was the only person who applied for the job. I did however earn the distinction of having MCNT after my name. As for Dr. Marsden, he opened his clinic but was banished out of Brighton labelled 'an Australian quack'.

I had completed a month's poultry farmer's course prior to my demob from the army and after being called up with the spivs and drones, I had applied for a government's sponsorship to learn how to become a poultry farmer. Apparently there was a waiting list, but finally I went before a committee at Lewis very close to the prison. They asked me a few questions and said they would fix me up on a poultry farm in the vicinity.

Some months later, out of the blue, came a letter to say I was to report for work at a poultry farm at Plumpton, a few miles outside Brighton. As it was a 7 am start, it meant I would have to find accommodation in Plumpton. A friend of the poultry farmer accommodated me. I had a small bedroom and full board 5 days a week.

The poultry farm turned out to be a collection of broken down sheds. I saw few chickens and was ordered to clean out some of the empty sheds. No mean task, as I am sure they had never been cleaned out for years. There was at least a foot of droppings caked to the floor. After the first day's hard labour, I was totally exhausted. The only manual work I had ever done was digging a few slit trenches. My dinner that evening gave me violent indigestion and I went to bed a very unhappy, disillusioned man. The second and third days were equally exhausting and I never saw the poultry farmer or his chickens at any time. On the Wednesday, the third day, I had just finished an equally indigestible meal when who should arrive at the front door, but my pal Ken Webb. We exchanged a few pleasantries and then he said:

"How would you like to go to Hanley and open a pools office on my behalf?"

"Where's that, never heard of it?"

"It's one of the five towns in Stoke-on-Trent" he replied.

"Ah, now I know Stoke. It's where Stanley Matthews comes from. What's the deal?"

"We have taken over a small connection from ITP. A Mr. Norman Black has moved to William Hills down south somewhere and ITP has sold out. There are half a dozen agents you may be able to persuade to change to our 'Fixed Odds' coupon. Then it will be up to you to go out and get more agents."

"How much do I get and where do I stay?" I enquired.

"A bit more than you're getting now and a good bonus scheme. I will book you into a small hotel for the first week, then it will be up to you to find your own accommodation. If you do well, we will supply you with a small car."

"I've had no experience with the job you offer," I protested. "I know I have run your coupons at the factory for a few months and that's all."

"I have a feeling you will do very well," he replied. "I am taking a chance too, as there are several other men interested in the job."

"When do you want an answer?" I asked.

"Now" he replied.

"That's impossible," I protested. "I must talk to Hazel first."

"I've already had a word with her and she says it's okay by her. Look, if you stay here, you'll be shovelling shit for the rest of your life, but if you join me you'll be able to own your own bloody chicken farm in 5 years."

I thought to myself something my elder brother Jim had said. 'In your life young man, you'll perhaps be lucky and get one opportunity. You must not hesitate. It may never occur again and the first £100 is the hardest to accumulate. After that it's easy.' I thought for a moment or two then grasped Ken's hand and said:

"You have a deal. I'll leave for Stoke tomorrow."

"Good, pack your bag and I'll take you back home." I told the landlady I was leaving and she said:

"You can't do that"

As it turned out Jim's advice was sound and Ken's forecast accurate and I could indeed have bought my own poultry farm within 5 years. But those 5 years were spent in a most extraordinary manner and I am sure my upbringing and years in the Guards helped me overcome the trials and tribulations that were to come.

Hazel was to continue to work at the Errol works until hopefully I got accommodation for us. She was a good sort and said she thought I would make it. We kissed goodbye that Thursday morning and it would be eight months before I was to see her again.

I arrived at Stoke station and made my way to my hotel, which turned out to be a very select country club on the outskirts of Stoke. That evening I met, for the first time, people from the Potteries, and what a revelation. Millionaires would mingle and be pally with the local milkman or window cleaner; so unlike some of the snobbish people down south. They made me very welcome from the start and wished me luck in my new venture. I was not allowed to buy a single drink that first evening. The pottery people of those days were a breed apart, very friendly and helpful.

Next day I met Mr. Black, who put me in the picture regarding the six agents I should meet as soon as possible. He also told me of a few pubs where gambling played a prominent part. He said I must find a new office as the landlord of his office had other plans now that ITP was closing down. Mr. Black departed for Plymouth later that day so now I was on my own.

To find an office was my first priority so I made my way to Charles Butters, the estate agents in Trinity Street. I stated my requirements to Bill Cooper who, with Mr. Parry, owned the well-established firm. Bill Cooper was most helpful and said:

"If you don't mind a first floor office, I may have the very place for you, 200 yards from this office."

159

He took me round to 41a Piccadilly, on the first floor over the Army and Navy Stores and next door to the Gaumont Cinema. There were two floors above but not tenanted at this point.

"How much?" I enquired.

"How's £3 a week sound, inclusive of rates?"

"Great," I replied. "I'll advise the boss in Hove and get you 3 months rent in advance."

Mr. Cooper had a crop of silver grey hair and was a fine example of an English gentleman. We were to be friends for a great many years. His son, Tim, followed his father in the business and, like his dad, has turned into lifelong friends, together with his delightful wife, Thelma. The office consisted of two rooms, one with a long counter and an inner office large enough to house six clerks.

I bought a street map of the area and was alarmed to find that four of the six named agents lived outside Stoke-on-Trent. No matter, another map supplied me with the information I sought. That evening I visited the two local agents and was happy to report that both would be interested in running 'Webbs Fixed Odds'. I told them they would be rewarded if they could introduce me to other contacts.

As I remember, the other four lived at Blythe Bridge, Cheadle Waterhouses, and Kingsley Holt. I had no transport so the following Sunday I trudged round on foot. My first call at Blythe Bridge was to meet the delightful family of Bert Wood. Mrs. Wood was kindness itself and she sported the finest pair of legs I had ever seen. Her two daughters were something to behold. As for Bert, it would take two chapters to describe his many talents. He was a retired coal miner and spent his hard-earned commission in educating his daughters to a high standard. After my last call at Kingsley Holt, I made my way to the Ash Bank Club, which Norman Black had recommended to me. It was 9 pm.

I was knackered, to say the least. Like the country club where I was staying, all the members were very friendly. Bill Rowley was very impressed with my hike and introduced me to Billy Carter who turned out to be a professional gambler.

"Where are you staying?" he enquired. When I told him he said:

"That's another 5 miles. I'll run you home at closing time." And so he did, in his Rolls Royce.

I did some good business from the Ash Bank Club for many years. The four agents I visited all signed up with me and when I telephoned Webb on Monday, he seemed delighted. I had signed up the six ex-pools agents, got myself a very central office at a very cheap rate, and arranged for a phone to be installed within the next few days. One agent led to another and with my sample coupon and its attractive heading: 'Win Weekly with Webb', I soon found that it was the coupon these people were waiting for. William Hill had agents in the area and these agents were my target. Their system of collection and pay-out didn't suit the majority of agents, so I was able to persuade several to change over to me, much to the annoyance of Mr. Brown, the Hills' main agent in the area.

Ken Webb visited me a few weeks later and bought with him Templegate Trio Tickets at sixpence a ticket, with numbers which corresponded with Templegate Horse forecasts in the Daily Herald, the much read socialist paper of those days. If your numbers were correct, you got three doubles and a treble up at £1 odds.

"Money for old rope" Webb said and I agree. However, my sub-agents were delighted with the chance to earn 25% commission on their total taking. Unsold tickets were returnable.

In the end, I was getting rid of £500 worth a week and the Webbs' were so delighted that they bought me my first car, an Austin Seven. It was a Godsend. Although I had driven 15 cwt. and 50-ton tanks in the war, I still had to take a driving test. I failed two and was beginning to give up hope, but luck was with me for at my third attempt the examining officer got into my car in a terrible state, shaking visibly. I asked him what was the matter and he replied that he had just failed a guy because he couldn't drive at all. The client had raged:

"I am Mr. Davies, MP for Leek. You have got to pass me"

"No I haven't," replied my new found friend. "You haven't got a clue"

"I'll have you sacked" bellowed Mr. Davies.

The row had upset my examiner a great deal and he said:

"Just drive where you like and find a spot where we can pull up and have a chat."

I did just that and he lit up a fag and talked away like an old partner. He said he would follow my career with interest and said if any of my family wanted testing, to make sure they got him. After a while, he said we had better get back to Longsdale Street. Needless to say, I had passed with credit. As for Mr. Davies, he must have passed some time or other, for some years later he arrived at my home at Foxdale courting my then ex-wife, Hazel. As he crept in the dark and left in the dark, perhaps he hadn't passed a test but was just chancing his arm. A typical M.P. Snot-gobbling, sanctimonious and two-faced creeps, as I would describe many of them.

My Austin Seven didn't last long and I will now describe its fate: Two of my friendliest sub-agents of this time were Ernie Wood of Kingsley Holt and Geoff Lomas of Huntley near Cheadle. Ernie collected bets and coupons at Boultons' Copper Works at Froghall and Geoff was a delightful banjo entertainer. He could play his banjo from opening time until closing time, sing along in perfect disharmony, and never repeat a ditty. Actually, he sounded quite awful to start with, but after a few pints and the evening wore on, his voice and banjo seemed quite pleasant.

Anyway the public liked him and he was always in big demand, so I thought I had better sign him up as my personal entertainer. He was happy to agree with my terms of £5 per year (in advance of course), which meant I had first call on him any Friday or Saturday night. I would take him with me on my weekly adventures into the unknown pubs of north Staffs. Everyone seemed to know him and I am including people who collected or invested on Webb's 'Fixed Odds' coupon. Dear old 'Steel Tonsils', as he was so lovingly known.

One Saturday night, we had been giving a performance at Jim Shaunessy's pub in Chesterton. Ernie Wood, Geoff, and I were returning home all under the influence from our successful evening in Chesterton. It was foggy and we made our way across the Potteries and finally got to Kingsley where Ernie suggested we stop at a pub in the town.

"But it's past midnight they will have been shut an hour" I protested.

"Not on your Nellie" he said. "They stay open all hours on Saturday nights".

So, in we went. The place was full of happy people singing and dancing to their hearts' content. We downed some more beer and at about 1 o'clock decided to call it a day.

Ernie, Geoff, and I climbed into the old Austin and made our way to Kingsley Holt. The fog had thickened, as indeed had my brain. We hadn't gone a hundred yards when there was an almighty crash and the old bus came to a standstill. We were all flung about and there was dead silence for a moment or two. Then old Steel Tonsils cried out from his front seat position:

"Is my banjo alright?"

"F—k your banjo", yelled Mr. Wood. "How am I going to eat my breakfast in the morning" and he spat his front teeth into his hand. They had been dislodged from his poor old gums when his head crashed into the head of Geoff sitting in front of him. We surveyed the damage and decided to make our own way home. I returned to Bridle Path and they in the opposite direction. The following evening, I returned to the pub we had been drinking at and as I stood at the bar the local policeman came up, put is hand on my shoulder and cried:

"Mine's a pint. When are you going to collect your car, Ray?"

"Oh, will tomorrow be alright?"

"Sure, take your time and I think I'll have another pint."

That was the village copper - turn a blind eye to anything for a pint or two. Another Saturday night's entertainment I well remember with 'Steel Tonsils' was at Halmerend, a small mining village on the outskirts of Newcastle-under-Lyme.

A publican of that village, with whom I had been negotiating to run Webb's coupons, telephoned me and asked if I would like to come to his pub next Saturday, to judge the 'Biggest Fanny Competition'.

"Bring Geoff won't you?" he added.

I could hardly refuse this interesting request. What I would have to do conjured up all manner of terrors in my mind. My fears were groundless however – for the judging was easy. The only thing the ladies had to do was remove their knickers and sit astride a school form, and roll up and down on a generous sprinkling of flour. My task was to measure the imprint with a tape measure. The eventual winner was the smallest competitor, which confirms the saying: 'Big woman - Big fanny- Little woman - All fanny'.

By the time the 1952 football season was to start, I had signed up over 100 agents to take the fixed odds coupons. The Webbs' were overjoyed, I can tell you. I had to organise the pick up of most of the agents' coupons before the 3 o'clock kick-off, sort out a staff of clerks to check the coupons and list winning clients to be paid out. To get honest, reliable personnel to do this would need some careful thought. Then I hit on the idea of civil servants who would undoubtedly lose their excellent safe jobs if ever they transgressed in any way, shape or form.

I made my way to the office of Social Security in Hanley and asked to see the manager. Johnny Hughes came forward and I immediately took a liking to this friendly Welshman. I told him my needs and he said:

"I am sorry, we civil servants aren't allowed to partake in any other part time employment. Against the rules. Incidentally, how much an hour?" he enquired.

"Five shillings an hour, tax free. How's that?"

"Five shillings an hour, count me in and how many clerks do you need?" I told him. "Fair enough, I'll be down at your office tomorrow with reliable staff for your inspection and to sort out final details."

Next evening, after office hours, into 41a Piccadilly trooped Johnny Hughes, Harry Baskeyfield, Douglas Philpott, Cyril Knapper and a couple more whose names escape me. I had advertised in the local Evening Sentinel for checkers and drivers and had an excellent response. From these I was able to employ Arthur Matthews, Stan's brother, Joe Baddley - a miner, and Les Wilburn a wages clerk at one of the Pot banks.

The football season kicked off and we got off to an excellent start, winning over 60% of the take. Mr. Webb Senior visited us from time to time and it didn't take me long to discover that the man was quite mad. More concerned with emptying his bowels than conducting his business. He was, however, a very clever man at picking his short list. The short list was a group of eight matches selected by Mr. Webb from any of the English or Scottish leagues. He offered odds of 8-1 for three homes or three aways. So his target was to get as many draws amongst the 8 matches as possible, thereby making it difficult for the punter to win.

Nearly every week there would be 3 or 4 draws amongst his 8 selections and it didn't take the punters long to realise that, if they permutated his short list, any 3 from 8, 56 lines at 1/- on the long list, if there were 3 draws up at 52-1, they would only lose four shillings. However, if there were four draws they would get four lines of 52-1, winning £6.34. And if they got five draws they'd win them 10 lines. I warned him of this, but he said:

"Don't be afraid, I've never had a losing season since I started coupons."

One day Ken arrived and said the boss wanted to start bookmaking in the Potteries. My heart sank. What next? I wondered. Bookmaking. I knew next to nothing about the game. I asked Ken what it would involve.

"You will work with agents and clock bags."

"Clock bags, what's that?"

"It's a device the agents operate with a single clock bag, which, when they have collected their bets on the works or factory, they put all the slips into a leather bag and screw on the clock which fits on top of the bag. At the point they clock-in, the pocket sized watch stops, letting the bookmaker know at what time the bets were secured safely before racing started."

The six-race bag was a much more complicated mechanism which allowed the bookies runner to clock in 6 times during an afternoon's racing according to the times of the races. These were issued to the bigger runners collecting in excess of £50 a day.

Webb Senior also made the dreadful mistake of going 'No Limit' on the bets collected. This was quite unnecessary as all the Potteries bookies had very tight limits which safeguarded their livelihood and which didn't upset the clients too much as they were terms they had been used to. To get better odds, they would have to get on their bikes and cycle to Birmingham, Manchester, or London.

Old Big Head wouldn't listen and instructed me to get cracking as he wanted to start business when the flat started in March 1953.

"Open a book on the spring double," he declared, "the Lincoln Handicap, and Grand National." And so we did, and took thousands of bets for which vouchers had to be issued confirming the stake's odds and what the punter would win. I had to employ a full-time clerk just to write out the ante-post vouchers. Old Big Head was just lucky and we got a turn up in the Lincoln that knocked out all but a couple of small bets.

After a shaky start, I soon got into the swing of opening the clock bags bought to the office by my drivers after racing had finished. The routine was as follows: Drivers collect the clock bags from the runners. I open them and check that there were no bets in the 2.30 bag containing the 2.0 and 2.15 winners, and so on. I then transferred the bets into a large brown envelope with the agent's name and code number written on the front. This would then go into a box to await being staked. In other words, checked-up on the total investments of the agent. This figure would be entered on the front of the envelope.

Next, the bets would be checked by our checking team, the real brains of the operation. They would sort out winning bets from losers. These, in turn, would be passed to the 'writers-in', who listed the name of the winning client and his return. This list was added up and deducted from the day's takings or, in some cases the stakes were deducted from the winnings, giving a balance of one way or the other. At the end of the day, all the agents were listed and we would soon see what had been won or lost.

The 'no limit' old Webb offered knackered the business, as every week a bet would turn up that would fetch hundreds of pounds. With a sensible limit, the client would have won much less. These odd

166

winning bets got up the nostrils of Webb Senior, who thought some skulduggery was going on between my staff and the agents. This could easily be done with dishonest clerks who, lucky for me, had been interviewed and selected by His Lordship.

I, too, came under suspicion when Martin Hamnett, who collected on the huge Steel Works of Shelton Bar, won over £500 on a bet. I had previously told old Webbey what a character Martin was. He had served in the parachute regiment during the war. Just because of my fraternisation with him, Webb thought I had stuck the bet in after time and shared the proceeds with Hamnett. I had done no such thing, but if I had been of a dishonest nature, I certainly would never get involved with a second person who would have you by the balls for ever.

I'm a funny old bugger, as you may have concluded so far, but stealing cash from a good friend would never interest me and young Ken was a friend. Come the Derby and a horse called Pinza, to be ridden by the maestro Gordon Richards, was favourite. We took thousands of pounds ante-post on the 1953 Derby, but very little on Pinza. The punters were looking for bigger odds and a turn up. Old Webb came up from Hove to conduct the running of the Derby. When he went through the ante-post books and saw we hadn't laid (taken many bets) on the favourite, he went berserk.

"What sort of book is this?" he yelled. "You haven't laid the favourite."

"Can't help it" I replied. "The punters aren't interested in short priced favourites."

He immediately telephoned Percy Cooper and offered him a point over the current odds, which Percy immediately accepted.

"Put me £300 on Pinza" he instructed.

How bloody clever. Pinza was an easy winner and we had a good day spoilt by the £1000 we had to pay the Coopers'. Webb was adamant after the race and declared

"You've got to lay the favourites." A theory I always ignored in the forty years of bookmaking I was soon to undertake. I preferred the best horse in a race running for me.

Relations between Mr. Webb Senior and me became very strained. I felt very uneasy and trapped in Stoke-on-Trent. The final straw was when he sent up one of his staff from Hove to conduct the running of the office. I think the guy was a Mr. Smullet, a snivelling short-arsed little creep whose very appearance upset my agents.

"Who is he? ", they declared.

He had no idea of public relations. Thankfully he could see no point in staying in Hanley as everyone ignored his silly orders, so he soon returned to Hove.

The second football season had started and, as usual, old Big Head was shrewdly getting the draws on the short list, three or four a week, and while he was winning on that list, the punters were copping on the three draws on the long list. One Saturday in November, he got six draws amongst the eight on the short list. I feared the worst. This meant that the clients, picking Webb's brains and gambling on the three draws with the aid of his shortlist, had a field day. Anyone doing the three from eight had 20 lines up. A disaster!

Webb Senior back in Hove saw the danger and telephoned Hanley and instructed Ken 'to put up the shutters, close the office, and return to Hove.'

"What does he mean?" I demanded.

"He ain't paying out," was his reply "and if I was you I'd close the front door and dismiss the checkers before the first agents begin to arrive for their returns."

I thought for a moment or two. 'If we close down now we shall never know the extent of our losses. They can't all win, not all the 100 odd agents, and if we win from some we can pay out on the smaller winning agents. It may not be as bad as all that, I thought.'

I told Ken I was staying and he had best clear off as soon as possible and leave me to my own devices. We bid each other goodbye and he said he would telephone me later.

A sudden calm came over me. I didn't panic, nor did I tell any of the checkers my predicament. As the agents coupons were checked, things didn't seem so bad as first predicted. In fact, we won from over 50 of the agents, which enabled me to pay out on 30-40 smaller

168

winning agents. In the end, only 20 agents were owed money, 15 of them in Crewe and only 5 in Stoke on Trent. I endeavoured to settle the Stoke agents first for obvious reasons. Many of the losing agents' clients could be paid out of their stake money. So my decision to stay and face the music was correct. I still had 80 happy agents and some of the unlucky ones didn't seem too bothered. In fact, a chap called Finny, who was owed £30 said:

"Well Ray, you had better get fixed up with another firm, pronto." I couldn't believe this man's loyalty.

The following Monday was very unpleasant; a day to remember all my life. Racing continued as usual, but as it was National Hunt Racing, business was greatly reduced. I had no ready money for payout in case we lost, so I thought my best bet was to go to Barclays and see if I could get a loan. I had dealt there through Webb's for a couple of years so I was known to the manager. I managed to see him and explained what had happened.

"Could I have a loan?"

"What collateral have you?" Never being in business before, I didn't know what he was talking about. "Have you a house or investments?"

"No" I replied. "I've just spent 5 years in the Guards and haven't had a chance to get a home. I am only 26 years old."

"I am sorry Mr. Fear, I can't help you," he replied.

"Not even £5?" I asked.

"Not even £5" was his answer.

Foreseeing a refusal, I had bought a pair of Zeiss Binoculars with me and hastened down Hope Street to the pawn shop who loaned me £3 on a six-month ticket, thank God. Hope we win today.

The big problems started after working hours that evening, when irate punters having won on the football, came to the office to demand their winnings. (A very unpleasant experience, I can assure you. One very angry miner came in brandishing a pickaxe handle. I told him I had nothing, only the clothes I stood up in.

"That will do me," he cried. "Let's try your jacket on." I flung my coat at him and to his satisfaction it fitted well.

"Now the trousers." he demanded, brandishing his fearsome weapon. I didn't hesitate. In fact I was being watched by my racing checkers, agents, and individual clients. I took off my pants and threw them in his direction.

"I'd have them dry-cleaned," I jeered. "I've just had a dose of gonorrhoea." This caused a laugh in the office at the expense of the guy who had just acquired my suit.

Things quietened down a little and my next problem was to get a sponsor for next Saturday's matches. The coupons had already gone out to the agents as usual, but at this point, there was no one liable for the payout. I had met a lively, likeable gentleman at the Ash Bank Club, whose name was Idras Isaacs, a Welshman and not a Jew in spite of his name. I made my way home with brown paper covering my private parts, a sight that Hazel found most amusing. After dinner, I got into my best suit and called at the Club. Luckily, Mr. Isaac was in and I quickly cornered him.

I told him what Webb had done and after a few enquiries he said he would have a word with his pal, Mr. Fenton, a local butcher, and a very nice gentleman he turned out to be. I was told to return next evening when they would give me their answer. I did just that after another unpleasant day when further unpaid clients called at my office to demand their rights. I told them all to come back in two weeks time and that if I had acquired any funds I would be able to pay them. This was always my contention and, funny enough, years later people were coming up to me to say I owed them a pound or two on their fixed odds winnings when Webb did a bunk. I always paid what they asked and no doubt some of the claims were false. But the rogues who caught me no doubt continued to bet and, in the long run, I got my money back.

The meeting with Mr. Isaac and Mr. Fenton was very jovial and they agreed to run the coupons for a trial period. On the following Saturday the results were not good but fortunately, because of the last week's scandal, our takings were halved. We won a few pounds but not enough to please Mr. Isaac, who had the wrong idea that bookies always won most of their take.

170

"That's enough for me," he declared. "I'm finished."

I had heard of a firm called 'Rays of Halifax', so I telephoned them and explained the situation. They had heard that Webb had failed to pay out in Stoke but was carrying on in other parts of the country. They thought that Webb should be banished from ever taking another bet. They were very interested and came to Stoke the same day along with a few thousand coupons for the following Saturday. 'Rays' lasted for about a month. As the takings continued to fall, the results were not good and in the end, the boss said:

"Sorry Ray, you'll have to get another firm." They were very fair and gave me a month's wages to keep me going.

All my sub-agents were getting a bit restless at this point and a few of them changed over to William Hill. I racked my brains for the answer, when somebody mentioned 'Shermans' of Cardiff. After a short conversation on the telephone, they said that they would let me have some fixed odds coupons, as long as I ran their pools coupons as well. To this I readily agreed and this was the beginning of my 40 years in Pools.

I met a Mr. Walker, a security guard at Shermans' and an ex-police officer, at Stoke station later that day. I took him to the small guesthouse where, for the next few years, he was to spend every Friday night during the football season. (No summer pools in those days!) He had brought me several thousand Pools and fixed odds coupons in a large blue suitcase, which I hastened to deliver to my numerous sub-agents. We got off to a slow start, but because of their regularity, Shermans' soon became very popular in Stoke-on-Trent.

Harry Sherman was a toff and every Christmas he would telephone to thank me for my business, to wish my family and me a happy Christmas and to enquire if a large box of Habana cigars would be acceptable.

"Yes Mr. Sherman." He really knew how to treat his main agents and get the best out of them.

It was a sad day for me, when he sold out to Littlewoods. When he did this, he telephoned to wish me luck in the future and that if he could ever be of help, to just telephone him. He gave me his home number and we bid each other farewell.

One day after the changeover, a guy called at my new office in Marsh Street to announce that he was the Littlewoods manager and that he had taken me over. I must report to his office in Stoke the very next evening to receive instructions. I was in no mood to talk to this little dictator during the middle of racing, so I told him to piss-off out of my office. I asked Mr. Baddeley, my manager, what the alternative to Littlewoods was. He reeled off a few firms and I said:

"We will try Vernons'."

I telephoned Liverpool and asked to speak to the boss. I was put through to a Mr. Bethell, the Collectors Service manager. I asked him if he was interested in my business.

"Well," he replied. "We only deal with agents through the post, but I suppose we will have to change our ways if we hope to expand."

When I told him I wanted 8000 coupons a week, he was most surprised and asked if I could furnish him with a reference. I gave him my bank number as I knew they were aware of my weekly take.

"I'll have a word and telephone you back" he said. Two minutes later, he was back on the telephone.

"I am on my way. Can you meet me at Stoke station?" He telephoned yet again with details of travelling arrangements.

He was a very nice gentleman of the 'Old school'. He said he would personally collect my coupons each Saturday and asked if it would be possible for him to sit quietly in my office from 10 am onwards to see how main agents operated. I saw no reason to refuse his request and felt quite proud that a firm like Vernons' were coming to me to learn all about collectors' service. That's how Vernons' started their main agents business.

The first year or two was great, dealing with Mr. Bethell, but things soon changed when they appointed regional, area, and local managers. I had dozens of these people to deal with over the years. Some were nice, some were bastards, but they all had one thing in common. They knew next to nothing about Pools. Breaking in these new managers was a problem and a waste of valuable time. But more about Vernons' Pools towards the end of my narrative.

Back to racing and my first Cheltenham was approaching. I had heard that it was a busy time for bookmakers and that soon after the Cheltenham Festival, the Lincoln and National would follow. I had earned a few bucks in my early months as a bookmaker, but not enough if I had a few bad days. Joe Baddeley said he would be interested in investing £50 in the business and that if things went well, he would pack up his job at the pit and come and work full-time for me. Mr. Wilburn also said he would invest £50, but would only want a share in any profit we had made at the end of the year. And so I stuck in my life savings of £100 and my two partners gave £50 each. I just hoped that Cheltenham would start us off on the right foot.

Fortunately we had a great 3 days and, in fact, won every day for the first four weeks, including good results in the Lincoln and Grand National. Joe Baddeley came to work full-time at a weekly wage; I also drew a somewhat larger wage and we three agreed to share any profits at the end of 12 months - they 25 % each and me 50%. At the end of the year, we had made a handsome profit. Mr. Wilburn decided to start business on his own and left to open up in Burslem. Joe and I had a long chat on the future and I agreed to increase his share to 33 %, as long as he left a certain amount of capital in the kitty. As business increased, I began to think about income tax and bank safe deposit boxes. Both Joe and I acquired two large deed boxes and had our names painted on the top of each.

My next port of call was the income tax office in Stoke. After a little while, it was my turn to approach the counter.

"Yes, Sir?" the girl enquired.

"I want to pay tax." I declared.

"How unusual" was her reply. "When did you start business?"

"Today." I said. A wry smile crept over her face.

"Just a moment" she said and disappeared to the manager's office. A few moments later, the door opened a little way and the manager peered out. Something was said to the clerk and I could hear a titter between them.

"I'll make you titter," I murmured to myself. "By God I'll make you titter." The girl returned to the counter, told me the routine, and told me I must return to their office in one year's time.

Each day my first job was to fill in my tax book; daily take winnings or losses. At the end of each week I concocted the expenses and deducted this from the winnings and carried the result forward. If we had a losing week, the losses were added to the expenses. This was a very simple way to keep one's books and within 24 hours of my year's end I could produce my books, all spic and span. So at the end of the 12 months I returned to the tax office and presented my tax book to them. The counter hand was a bit reluctant to accept them, but I pointed out that I had been instructed to return after one year in business. A short while later, the income tax people telephoned me and said they had examined my books and I must employ an accountant.

"That will cost me money," I replied "and I can't afford an accountant. I'll do my own books if you please."

"An accountant will save you a lot of money" she replied.

"In that case name me one" I said.

"Not allowed to do that." she replied

"Miss, do you deal with accountants?"

"Yes all the time"

"Well name one"

"Where is your office, Sir?"

"Piccadilly" I replied.

"There's a J.C. Barker & Son in Pall Mall" she advised me, and that's where I took my books and where I stayed for 40 years.

I thought the tax inspectors were hardly likely to recommend an accountant other than a respected one. As it turned out, I had no problems with the taxman and they accepted my figures annually without a murmur. So I got my own back on their tittering. Each year I would spend an hour or two with Mr. Barker Senior and books would be cleared within two weeks, but as the years rolled by taxes became more complicated and towards the end of my business career it was over a year before the firm were able to complete my books.

174

A couple of incidents are worth recording. One year I had a tax demand of £4.50. I immediately telephoned J.C. Barker and demanded to know what he was playing at.

"But it's only £4.50" he protested.

"Yes Mr. Barker, but it's the thin end of the wedge"

"Okay" he agreed, "I'll see what I can do, but pay what they demand."

Some while later I had a letter from Longsdale Street to say there had been a mistake and that they would hold £4.50 to my credit. I telephoned the tax office straight away and asked to speak to the boss.

"I can deal with you" the clerk replied.

"I want to speak to the boss, not his hirelings." I snorted.

I was put through to His Lordship and I told him the problem. "It's normal to hold small amounts to the client's credit" he explained.

"That may be, but you have no right to hold my hard-earned cash. Please send me a cheque immediately." I put down the telephone before I received an answer. A little while later, I got my cheque for £4.50. Old Joe Baddeley said:

"I don't know Ray, you've got a nerve."

Some years later, I had to pay about £60 for the year. This infuriated me and I had a word with the inspector of taxes.

"I can pay a bit each month." I announced.

He gave me the address of their new offices in Stoke and I duly called in my nice blue Mercedes Coupe. I took off my expensive leather coat and exchanged it for my old gardening anorak. I gave the girl behind the counter my tax demand and said I could pay £1 on account.

"That's not enough Sir, can't you manage a little more?"

"I am afraid not."

"Okay, but you must call again next week." She was about to write out my receipt when I suddenly thought of an angle on how to reduce my payment.

"Oh, Miss, I am sorry, my wife has asked me to get some ostermilk for the baby and I haven't any more money"

"Oh, dear me, I'll reduce your payment to 10/-, but please make sure you have at least £1 next week. How old is the baby?" I thought I had better not say he was 7 years old, so I said:

"Just six months, my dear." I laughed to myself as I descended in the lift and thought to myself, I'll make you titter.

While we are on the subject of tax, it is interesting to mention that poor Joe Baddeley was killed in a taxi returning home after night racing. I visited Olive Baddeley the next day with my condolences and explained about Joe's deed box at the bank. She knew about it, but not how much it contained. I said she must hasten to the bank and ask the manager if she could have access to the box. This she did but the manager said because of the death of Mr. Baddeley, the box must be opened in the presence of the manager, a solicitor, and a tax inspector. When she told me this I was very concerned, so I called at the bank and asked if Mrs. Baddeley could just have 30 seconds to unload any cash into her shopping bag.

"Not possible, more than my job's worth."

"No one will know if you and she go to the vault alone"

"Sorry." was his reply.

I then had a word with Ben Brereton. Ben was a close friend of mine and I asked if he could nip down and grab a bag of notes if I gave him the key to Joe's box.

"That's impossible as I have no authority to ask for the keys to the vault." And so it all happened and in the end the box was found to contain over £10,000 which, in the 1960s, was a great deal of money.

The tax inspector telephoned me and asked how my manager, earning £15 a week, could have accumulated so much money.

"I am amazed," I replied. "He must have won it on the Pools."

"No" was his reply. "Mrs. Baddeley said this and we have checked with the pools firms."

"Then he must have stolen it from me, worked it with one of our runners, the bastard. No wonder our winnings have been so low over the years."

"That's more like it," said the inspector. "Anyway, thanks for your help." Mrs. Baddeley finished up with less than half of the

176

windfall after the tax bodies had taken their share. Mr. Joe Badderely was a fine, honest, man and I was fully aware of the contents of his deed box. My business was never quite the same after his untimely death.

In about 1963, the government stepped in and announced that they would legalise betting and we bookmakers would have to apply for a license for ourselves and a license for each of any betting shops we may acquire. These would have to be applied for through the courts, a lengthy and time absorbing business. At the first hearing, I had applied for 16 betting shops. I was granted one license and three shops, being turned down on 13. Seemingly, the local licensing committee didn't want me to have a monopoly in the Potteries. Anyway, I objected to their decision.

On six of their refusals I took them to a higher court where we had to employ a barrister. The man we employed was Mr. Stephen Brown from Birmingham. He was brilliant in cross-examination and we got on very well indeed. He once said I was the best witness he had ever cross-examined in the witness box. We won our six cases with costs. So my regard for Stephen Brown didn't diminish because of large fees borne by the licensing committee. I applied for several more shops without any hindrance and finished up with 15. I also bought a few shops from other bookmakers, and at my peak had 20.

The 'powers that be' had laid down some laws and guidelines that we bookmakers must follow and the one that sticks in my mind most vividly was that the client must place his bet and leave the premises. The bookmaker must not provide newspapers, pencils, betting slips or anything else that may encourage a client to bet, and there certainly must not be any race-to-race payout. In my wisdom, I thought a small room would suffice and the best of my old runners could run the offices. If the government had stuck to the laws that they had made, all would be well and I would have survived, but it was not to be.

When the customs and excise saw what could be earned from betting, a blind eye was turned to the laws and very soon the large betting shops began to appear where every law in the book was broken so that people could spend a whole afternoon in a betting shop investing in every race and thereby doubling or trebling the stakes they would normally invest. This spelt the end of my days as a very wealthy bookmaker and as only a couple of my shops were big enough to conform with the new large betting shops, my weekly turnover was reduced by two thirds.

When I first started bookmaking, I had applied limits on what a client could win. 60-1 for a double, 80-1 for a treble, 100-1 for accumulator and a kick up the arse to anyone who exceeded these odds. I recall once a regular daily client who had his bet at HQ, having a sixpenny yankee up, 6 sixpenny doubles, 4 sixpenny trebles and a sixpenny accumulator. 5/6 invested, he had four big priced winners and his winnings should have been £460. Instead, with our limits, he won £16.1s., and I saved myself £445. My staff suggested I should face the client next day when he came for his winnings. I didn't fancy the job but reluctantly agreed. Next day our client arrived all bright and breezy.

"You had a bit of luck yesterday" I declared.

"Yes Sirrrr! What do you make it?" I hesitantly answered, my voice full of trepidation:

"Sixteen pounds and one shilling."

"Correct, that's what I made it, with the limits." I gave him the winnings and to my surprise he returned the shilling to me.

"Get yourself a pint." he laughed.

I thought to myself, I've done well coming to Stoke-on-Trent. In Brighton they would have killed the bookmaker. I had sensibly had thousands of rule cards printed, which all my agents distributed amongst their clients, so there was no argument when the punters hit the limits. These rules saved me a fortune.

To give the reader some idea of a 'Bookies Runner', I will endeavour to give my observations. In most cases, he was 100% honest and trusted by his workmates. He could work out the most difficult bets in his head and could hold his drink. But above all, they were all comedians and rare characters. I'll describe a few of these comedians.

Bill Hollins was the Potteries biggest runner. He lived at the Meir and collected all his bets in his kitchen in Cobham Place. He dressed in a most peculiar manner. Boots, bus conductors' trousers with red piping down the seams, an ARP overcoat (an air raid precautions warden's issue), and a cap. His nose had been bitten off by a savage dog when he was a lad and the wound had never healed, so he was constantly wiping what was left of his nose with a large, coloured handkerchief. He was a brilliant checker of bets and could give you the answer to any yankee in seconds. We gave him a six-race clock bag for a normal day's racing and two for big races and Saturdays. One Derby day he telephoned me at about noon and said he had used up his bags.

"But you had two six race bags" I declared.

"Filled them all" he cried.

"Then stick them in a sock!"

That evening he arrived at our office at 7 pm. In one hand, he held a straw fisherman's bag containing the two clock bags, and in the other a large carrier bag full of bets with an old newspaper over the top to hide his merchandise that he always used when travelling on the bus to get to our office. My offer to have one of my couriers pick up his bets had always been turned down as he insisted that he didn't want his business out of his hands. So now we have it, Bill arrives four hours after the big race with a large bag of bets.

There was nothing to stop him from taking out all the losing bets and putting in a few winning bets. Nothing at all. But Bill was 100% and was content with his commission. That Derby Day, Phil Drake won. Last round Tattenham Corner, he sped up on the outside of the field to win comfortably at 33-1. A French outsider, which few had backed. There was money to go back on the second and third and the other races run that day, but we won over £1,800 from Bill who paid up there and then with a smile. We had a brilliant day and decided then to have an agents' party later in the year.

We only had poor old Hollins for 3 or 4 years. One morning, as soon as our office opened, the telephone rang. It was Bill's brother who announced that Bill had got out of bed in the middle of the night, descended the stairs, and had a fatal heart attack in the kitchen. He was only 50 years old. I was dumfounded and rushed over to the Meir to see what was to be done about payout of his yesterday's bets, and who would collect this day's business. Apart from the money to be paid out, no other money was found according to the brother. Very strange, as Bill had been earning between £100 and £200 a week commission, when the average weekly wage of a man was £10-£15. It was always a mystery as to where the money went, but Bill's nephew seemed very affluent when I met up with him some years later. A nice, respectful lad.

I managed to get one of my smaller runners to take over the Meir round, a certain George Riley. What a card! YKM was his 'nom-de-plume.' I often wondered who YKM was when I opened his clock bag.

"Something fishy here," I told Joe Baddeley. "He always bets in fivers and tenners." I asked Riley one day who this punter was. All he replied was:

"You know me." It was him betting. He didn't win in the long run so we let him get on with it. If he wanted to lose most of his hard earned commission, that was his business.

When they legalised betting I opened a shop in Western Road. At first, it was a gold mine. In fact, we opened it before betting shops were legal, but I had a word with the police and they had said:

"Go ahead, no problem."

On our first Grand National at our new, and only, betting shop in Stoke-on-Trent, there were police controlling the queues waiting to place their bets. Mrs. Anne Riley would assist her husband, and what a hero she was. Educated to a high level, she could have run the shop herself. She worshiped George and fetched and carried for him. She always accompanied him to the office after racing and waited with him for their returns.

One afternoon a strange thing happened at Newmarket. A horse called Good Men are Missed, ridden by Doug Smith, won at 20-1 Now Doug Smith was second only to Gordon Richards and a top class experienced jockey, but on this occasion he failed to 'weigh-in', something all winning jockeys have to do after a race. So he was disqualified and placed last. Riley arrived at the office and I could see by his countenance that he was not in a good mood. When I opened his bag and was checking through them, I was surprised to see £10 each way on Good Men are Missed, and who was the unlucky punter? None other than YKM. Joe and I had a laugh behind George's back but pretended to be sorry for his bad luck. He grunted something about the unlucky jockey. The rest of this tale was related to me by the publican of the Unicorn, just opposite my office.

It seems that Mr. and Mrs. Riley seated themselves in the saloon bar and she ordered a pint for George and a half for herself. He sat there very quiet and she very wisely didn't disturb him from his thoughts. After a while, she said:

"Don't worry Duck, what would you like for your supper?" Without hesitation George replied:

"Doug Smith's balls on toast!"

George never had the best of health and Annie would look after the shop when he was unable to get to work. One of his illnesses was a little more serious, so I decided to visit him at his upstairs flat on Bentile Estate. I knocked on the door and his young daughter answered.

"Dad, Mr. Fear's here" she cried out.

"Don't let him up here" he said.

However, I decided to climb the steps and see how my dear George was feeling. He came to the door and seemed a bit distressed, but I insisted on entering his home to have a chat. I was amazed to see on his large dresser, dozens of white £100 bags used for silver. In each bag, there were normally twenty £5 bags of large coins. There must have been at least 30 of these bags. When I enquired the reason for this great store of money, his only reply was:

"I need to keep a bit of change about me in this business." Comedian? I should say so, and he was no. 1.

Harry Baker lived in Abby Hulton, one of the many council estates in Stoke-on-Trent. He was a founder member of the Workingman's Club in that area and played a big part in running that establishment, including handling the bets and football coupons. No one else was allowed to take bets or coupons at the club.

While still at Piccadilly I had got the floor above our offices made tenantable, lining the walls with hardboard and dividing the biggest room into two rooms and having a spy-hole cut so one could observe what was going on in the 'shaggery', as the one with the single bed was called. At one time, I installed a brooder for 50-day-old chicks. When they were about 6 weeks old, I transferred them into my garden. Harry Baker asked if he could have a dozen to rear up for Christmas. He said he would wire up half his garden and construct a hut for them. A couple of days later he took delivery of the twelve chicks.

About three months later I was travelling through the Abbey and decided to call on Harry and see how the chicks had grown. I remember well that although it was noon when I called, Mr. Baker was still in bed. I shouted that I had come to see his birds and he bawled back:

"Help yourself." I still can't believe what confronted me.

Of the 12 chicks, only 3 remained alive and I swear they were smaller than when I had given them to Harry three months earlier. The run was bare except for a handful of bones, the only thing left of the other nine birds.

"What in God's name have you been feeding them on?" I demanded.

"Feeding them?" he replied. "Didn't know you had to feed them. Thought they lived off the land."

I gave him a telling off and told him what to buy for the poor chickens, but they were too far gone and all three died within the week.

After he had been running for me for about 3 years they legalised betting and I managed to get a small room behind the chip shop at the abbey. I installed Harry there as office manager. His normal takings went up considerably and he seemed quite settled. As there were no big betters, the office was no worry to him. One Saturday night he arrived at the office in a right mood and I could see he was very agitated. As was the custom, the office managers settled one way or the other on a Saturday night. When we had checked the abbey's bets, we arrived at a figure and Harry had to pay in £120. He took the statement and settled down with a pen at a table the other side of the counter. A few minutes later, he called me to the counter.

"Here," he cried. "If you give me £1.50, we'll be square and I have finished working for Piccadilly Racing."

I couldn't believe my ears and picked up the slip of paper he had chucked at me. What I read was a classic, typical of my office manager. It read:

Two bicycle tyres £4.50

3 years Midday Chronicles £48.00

Shoe leather £10

Puncture outfit 50p;

New pair of trousers savaged by dog while collecting bets £3 .50

And so on...

The list was endless and when totalled up came to £121.50. So, according to him I owed him £1.50. What a giggle. So as to ensure he wouldn't talk about me, I paid him what he demanded and asked him to put a notice in his office window that the office was closed permanently and that clients could bring their bets up to me in Hanley or take them to Ernie Williams, the other bookmaker in the abbey. This he agreed to do.

I cannot record Harry Baker without telling you about his early days in Abbey Hulton. According to him, he was the local midwife and he had brought dozens of babies into the world. He once told me that if the baby was male, he would circumcise them at birth.

"How?" I enquired.

"With my forefinger and thumb." And he went through the motions of pinching off the poor unfortunate baby's winkle. What a lad he was. He continued running the coupons for me but I never allowed him to bring any of my offspring into the world, neither did I entrust him with any more chicks.

A word about my biggest telephone agent. I was motoring from Biddulph one Monday morning and drew into the garage of Geo.

Rhodes, situated a couple of miles out of town, to fill up. I was confronted by a man of about my own age whom I had never seen before. He addressed me as follows:

"Hello Ray. My mother's bookmaker, Mr. Darnley of Cangleton, committed suicide on Saturday night after a very bad day's results. You may be able to sign her up."

He gave me the address, 4 King Street, and I retraced my steps to visit the redoubtable Mrs. Elizabeth Rhodes. It seems I had been pointed out to George Rhodes by a friend at a recent bookmakers' dinner where our worthy president George Follows turned up in gum boots and a well worn Harris Tweed suit. It happened to be a black tie job, but George Follows was a law unto himself.

I knocked on the door of 4 King Street and was greeted by Mrs. Rhodes. I introduced myself and offered her my services.

"Too late" she cried. "I've been in touch with Knocker Holland of Tunstall. However, I'll take your card and give you a call if things don't work out.

Two weeks later the phone rang in my office. It was Elizabeth Rhodes.

"Can you believe it, Mr. Fear? They have sacked me! Never been sacked in my life. True I have had a couple of winning weeks, but not much."

"I shall do my best to accommodate you" I replied.

For many years she was a top agent and according to my records we won in excess of £35,000 (today's value £455,000). Her business came from her relations and business associates in the area. According to son George, she always referred to me as her Indian Prince. I fancy the Hollands, fearing the same fate as Mr. Darnley, got rid of Elizabeth before she ruined them.

Chapter 8

My Employees

There is a saying amongst my friends and business associates to wit:

'The Lord makes 'em and Fear takes 'em.'

I think this applies to some of the characters I employed. I've already mentioned my manager Joe Baddeley, and now I shall give you a write up about the lesser individuals I employed. The youngest and most interesting must be David Scrivens. I first met him when he used to bring his mother's six-race clock bag to the office daily at the end of racing. He was a cheeky varmint to say the least, but most likeable. After a few months he announced that he had been expelled from school for exposing his penis to his form mistress whom he had taken a fancy to.

"I'll be able to bring Ma's clock in a lot earlier now I don't have to go to school."

This suited us as it gave me a chance to open the clock and check the bets and see there were no winners of the 2 o'clock race in the 2.15 bag and so on. Occasionally his mother called at the office and one day asked if we could employ young David. I conferred with Joe Baddeley and we came to the conclusion that an office boy would be most useful. At the tender age of fifteen, David started full time employment with the Piccadilly Racing Service.

From the start, he proved to be a likeable pain in the arse, and I spent a lot of the time checking and re-checking the simplest of tasks I had asked of him. As his penis was above average in size, he would occasionally flash it to the rest of the male staff. When he misbehaved, I would order him to produce his dongle and lay it on an ashtray. I would then give it a couple of light taps with a ruler. As time went by my taps increased to quite a whack and accordingly the end of his dongle resembled a serpent's head. To this day, he relates these happenings with great pride and when under the influence of drink he startles his audience by showing them his serpent.

When betting was legalised we moved from our upstairs offices in Piccadilly to Marsh Street. Our toilets were across the yard at the back of the premises. On cold mornings, if I wanted to relieve my bowels I ordered Scrivens to go and warm the toilet seat. On the first morning, he shouted that he thought the seat was warm enough. I hastened to the W.C. to find Scrivens sitting on the seat with his trousers on. I was horrified.

"Get your pants off and warm the seat properly," I demanded. "You can't do the job correctly with your trousers on." A little while later he announced he thought the seat was to my liking.

"Okay." I said, "Stay where you are."

I crossed the yard and David was about to rise from his sitting position when I bawled out:

"Sit tight. Wait until I have dropped my pants." This done we quickly changed places. It was truly comfortable and I told him that is how I wanted it done in the future.

"Okay Boss." he replied with a smile on his face. Now that's discipline if you like.

Imagine what might happen today if one ordered one's staff to do likewise. You would be charged with anti-bum freezing, and be sent to jail for a lengthy period.

At the end of three or four years, David was still earning the same as when he started. Joe and I didn't think he ever earned his wages, small as they were. In the end, he left us and joined the Staffordshire Police. He was very popular and landed a nice cushy job from the start selling boxing tickets for the annual Army vs. Police at the Victoria Hall. He never did much normal duty expected of a young police officer and as the years went by he continued to skive and get all manner of odd jobs. Now he has retired, believe it or not, and we have remained good friends for all these years, exchanging letters and

Christmas cards without fail. He claims he learned more at Piccadilly than he would have done at any University.

You could hardly class Bill Potts as our employee as he was eighty-four years old, but he ran errands for us at Piccadilly before David had started. He would arrive at the office at 11 am daily and stay for several hours seated at the other side of the counter. He would make tea, post the mail, and fetch us our lunches from nearby Boyce Adams.

He was a real character. Short and fat with a bowler hat and brown suit that had not been washed or cleaned in a lifetime. He had a round, cheery face and resembled a cross between Winston Churchill and Mr. Pickwick. His waistcoat was something to behold, encrusted with bacon fat and gravy. I swear, had it been boiled, it would have made a tolerable soup. Across this monstrosity, he wore a gold watch chain attached to a gold Hunter pocket watch, which he claimed his employees had given him for fifty years service on his retirement. To ease the boredom of waiting for racing to start we played all manner of tricks on poor old Bill.

One morning at around 10.30 am I spied Bill standing on Burton's Corner, at the junction of Piccadilly and Stafford Street in Hanley. He looked quite peaceful. As I passed him, I very quickly thrust half-a-crown (12 ½ pence) into his hand. I am sure he didn't recognise me. As I passed Grays, the electrical shop, I saw the owner Cyril Barker having a breath of fresh air. I said to him

"You see that old guy on the corner, rush by and place half-a-crown in his hand. Don't stop and talk. Just be as quick as you can."

Cyril didn't hesitate and did what I bid. Old Bill looked bewildered but didn't move. Come 11 am he didn't come to our office. Nor did he call all day.

Next morning I was ready for him and when he arrived at his usual time I bollocked him up hill and down dale for failing to attend to his daily tasks of the previous day.

"No tea, mail not posted, I don't know."

"Dust yer surrey. I were standing at Burtons Corner when a very fine gentleman passed and put half-a-crown in my hand, and low and behold, five minutes later, another gentleman passed and put another half-a-crown in my hand. I thought it was my lucky day and I stood there until 6 o'clock. Sorry about the tea." We did laugh.

Joe Baddeley asked me if he could borrow my lawn roller to roll his new lawn next day. With the help of a neighbour, I managed to get it into the boot of my car. I parked outside the Theatre Royal about one hundred yards from my office. I told Joe I had brought the roller.

"Sorry Boss, I've decided to buy one." he replied.

"Doesn't matter, we will get old Bill to bring it to the office. Should be good fun."

Bill was none too pleased when I instructed him what to do. Two minutes after he left the office I followed him and took up a vantage point where I could watch his performance. It didn't take him long to realise that it was too heavy for him to lift out of the boot of my car so he wisely got the commissionaire from the theatre to assist him. Then the fun began. He pulled the roller behind him holding on with both hands and made his way very slowly up the slight hill of Pall Mall.

On reaching the junction of Piccadilly (I had already dashed back to the office and opened the window to get a clear view of Bill's progress), he stopped at the zebra crossing and hesitated to get his breath. Then after a lot of puffing and blowing, he managed to get the roller into the gutter. After another rest, he started to pull the hundredweight roller across Piccadilly. There is quite a camber in the road and after he had gone halfway, he stopped and that was his downfall, for at that moment the roller started rolling backwards gathering speed with every yard and dragging poor Bill with it. When it hit the kerb, poor old Bill went arse-over-tip and he landed on the pavement. Several passers-by rushed to his assistance. Not us however, we were doubled up with laughter.

A while later he called up the stairs that he had brought the roller.

"Oh sorry Bill," I shouted, "Joe doesn't want it now, please take it back to the car."

"F--k yer!" was all I heard from him.

188

41A Piccadilly had three floors, the ground floor housed the Army and Navy Stores and we occupied the second and third floors. Bill Potts was quite a ladies man. One day he asked if he could invite his lady friend to the 'Shaggery', our den of iniquity on the third floor. It seems his sister, whom he lived with, didn't take too kindly to her brother entertaining loose women on Wednesday afternoons.

Come his first engagement with the lady, he arrived at the office sharp at 11 am and asked if he could prepare the bedroom. While he was collecting our mail from the post office, I checked his labours and was surprised to find he had laid out clean newspaper on the camp bed, and on the small bedside table, he had arranged a glass and a medicine bottle full of port.

I adjusted the bed so I could get a clear view from my spy hole in the next room. Racing started as usual with the early mad rush of telephone calls but by 3 pm things got a bit quieter. Soon after 3 pm Bill popped his head around our office door, winked and said

"Everything okay?"

"Yes, enjoy yourself." I replied. We then heard the patter of tiny feet race up the stairs followed by the slow methodical clump of Bill's boots.

I gave them about ten minutes and entered the spare room. I peeped through the spy hole in time to see Bill remove his trousers. They were so grubby they appeared to stand to attention once he had removed them, like two drain pipes standing erect. What was to follow was the biggest laugh of all time. His lady removed her knickers and they both sat on the side of the bed to enjoy a glass of port so thoughtfully supplied by Mr. Potts. Then the fun began.

She let us call her Carmen for she looked the part, lay on the bed, and raised her skirt revealing a very pleasant sight. This must have had an equally agreeable effect on Bill for he was on top of her in a flash complete in Long Johns, waistcoat and bowler hat. There was a lot of puffing and blowing from Bill. I couldn't see much of Carmen at all. The only words spoken were

"Is it in darling?" and "Yes, isn't it lovely." I had seen enough and rushed down to tell Joe to hasten upstairs to see the grand finale which happened just before the climax was reached, when Bill's bowler dropped off and according to Joe, a pillar of steam clouded the room.

The patter of tiny feet announced the departure of Carmen who no doubt was delighted to earn 50p, the amount Bill told us he paid the lady for services rendered. Later that afternoon he thanked us for the use of the room and asked if it would be okay for next Wednesday, to which we readily agreed.

Bill once confided in me that he had £1,000 in a savings account.

"Good-o, Bill. Leave it to me," I insisted. "Get the name right, Raymond Charles Sebastian Gigor Fear."

This is how I greeted him daily for at least two years:

"Morning Bill. How about the Will? Get the name right." In the end, it nearly drove him mad and said he had adjusted his will in my favour. My tactics changed and I was forever thanking him for his benevolence. He didn't however pay me in advance. Soon after, he became ill and bedridden.

I visited him once at his sister's home in Well Street. As I entered his bedroom, he recognised me and his little hand crept towards his gold watch and chain on his bedside table. In one quick movement, his valuable belongings disappeared beneath the bedclothes. So that's what he thinks of me, I thought. I stayed with him for a few minutes. It was the last time I saw him alive.

When his death was announced in the local paper, I got in touch with La Margarets and ordered a wreath. It was to be a six-foot horseshoe in red carnations and inscribed 'In loving memory of a good and faithful servant - from his friends and admirers at Piccadilly Racing'. When the bill arrived, it was £15. In those days one could get a reasonable wreath for 50p, so I had really gone to town, but it was a small price to pay when one was about to inherit £1,000. Wrong! When his will was read he left all his cash to a nephew I had never heard of.

I hastened to send the bill for £15 to him, care of Well Street. I enclosed a message to the effect 'You got the cash, you pay the bill.' Wilf. Evans at La Margarets was tickled to death. He never was paid nor did he ever ask me for the money. I'm sure it was one of his favourite tales and to this day. His daughter Jill recalls the incident with much merriment.

Ross Wilkes was one of our most faithful agents. He collected his bets on a big Pot Bank in Etruria. When he first started with us, he was normally upright but as the years went by he got very bent and his chin was permanently on his chest. This called for comments from young Scrivens.

"If you don't break them you bend them." However, Wilkie, as he was known, won a few thousand pounds on the football pools.

He came to me one day and asked what I thought of his idea to go to a specialist in London and have his back straightened. I asked if he was happy as he was and he replied yes, but was having great difficulty drinking his pint of ale.

"I would leave it, I wouldn't have surgeons experimenting on my back." was my advice.

Nevertheless, he went to London and apart from the days of the operation, he phoned us with his daily bet, which incidentally had grown in size since his good fortune. At first he was quite happy with his progress then he became depressed and wished he had taken my advice and left well alone. He continued to phone daily until one day no call from Mr. Wilkes. We soon learned the reason, for his wife telephoned to say the worst had happened.

After the funeral, the truth came out. Apparently he was all wired up and had reached out of bed to get his Sporting Life when he toppled out of his cot onto the floor. He died a few hours later. Poor old Wilkie. If he hadn't won the Pools he would have lived a few more years, bent or not bent.

'Sampy Dyke was also a faithful agent until he met a woman who led him astray. One Saturday afternoon my courier reported that there was no answer from his home when he went to collect the clock bag. We telephoned the pub where he collected most of his bets and they confirmed he had collected as usual. Later that evening I called at the pub and a friend of 'Sampy' suggested that he had done a bunk with his takings and gone to Blackpool with his girlfriend. Later that evening I called at the Abbey Inn.

Settling the winning clients was very difficult, as I had to take their word for what they had coming back, and made more difficult as many couldn't work out their bets correctly. In most cases, I gave them the benefit of the doubt, and estimated that 'Sampy' had run off with about £160. Occupational hazard!

Days later, he returned to Abbey Hutton broken-hearted. His woman had deserted him as soon as the cash ran out. He attempted suicide by sticking his head in the gas oven. He very nearly succeeded and if his neighbour hadn't called round for his last week's returns he would have died.

Mr. Dyke was carted off to hospital where he remained for some time. On his return home, we discovered he had turned a golden copper colour and resembled someone suffering from yellow jaundice. The general feeling was 'serves him right'. I couldn't help feeling sorry for him and if he had only come to me and asked for a few pounds to take his bird to Blackpool, I would have obliged or given him some fatherly advice.

The Hunt brothers, Jack and Robert, also came from the abbey. Bob I could understand but Jack never. He spoke in a manner only understood by himself and some members of his family. Doing business with him was quite an ordeal and we normally would communicate with hand signals and written notes. It was a relief to me when he passed on. I wonder?

Dear Mrs. Hunt sent a message for me to call on her. This I did post haste. After offering my condolences she said that as she had no experience of funeral arrangements, would I do the job? I could hardly refuse the good woman. Being staunch Roman Catholics presented a problem, but with the help of Wilf. Evans of La Margarets, I arranged the service for 9 am the following Monday morning and the wake at the Sneyd Arms at 11 am.

It suddenly dawned on me whether or not Mrs. Hunt had got the death certificate. I rushed down to her home once more where she confirmed my suspicions. No she hadn't got one, nor did she know how. This was Saturday and the registry office would be closed until Monday. The priest certainly wouldn't be able to bury poor Jack until he had received this vital paper. I saw him and explained the situation.

"Don't worry. I'll carry out the service at 9 am and by the time you have been to the registry office, I'll be ready for the burial. Make sure you're there sharp at 9 am."

I got to the office on the dot only to find it didn't open until ten. What to do now? Only thing to do was to wait and hope the registrar would be early. At least I would be first in the queue. The office didn't open until 10.10 am so I was off to a bad start. Worse was to follow, for the first question I was asked was

"Are you a close relative?" Guessing the death certificate would only be issued to a relative I answered:

"Yes, his Son."

"What are your father's Christian names?" I quickly glanced at the doctor's certificate and answered

"John Bertram Hunt"

"Occupation?"

I didn't know so I guessed. "Miner"

"What did he do in the pit?"

"He dug for coal"

"Yes, but how would you describe him?" I thought for a moment

"Face worker." I replied.

"That's better." said the registrar.

A few more questions were asked and I guessed the answers. After I signed myself Ray Hunt, I looked at my watch. It was 10.35. I sped to the Crematorium in a downpour of rain and was horrified to find nobody in sight. I looked around the graveyard for a while and suddenly the priest appeared from behind some tombstones where he had been sheltering from the appalling weather. I waved the death certificate at him and he cried out

"Praise be to God!"

This was the signal for about fifty people to rise up out of the ground as if by magic. We followed the priest to the graveside and the service commenced, or should I say, the comedy commenced. The rain had stopped but the place was shrouded in a grey mist. The first thing I noticed was Bob Hunt's dewdrop, which was going up and down like a yo-yo on the end of his nose. I nudged Joe Baddeley and we had a quiet giggle. Halfway through the service, a gust of wind caught Mrs. Hunt's hat and it went on top of her late husband.

"My best hat" she wailed, and attempted to climb into the grave to retrieve her Sunday best. In the end, a grave digger was able to rescue the hat, much to Mrs. Hunt's relief.

Near the end of the service, the Priest sprinkled some holy water on the coffin and offered the bottle to Nellie Hunt.

"I've got my own" she announced and produced a Double Diamond beer bottle from her handbag, and sprinkled it vigorously onto the coffin.

After many farewells to our beloved Jack, we headed for the spread. Not before I had tipped the gravediggers, however. Joe and I could only stay until noon but by that time half the mourners were well on the way to being pissed. And from what I heard from John Lawton, the publican, they all refused to go home at 2 pm., normal closing time, and stayed on until midnight. All I can say is I'm glad my agents didn't die every week or I surely would have finished up in the work-house.

Who have I missed? Who is worth mentioning? Oh yes! Wacker the Tacker, alias Harold Walker, son of Jack Walker, who was one of the first agents who came to me in spite of the fact that like Jack Hunt, I could hardly interpret a word he said.

I remember on first meeting him he grunted:

"If yow'll gil may 'alf odds wan tow, I'll take for thee." I agreed to these terms, not realising what they were. Translated, he was asking if I was prepared to pay half the odds, one horse to finish first or second instead of the normal quarter odds on the horse finishing first, second or third.

This kind of bet was only familiar in north Staffordshire. I had never heard of such terms in any other part of the country. It was a fair bet and I don't suppose it cost us much at the end of the day. I do remember on one Grand National, a very well backed horse came third. We went to the trouble of checking the bets to see how much it had saved us with the punters who had backed it first or second. We were delighted to learn it had saved us some £800.

Jack died soon after starting with us, and his wife and Harold decided to carry on the very lucrative business. Harold soon learned the trade and after a couple of years took over the round completely. Over a drink one evening, he confessed he had never been with a woman. Sad really, as he was what one would describe as a dwarf, well under four feet, but a happier more likeable chap would be hard to find.

I listened to his tale of woe and promised him I would fix him up with a bit of crumpet pronto. I got in touch with Elsie, a nice lady from the Exchange Telegraph company. She and I had had one or two encounters recently. She was definitely a sex maniac and frightened me to death. I telephoned her and asked if she would do me a favour and entertain little Harold.

"Of course Ray, when?"

"I'll get it fixed up in a day or two." I assured her. Harold was overjoyed but said he felt a bit nervous.

"Don't worry," I told him, "I'll prepare her for you and all you'll have to do is pop it in."

A date was agreed and Fat Al, as we so rudely called her, arrived half an hour before young Harold. I took her upstairs into the storeroom, which housed a trellis table and all our stationery reserves. I laid a blanket over the table and got dear Elsie to lie on it after removing her underwear. I thought it better for Harold if I warmed her up a bit. This thrilled her no end and she begged me to 'stick it in'.

"No," I said, "This is Harold's big day. Don't let's spoil it for him."

I had arranged with Joe Baddeley, that when he heard me stamp on the floor twice, he was to send up Harold. The crafty old bugger had other ideas and when I stamped the signal he said to Mr. Cruxley, (a church-going Christian),

"Please go upstairs to the store room and get me some writing pads"

Old Cruxley hastened upstairs and as he approached, thinking it was Harold, I stood aside ready for him to take up the vantage point as he entered the room. There was a gasp of disbelief from Mr. Cruxley and he fled down the stairs to Joe, where he bleated out:

"Ray's got a woman on the table and she's got a fanny like a hedgehog"

Harold, learning this, rushed upstairs to tackle the hedgehog, and once again, I stood aside so he could enter the Promised Land. Alas, no! I had forgotten that Harold was a dwarf and was at least a foot short when he endeavoured to pop in his enlarged dongle. I hurriedly set up packets of writing pads that Harold could stand on. Seemingly all went off well and Harold thanked me many times for introducing him to Fat Al.

He had a small car and used to take Elsie out on many occasions. She confided in me once saying,

"He's the only man I have ever had who can stand up and poke me on the front seat." Dear Elsie was a good egg and could always be relied upon to entertain any of my more intimate friends.

I remember on one occasion, my dear pal Jack Gardner coming over for a couple of weeks on his own. Anyway, after a few drinks with Elsie and another dame, we retired to Elsie's home in Weston Coyney. As soon as we got settled in, Elsie invited Jack upstairs. A few minutes later, I followed them to the bedroom and listened outside the half open door. There was a lot of snorting going on and Elsie cried out a couple of times

"Oh Sam! Oh Sam!"

"I'm not Sam, I'm Jack" was my friend's reply.

I waited until the appropriate moment when they were both in the throws of sexual delight, then stormed into the bedroom and in a disguised voice demanded,

"What are you doing to my wife?"

When the two love birds finally joined us downstairs, they were none too pleased with my intrusion. We have had many a laugh about the incident years later. With some of the pranks I played on my friend I often wondered why he tolerated me.

A couple of years after I had introduced Harold to Elsie, he announced he was getting married. I heard this with mixed feelings, thinking to myself,

"Ah, more expense!" However, what followed was worth every penny it cost me. The marriage was to take place at 10 am at the registry office at Stoke. As it happened, Sam Small, my old army pal, was visiting me with his brother and two friends. So with Joe Badderly and myself, it made six guests. Harold and his wife had nobody in attendance. Joe and I were to be witnesses.

We were all ushered into the registrar's office and the questioning began. When the question was asked,

"Occupation?" Harold answered without hesitation,

"I'm a runner." The Registrar looked up with some surprise.

"You're an athlete then?"

"No, I'm not," snorted Harold, "I'm a bookies' runner and don't take the piss out of me if you don't mind."

We could hardly contain ourselves and hid our laughter behind handkerchiefs. There was more merriment when Harold couldn't remember much of the dialogue one has at a wedding. We observers of this fiasco were addressed by the registrar who stated that if we didn't conduct ourselves in a proper manner he would clear the room, which would have meant no wedding.

As we left the office, I turned to Harold and asked him where we were having the wedding breakfast.

"Wedding breakfast? I've had my breakfast" was his innocent reply. I telephoned Hazel and explained the situation.

"Give me an hour," she said. "How many?" I said there would be nine altogether. She knocked up quite a spread.

We left for the office at 1 o'clock sharp. Harold advised us that he had told the manager of the Fegg Hayes Working Men's Club that he would be entertaining a few friends that evening and Mr. Fear would be paying.

After racing, we sped off to Fegg Hayes. On the way, we picked up Brian Hinds, an ex-grenadier who was in the Hanley Police Force. I thought it a good idea to have a copper aboard on our return from the big piss-up. He had been a sergeant in my company in the Fourth Battalion and had been a decent NCO.

As we entered the Club, about a hundred residents of Fegg Hayes rose to greet us, many with empty glasses in their hands. All went well as one would expect when free beer flowed. At closing time, Harold suggested we took a couple of crates of beer back to his home. His father-in-law was a cripple and wheelchair ridden. Not for long however, for Harold tipped the poor drunken fellow out of his wheelchair onto the bar floor and proceeded to load the crates of beer in his place. Joe Braddeley pushed the wheelchair back to Harold's home. I asked Harold if he had any glasses.

"Only a couple," he replied, "but we will manage with cups."

He started his collection by reaching onto the mantelpiece and retrieved a handle-less mug. He removed a pair of false teeth, threw the water onto the fire, and proceeded to pour a beer for some poor unsuspecting guest.

Sam Small called me to the kitchen where I perceived a large block of cheese.

"Did you see that?" he yelled, "A bloody mouse"

To be sure, there was a large fat mouse happily nibbling a hole into the cheese. By the size of the hole and the mouse's belly, he had been tucking in for some time. No doubt, his friends and neighbours had also enjoyed the treat.

As for the bridal suite, Harold and his bride were to share the rear bedroom with other members of his family. All's well that ends well, for Harold and Lucy lived happily ever after and she turned out to be a good mother to their four children and an excellent wife for Harold. I also gave them the little betting office he obligingly ran for me in the village.

Douglas Philpot was one of my original selections to help check the bets. As he had no racing experience but was a very good writer, he spent the next few years 'writing in'. This entailed copying down on the return pads the client's winnings, finalising the total at the bottom of the list and then declaring you win or you lose, as the case may be. Doug was very distinguished looking and always immaculately dressed as I thought a Harley Street specialist might appear.

A grubby little man who was a washer-upper at the Grand Hotel would bring the manager's bet to us daily. We all thought Horace was a bit queer (gay). One day he complained that he thought he had 'piles' and without a thought of the consequence I told him I would have Doctor Philpot have a look at him at 6 pm.

When Doug arrived at the office at 5.45, I explained to him his new role as medical adviser to the Piccadilly Racing Service. In the meantime I had called at Mott's the chemist opposite us and asked Mr. Mott to knock up a small pot of Wintergreen which, as you should know, is for athletes to put on troublesome injuries. He refused to put a label on the tub, instructing the patient to rub gently on the effected part of their bum, but he did give me a blank label after he had removed his name from the top. I filled in the appropriate instruction for poor old Horace. On his arrival at 6 pm. sharp, I introduced him to Doctor Philpot and left them to it.

"Good evening Horace, I understand you have piles."

"Yes, Sir, very painful."

"Just drop your trousers old chap and turn round so I can get a better look." This all went on the other side of the counter and in full view of the two or three agents awaiting their returns. This didn't worry our Horace who seemed to enjoy exhibiting his arse to all and sundry.

"Ah yes," said Doug, "you have piles alright, just trot upstairs and rub some of this ointment on the whole area of your anus."

A few minutes later there was series of screams of anguish from the upstairs toilet and Horace rushed downstairs with a look of horror on his face.

"You rotten swine!" he screamed as he disappeared into Piccadilly, never to return. The guy who took over the job of bringing the bets from the Grand Hotel said Horace had suddenly left his place of employment without any explanation.

Mr. Philpot's mother was quite a lady and held herself in high esteem. She very courageously assisted me when I was courting my second wife Rita. She loaned us her bedroom on several occasions, where Rita and I exhausted each other after a hard day's work.

Many years later Doug and I met in Newcastle-Under-Lyme where he was manager of the newly named DSS offices. He looked the same but for a few grey hairs. We had a drink together and recalled old times. He asked me if I remembered how much an hour I had paid him during those fifteen years as a 'writer in'.

"25p an hour." I replied.

"That's right," he declared, "25p an hour for fifteen years. Never a rise for any of us. But my friend, I would have worked for nothing for all the laughs we had at the Piccadilly Raping Service. They were very happy days!" I told him that all that had changed since the politicians had legalised betting.

"Now it's dog eat dog and pay up to the Customs or get out." We parted and I've never seen him since. I remember Doctor Philpot with much affection.

Chapter 9

Jack Gardner

I think this a good time to relate some of the happy times that Ben, Jack Gardner, and I spent together.

It was fortunate that Jack came to Brighton to train. As I lived only a few minutes from the gym, we could meet up most evenings. A couple of years later when I went to Stoke and he lived at Market Harborough, it was less than two hours to exchange visits to each other's houses. When he left the army, he went to live at Overton near Basingstoke and it's there I once cycled from Brighton. My advice to the reader is never to try to do such a trip on an old one-speed ancient policeman's bike. As I had done no cycle training, it was one hell of an awful experience.

Towards the end of my journey, I found I could only manage to cycle on the flat or downhill. Hills became a nightmare and when I was nearly there, I parked my bike and started up the hill with my pack. When I reached the top of the hill, I dumped my pack and returned downhill to bring the bike up.

At about 6 pm I was getting very hungry and decided to have a fry-up. I had ignored my wife's advice to take sandwiches and easily prepared dishes. Not me. I want a hot cooked meal every evening. Several cars passed me as I devoured my tasty morsels and after a short nap, I continued on my journey. A while later a car pulled up alongside me and the driver got out. I was overjoyed to see my dear old pal. He had been out looking for me for over three hours and feared I lay dead in some ditch or other. How could he have missed me? He enquired.

"Well the only time I left the road was to have a fry-up" I explained.

"Oh, so that was you I passed, someone huddled over a fire ages ago. It must have been you I mistook for an old tramp."

He put my bike in the boot of his car and proceeded to his cottage where I met Grace for the first time. She made me welcome in a condescending sort of way and I guessed Jack had told her of some of my escapades in the regiment, which she, as a staunch conservative and 'King and Country' woman, found quite revolting. On the other hand, I fancy she took a liking to me physically.

I spent a few days at Overton where we did some rabbit shooting and drank large amounts of the local brew in the evenings. When it was time to leave, Jack took me more than halfway back to Brighton in his car and I found the last few miles through beautiful Sussex a pleasant end to my holiday.

You have heard in an earlier chapter, how Jack won the British European and Empire Heavyweight titles. Soon after, he bought a nice farmhouse with sixty acres of land near his home town of Market Harborough, where he lived for the rest of his life.

In 1958 we decided to take a holiday at the Sandbachs Hotel in Poole. It was a lovely hotel right on the beach and, as it was late May, the hotel had few guests. Added to this, our first-class service was even more satisfactory, especially when they recognised Jack.

One evening he told me he had always wanted to swim naked in the sea.

"No problem" said I, "In the morning before breakfast we will do just that." So early next morning we walked to the water's edge, took off our shorts, and plunged into the very cold English Channel.

I didn't stay in long and quickly threw a towel round my waist, picked up Jack's shorts and towel and ran up to the front windows of the restaurant, where the waitresses were busy laying out the breakfast eating irons.

In the meantime Jack had come half-frozen out of the sea and shouted all manner of threats at me if I didn't return his shorts. I completely ignored him and hammered on the window of the restaurant. By this time, a group of waitresses were observing the fun and I demanded that they should call the police as there was some idiot person exposing his private parts on the waterfront. The girls did laugh, but Jack didn't. He was dancing up and down like the wild man of Borneo waving one fist in my direction and clutching his shrunken penis in the other. I decided to forfeit breakfast to give him a chance to cool down, not that he needed much cooling, considering he nearly got frostbite earlier on!

Towards the end of the holiday, it rained all day and as we peered out of the window we observed a couple of road workmen sitting in a little portable hut eating their lunch. We had seen them working every day since our arrival and were bemused at their behaviour. One was a giant of a man and the other rather a small fellow. It seemed the big guy was doing all the hard work digging and mixing cement and so forth, and the little guy was doing all the talking and giving instructions. As it was still raining, we decided to join them in their open-fronted hut.

"Good morning lads, how goes it?" was our first words. They were a bit taken aback at the sudden appearance of two such fine looking gents.

"Can we join you?" we asked.

"Certainly, Sir. Would you like a mug of tea?" They had already recognised Jack and he introduced me as the Welterweight Champion of South Africa. We had a good long chat and visited them on a couple more occasions. The big fellow's name was Ben and the little chap was Neddy. Sometime later, Jack commented on our recent meeting with the two roadmen.

"You know Fear, they were a bit like us. Ben was like me, big, strong and doing all the work and Neddy was like you, skinny, undersized and giving all the orders. I think from now on I will call you Neddy." This suited me as I can never remember Jack calling me Ray, it was always Fear. So at last, I had a Christian name.

"I'll call you Ben," I said. "How's that?"

"Suits me" he replied. So from that moment and for the next thirty years we always addressed each other by these new names. Naturally, it confused our friends and neighbours but I suppose they got used to it in the end. The name Ben always suited Jack, but I always thought Neddy was not my cup of tea, and is usually associated with donkeys. However, when Jack called me Neddy, it had a certain ring of affection, I can hear him now

"Hello Neddy"

"Come on Neddy"

"Your turn Neddy"

I think changing our names and becoming blood brothers (by cutting each other's wrists with a razor and allowing the blood to mingle), cemented our friendship, which apart from one misunderstanding, was to last a lifetime. Let me tell you about the misunderstanding:

It was during the period when I was living with No. 2 wife. Ben telephoned one day and asked if he and Grace could come for a few days holiday at the Haven.

"By all means, when would you like to come?" I asked. We fixed a date in the near future but No. 2 wife was none too pleased at the news and settled into a period of remorse.

"Why did you have to ask them?" she enquired. "I don't even know them."

"Well now's the time to get to know them" I said, and tried to explain my relationship with my former army comrade. "I've visited them on so many occasions and Ben is keen to meet you."

As the day of the visit grew closer, so did Rita's moods worsen. So after a real bust up the day before Ben was due to arrive, I telephoned and spoke to Grace. She was none too pleased when I asked her if she would mind putting off the visit.

"Mind?" she cried. "Of course I mind. We're packed ready to leave and have arranged for people to come in and feed the animals." With which, she slammed down the phone.

Months passed, during which time I had made up my mind to replace No. 2 wife and seek No. 3. When these arrangements were completed, I wrote to Ben enclosing a peace pact that read:

'I, Raymond Fear, promise non-aggression with Jack Gardner for a term of twenty years. Signed R. Fear – 3rd September 1963.'

A few days later, I had a letter from him enclosing terms to my Pact, and I must admit my undisguised astonishment at the length and variety of his vocabulary, as he, like me, had left school at thirteen. His terms read like this, and I copy the exact text, which I hold in front of me;

I, Jack Gardner, promise non-aggression providing fulfilment of clause 1, 2, and 3 by Raymond Fear in definition of Jack Gardner.

Clause to peace pact

1. Raymond Fear, hereto known as the Lesser, shall at all times of meeting Jack Gardner, hereto known as the Greater, prostrate himself mumbling in a loud voice 'Thou art the better man.'

2. The Lesser, on visiting the home of the Greater shall not use Brylcreem, aftershave or other toiletries with such great abandon as has been his wont.

3. The Lesser, on occasions of meeting, shall provide cigars for the Greater.

I wrote back eagerly agreeing to his terms. I also told him I had found No. 3, a sixteen-year-old well brought-up ballet dancer. On receipt of my letter, he telephoned me.

"Bring her over as soon as possible. I can't wait to meet her."

One summer when the Australian cricket team were touring England, we decided to have our own test match. Ben decided to hold the match in one of his fields and spent the next few days preparing the pitch and outfield. The pitch was full sized and had three stumps and bails at one end but only one stump at the bowlers end. He erected a large wire net behind the stumps to act as the wicket keeper. A white cord marked the boundaries.

To score one run you had to reach the boundary, and over the boundary for two runs. For every wicket taken, six runs were deducted from the total and an 'over' consisted of eight balls. The hours of play were the same as a real cricket match and our match was to last five days, Monday to Friday. We were to use four new balls. Pads were to be worn by the batsman and an innings was judged closed when the bowler took eleven wickets. The batsman would retrieve the ball and return it to the bowler if it hit the net but all the rest of the fielding was done by the bowler. As there was no umpire, there were no LBW decisions or 'no balls'.

Halfway through the first day I realised that I may have bitten off more than I could chew for I felt quite exhausted. I was exceedingly thankful when stumps were drawn. After dinner, we went to the pub and entertained the locals with our exaggerated stories of the day's play. For the rest of the week we were greeted on our arrival at the pub with 'How's the Test Match going?' They were not referring to the England Australian game, but to our match.

Ben was a medium-fast bowler and I, slow spin so in actual fact, his efforts were greater than mine, but the fact that we had to do all the fielding, evened things out a bit. By the end of the third day, I was knackered and was overjoyed when I crawled into bed. As I lay there thinking, an idea came into my head. I set my alarm clock for 4 am. When I was awoken, I crept out of bed and made my way to the pitch. On the way, I collected a huge drum of water on wheels normally used for filling the animal troughs dotted around the farm. I hastened to the batsman end of the wicket and slowly emptied the hundreds of gallons of water over and around the crease. 'That should fix him.' I thought and made my way back to bed.

When play began next day, Ben was batting and I can see him now prodding the ground with his bat.

"Been a heavy dew in the night Neddy. Should help your spin." So it did, and I took a few wickets in quick succession which cut down his lead. When it was Ben's turn to bowl, the soft pitch greatly helped my batting.

Towards the end of play I thought a bit of gamesmanship would do no harm so I pretended to be sick halfway through an over. That night, my lifelong friend took great pleasure in telling everyone how I had spent half the afternoon grovelling around spewing up my breakfast and lunch. Nevertheless, he had to admit that at the end of the fourth day the match was even and all rested on the final day. What to do? What to do? I lay awake wondering how I could cheat my illustrious opponent. An idea came to me, so I turned over and slept soundly.

Next day I was up and about early and visited the pitch, making sure nobody was watching. I moved the wicket forward two paces, thereby shortening the pitch by two yards. I scuffed around a bit to camouflage my handiwork, and as Ben was continuing his innings and I was bowling, I had plenty of opportunity to disguise my treachery. For some reason the shorter wicket helped me no end and I quickly finished off Ben's second innings. I needed to get a lot of runs to win and at lunch I thought my goal was out of my reach. But no. When Ben commenced bowling, his balls were coming down head high, and I was able to hook and swipe at every ball knowing full well if I missed, the ball would go well over the top of the wicket. Ben was bewildered and mumbled something about my lucky Jewish background. In the end I won by a couple of wickets.

That evening I gracefully received the prize money from the publican who was always delighted to serve the ex-British heavyweight-boxing champion and his ex-company commander, the title Ben sometimes used when introducing me.

As I lay in bed that night, I felt a bit guilty at my tactics in the match but consoled myself with the fact that I was 'playing away' on a pitch Ben had prepared. He was bigger and stronger than I was and, I fancy, a better cricketer, so I had to do something to even things up a bit. Besides, the winnings would come in very useful.

The East Laughton Steeple Chase was held annually on Boxing Day. Ben suggested we should both enter.

"I'll fix you up with a horse"

Steve turned out to be an ex-milk float pony barely fifteen hands, but Ben had a grey seventeen and a half hands. Our first encounter was a disaster. Ben fell at the first and to ensure I beat him I endeavoured to get Steve to land on top of my friend. To no avail.

Horses are clever and avoid landing on anything other than the ground. By the time Ben re-mounted, I had a healthy lead, but his faster horse and superior riding soon shortened my advantage.

As I jumped the last fence, I was still a few lengths in front. Unfortunately, as Steve was not fit, the exertion of racing about three miles saw his belly reduce in size and consequently, his girth began to get slack, with the result that I very slowly began to slip towards the ground. I clung on desperately but finished up nearly underneath the bloody horse with his flying hooves just missing my head by inches.

Steve by this time was only managing a canter and Ben in the long run-in, soon overtook me.

"What's up Neddy? Got problems? If I were you I'd buy a bike" he shouted with a smirk on his face. By the time we weighed in, all the other riders were on their way home. Gardner bought himself a handsome silver cup and had it engraved as follows:

East Langton Steeple Chase
Winner Jack Gardner
By 117 lengths.

When the jeweller told him you can't say 117 lengths, you must give a distance, Gardner flatly refused to take his advice and insisted that 117 lengths was engraved. I know how far it was, I measured it out. To think of the lengths he went to, when by sheer luck he beat me.

In the early 1950s, one could purchase gold sovereigns for twenty-two or twenty-three shillings, so when I began to get affluent, I would buy a dozen at a time. I mooched around all the second-hand jewellers and pawnbrokers looking for bargains. In the end, I had collected 500. I had thought to myself that when the revolution comes the pound won't be worth a light, but with a bit of gold one could buy a sack of potatoes or the odd chicken and survive.

In the meantime, the law had changed and betting had been legalised so I reluctantly had to open betting shops. At my peak I had about twenty. Then came the very hard winter of 1963-64 when, due to frost and snow, no racing took place for nearly three months. I continued to pay my staff their weekly pittance whilst most other bookmakers had put their staff on the dole.

Each week I thought racing would start soon but it never did and money began to run out. Instead of seeking an overdraft from the bank, I sold my sovereigns. As the price of sovereigns had increased considerably, I made a small profit but nothing to what I could have made these days. At the peak price of gold, my 500 sovereigns would have fetched £50,000 to £60,000. Had I sought an overdraft, I doubt if Mr. Stevenson the bank manager would have loaned me a carrot after my tadpole episode.

While I had the sovereigns in my possession, I would take them to Market Harborough on my frequent visits. On arrival I would hand Ben 250, the idea being that we would play cards for gold and at the end of our visit the one who had the most sovereigns would receive £5 from the loser. I can see us now sitting there each armed with a weapon, Jack a large dagger and me with my Luger pistol. These were to deter any cheating. Ben was always honest as far as I could tell but I as the underdog took advantage of any possible ways I could use to beat my lifelong friend. As we sat there smoking our St. Bruno we wondered how many people in the world today would play pontoon or brag for gold.

Midway through the 1970s, whilst on holiday at Abersoch, we had walked to the end of the beach and were about to climb the little mountain at the far end.

"I don't think I'll come today" said Ben. I ridiculed him for not coming, saying something to the effect that he was getting cowardly in his old age. But so as not to disappoint the children, I continued the climb and Ben returned the way we had come. On our return to the chalet I questioned Ben about his refusal to accompany us up the mountain.

"Well Neddy" he said in a subdued voice. "I've been getting a lot of headaches of late and dizzy spells." I suggested he went to the doctor. "I've already been and had tests," he replied, "and I'll get the results when we return from holiday." I reassured him that all would be okay. I was wrong, as a few days after our return Ben telephoned me to say that a tumour on his brain had been diagnosed. I was thunderstruck and didn't know what to say.

"I've to report to Leicester hospital in a couple of days, I'll phone you from there" he continued.

I cannot remember ever being so upset at hearing the news and knowing full well that there was little chance of a cure for the big 'C'. I telephoned Grace daily for reports on his progress, and was relieved to learn he had accepted the position and was outwardly quite cheerful. He had asked for me to visit him, which I did.

"I've got to have an op on my head to remove the tumour" he told me "and with luck I'll be up and about in no time."

"Thank God" I replied. "I know you have left me a handsome legacy in your will but I'm in no hurry to collect." We parted and I told him I would visit him again the following week.

"Bring some 'Tiger Milk'," he said, "can't get it in here." I assured him I would bring him a case.

On one of my visits to the hospital, I had a word with the surgeon who had operated on Ben. I introduced myself and asked him "Do you think boxing was the cause of the tumour?"

"Mr. Fear" he replied, "I'm dealing with over fifty such cases, half are women and children, the rest are men of all ages. Mr. Gardner is the only one that has boxed so how can I say boxing is the cause?"

"How long has he got?" I enquired. He was reluctant to answer my question but said,

"Please don't repeat what I'm going to say, but probably about six months to a year."

I just couldn't get his reply out of my mind and I was determined to visit my dear old friend as often as it was possible. But he surprised us all. No doubt, because of his iron constitution, he lasted four years. We even went on holiday together and visited each other regularly. He wasn't allowed to drive but Grace took over that quarter.

During the last year, he began to lose his sight and it was heartbreaking to see such a fine specimen of a man so struck down. I would endeavour to make light of his condition and said that when he could no longer see me, we would have an overdue boxing match. I can well remember his answer to my challenge.

"You know Neddy, ever since the day way back at the Guards Depot when you threw me over your shoulder and won that 100 yards race, I've always been a bit scared of the result of an encounter with you. You have always treated me as inferior to you and now we will never know."

I was somewhat embarrassed at his statement, as I had always known inside, that he was ten times the man I was. After the operation, Ben insisted on returning home to his beloved farm but for the last few days of his life, he was a patient at the Market Harborough Cottage Hospital. I decided to visit him on the Friday and called at Hammond's fish shop in Tontine Street for a lobster. I also acquired a couple of bottles of Tiger Milk.

On arrival at the hospital, I asked the nurses to prepare the lobster for his lunch and to bring a couple of glasses. Ben was very glad to see me and we talked about old times and how he was looking forward to being home again for Christmas. When the nurse brought his tray, I took it from her and said

"See, I've brought you your favourite food, lobster from Abersoch."

"Oh thanks Neddy" and he reached out for the tray. I quickly withdrew it out of his reach and said

"Repeat after me"

"What?" he asked.

"Repeat after me" I said for the second time.

"I, Jack Gardner"

"I, Jack Gardner" he replied.

"Think Winston Churchill was a fat old pompous pig."

"Think Winston Churchill was a fat old pompous pig" he mumbled. "Now give me the blooming lobster."

Halfway through the meal he dozed off for a few minutes, enough time for me to polish off what was left of the lobster! When he awoke he reached for the tray from his bedside table.

"Where is my lobster?" he enquired.

"I didn't think you were hungry" I lied, "so I finished it off as we didn't want to waste it, did we?"

"You had better bring me another next time you come" he answered. But there was not to be another visit, and as I parted from him we shook hands and his grip was as steel-like as in the past.

I knew I would never see him again. When I reached my car, I'm not ashamed to say that I cried for some time. We had been good pals for over thirty-five years. We had many good times together since the day we both lied about our ages and said we were older that we were, to join The Grenadiers.

He died the next day, Saturday 12th November, just a few days after his fifty-second birthday. The funeral was the following Saturday at the church in Market Harborough. Tom Frost, the secretary of the Northampton branch of the Comrades Association got in touch regarding the funeral arrangements. He thought the pallbearers should be former grenadiers and asked me to be right hand man as Jack's oldest friend. The others were Tom himself, Alan Higgs, Frank Harris, Jack Spiller, and Tom Simpson, all serving policemen.

My ex-wife and I stayed overnight at the farm so we would be ready for an early start on the morrow. The pallbearers were to have a dress rehearsal in the morning and the funeral service was to take place at 3 pm. The dress rehearsal was to show us pallbearers the drill for the proceedings. As Tom and I were the short arses, barely 5 foot 10 inches, we were to hold the head of the casket, then the two who were 6 foot 2 inches would be the middle men, and the two 6 foot 4 inch giants would take the rear. The vicar suggested we pushed our dearly departed on a trolley.

"On a trolley?" was our outcry, "Not likely. We're Guardsmen and will do the job properly."

"It will be very heavy for you to carry and all due respect to you gentlemen, you aren't as young as you used to be."

Having overruled the vicar we proceeded from the road to the church entrance. There I saw the narrowest entrance to a House of Worship that I had ever seen, with two steps up to the porch.

"This will be the problem" said the Reverend. "One of you will have to take each end of the casket because the entrance is only wide enough for that, then the other four will raise it up onto your shoulders once you have got up the steps and into the church." At the heavy end, it was either Tom or me.

"You can do it" said Tom, "You're fitter than me."

"Ah, but you're stronger" I replied. After a bit of arguing I accepted the job as the dummy casket was only made of plywood.

"When you get to the altar you will lower the casket onto the trolley which will be there in position. You will then take a seat in the choir stalls, three of you each side."

"You don't mean to tell us we have to sit down?" exclaimed one of us, "We are all grenadiers, and will stand to attention around the body of our comrade."

"Suit yourselves, but the service will last nearly an hour" the Reverend continued.

"We have stood a lot longer than that back in the old days" piped up Mr. Frost.

Back at the farm for lunch and my daily nap. Come to think of it, I had overslept and missed the ordeal I had let myself in for.

The hearse arrived at the church spot on 3 pm, where we six smartly dressed ex-guardsmen lined up in dark suits, highly polished black shoes, white shirts, and regimental ties. The undertaker wheeled the casket out of the hearse into our waiting arms and the first thing that struck me was how heavy it was. I suppose it was to be expected when one considered that poor Jack weighed around sixteen stone and the oak casket a lot more. It was heavy enough with six of us sharing the weight but what would happen when there was only one of the giants at one end, and little me at the other end having to walk backwards up two steps. Panic set in.

"God help me" I breathed softly to myself.

When we reached the church doorway, I managed to move round to the head of the casket where all I could do was hold it by my fingertips. I didn't get a good grip in the first place, but it would be impossible to change my position without fatal results. We were at a standstill when suddenly the giant who was glaring at me in the most unfriendly manner, cried out 'Gerron' and started to push in my direction.

His expression, no doubt, was recording his terror of the fear of dropping his end, but at least he had the lighter end and he was much bigger than I. Backwards I went, blindly feeling for the steps. Up the first, I nearly dropped the casket, but thought if I do, I'll smash my toes for good. I am sure the corpse inside the casket was enjoying the fun and I'm convinced it would have slid from my finger tips had not the guy at the other end continued to shove in my direction. I felt quite sick inside and I had a terrible pain in and around my testicles. I thought to myself 'The old bugger has had the last laugh for me stealing his lobster. He's ruptured me!'

The six of us made our way to the altar and stood to attention, three each side. Thankfully, I was nearest the altar so the mourners who filled the church could not see me swaying about after the first five minutes. Imagine standing there smartly to attention with your testicles somewhere in the region of your knees for one hour. I wouldn't do it again for a fortune.

I took little heed of the funeral service and all the nice things that were said about our ex-heavyweight champion. All I prayed for was that the service would end without me fainting, and the only tears I thought I might shed would be for my own gross discomfort.

When thankfully the service was over, the vicar indicated that we should then carry the coffin out through the rear entrance, which was much wider and had no steps.

"Not bloody likely" was our unanimous response, "we'll wheel it on the trolley, thank you."

Jack was cremated and on a later visit to East Langton, Grace and I spread his ashes on one of his fields, as he had requested before he died. Incidentally, I was ruptured and had a hernia operation in the North Staffs Infirmary a few weeks later. There was no waiting list as I was very friendly with the secretary of one of the hospital's surgeons, dear Mavis Bevington. She was also the wife of the chief of Stoke-on-Trent C.I.D., Malcolm Bevington, an old donkey-walloper with whom I had struck up a friendship, which lasted until my office was held up by bandits with sawn-off shotguns.

As for pall bearing. Forget it!

Years later, when on two occasions ex-guardsmen died and I was organiser of their funerals, their old comrades wanted to be pallbearers. I highly recommended, in spite of their protests, that we let the trolley do the work. Thankfully, on both occasions my advice was taken.

Chapter 10

Unpleasant Memories

At this point in my book, I had better introduce the reader to the first of my four wives. Her name is Hazel and I met her at The Errol Works, where we both worked. It was a large clothing factory and we worked at either end. I first noticed her as she was getting a drink from the factory fountain. I thought to myself. What good childbearing hips. I chatted to her and finally asked her out.

"No," was her reply. "I am fully booked."

I was a bit crestfallen, but some time later, she agreed. Thus began a very stormy 2-year courtship. I always wanted to marry her, but she wasn't too sure. She was only 16 anyway and I was 23. We had some fun together and plenty of sex, when possible.

I remember, to celebrate her seventeenth birthday I took her to London where we could book into a hotel without being recognised. We finished up in a sleazy boarding house, a bed and breakfast job. I had brought two double-yoked eggs, which I instructed the landlady to cook with the normal breakfast. Needless to say, we had to pay our bill in advance when registering.

In the middle of the night, Hazel wanted to spend a penny and as the toilet was some way along the passage, I suggested she should pee in the wash basin. She managed to sit astride the basin, but half way through this operation, the basin came away from the wall and she slowly descended to the floor, balancing on the end of the lead pipe. We did laugh, but hastened from this doss house early next morning. The landlady saw us leaving and shouted out:

"What about your eggs?"

"You can have them, darling." I replied as we sped our way to Victoria Station.

Yes, Hazel was a good sort, but we were not compatible. I remember one Saturday, a day in my life I shall never forget. I had heard of a flat going in Walpole Terrace, overlooking a large playing field. It was nicer than Dorset Gardens and the same rent, so we decided to move. In the 1950's one could only rent a furnished flat, as in the conditions, the landlord could always turn you out. If you had your own furniture in, they would have great difficulty expelling you.

So on this Saturday morning, I hired a small hand cart for 1/- and loaded it up with our few possessions and pushed it through the streets of Brighton to our new abode, humped everything up to the second floor and returned to Dorset Gardens. That afternoon, I ran in a 9 mile cross-country race for the Sussex Walking and Athletic Club, and that evening I boxed at 7.30 at Hove Town Hall for the Hove ABC.

As it happened, Ken Webb had given me a part time job of a Saturday night. It involved catching the 8 o'clock train from Brighton to Victoria, London. From there I had to proceed to four main line stations and pick up hand luggage containing 'Fixed Odds' coupons. When this job was completed, I caught the midnight train to Brighton, arriving there at 1 am. I met several of the theatre crowd on the train; the stars who were performing in the West End and who were returning home to Brighton and Hove. I sometimes got a lift in one of their taxis but on this occasion, I was out of luck. I decided to walk to save the 2/6d charge by Cream Line Taxis.

I deposited the four valises into Mr. Webb's safe and walked home another 3 miles, It was about 2.30 when I let myself into our new home and was greeted by Hazel's cheery voice as she sat very comfortably in front of the fire.

"Hi darling, make us a cup of coffee while you're up." I shall never forget her words.

I had moved house, ran 9 miles, boxed at Hove Town Hall, rushed around London's main line stations, walked heavily laden with coupons back to Webb's office and walked all the way home to save myself a buck, only to be greeted in that fashion. I thought to myself, she's not the gal for me. I made the coffee without comment.

I had been scheduled to box half way through the programme and because of my opponent's reputation, was near top of the bill. He was from a good East End of London club and had been schoolboy welterweight champion of Great Britain. This was his first senior fight, so they didn't intend to over-face him and chose me for him to work on. I don't suppose I did too badly, as the referee said:

"Let's give a big hand to a very good loser"

As I had had to catch the 8 pm from Brighton to Victoria, I had told my manager I must be first on the programme and box at 7.30. The sponsors were none too happy, nor was my opponent, as the first fight was normally for the less experienced fighters. Ken got me to Brighton station in time to catch my train, but I was very sore and continued to perspire the whole journey to London. When I finally arrived home I had hoped for a more cordial welcome!

Another incident that springs to mind was when all the Jaeger factories throughout Great Britain competed against each other at the Crystal Palace in London. It was a glorified Garden Party with several sporting events. I had qualified for the 100 metres sprint and finalists were being called to the start. I managed to locate Hazel in the crowd.

"I'm in the final" I said. "It's off in a minute"

"I shall miss it then," she declared, "I've just got myself a seat in the beer tent." I do like a bit of hero worship, but none was forthcoming.

On our way home, she refused to leave the bus when it stopped halfway at Peese Pottage. I was rescued by a fellow runner, Anita Titteral. I remember her words

"Come on Ray, don't stay in the bus with that miserable cow." Anita and I were great friends. We worked together in Burgess Hill where she lived.

One day I suggested we meet in Falmer and progress to Newmarket Copse to hear the birds sing at sunrise.

"Good idea" she said. "What time?" She had to cycle about halfway and me likewise from Brighton, so I suggested we leave home at 4 am. We met as the sun was rising and proceeded to the wood high up on the South Downs. The chorus was magical, one

218

could hardly hear the other speak. I look back on it as one of the happiest moments of my life.

Years later, I called on Anita who was now married. Her understanding husband had no objections to me taking her out for dinner. We dined at Rottingdean and spent a very pleasant evening together, talking about the past and our new roles in life. Thank you Anita. She was as different to Hazel as chalk and cheese. Oh to have married someone like Anita

A few lines about No. 2, as I choose to call my second wife. I met her at one of our work's parties, and after a few drinks she asked me to dance, a 'Ladies Excuse Me' had been announced. After a few pleasantries and out of sight of No. 1, she drew me to her and whispered

"Darling, you bring out the animal in me!" There is no doubt, that statement, as well as causing my dongle to twitch, was to change my whole life and cost me no end of dosh.

Her declaration to me was quite out of character as Rita was a shy person but I suppose drink had played its part. She told me where she worked and next morning I was there like a shot. She was most embarrassed and asked me to leave. I persisted and she agreed to meet me one evening later in the week. Although over forty years ago, I can remember where and how we spent the first evening together, finishing up in my office where she said she felt safer, away from preying eyes. She was married too. Then began a very hectic passionate courtship.

I remember well the 6th January, when we spent a very enjoyable evening together at Fat Al's. Elsie had left the house in good order and even changed the sheets. Nine months later, on the 7th October, Rita gave birth to a lovely little girl she named Beverley. At the time, Rita's husband thought the baby was his. Rita assured me it could only be mine and after seeing the child, I was convinced. As Beverley grew she had the Fear look about her and now she has my character too, which in these days of cut and thrust, can't be bad. She grew into a very attractive and loving person.

When Beverley was about two years old her mother announced one evening that she had left her husband and had moved in with an aunt in Porthill. My heart sank, as I had never anticipated her doing such a thing. Now I felt responsible for her. To add to my problems my No.1 locked me out of my home in Bridle Path. It was rather late on this occasion as I returned from my outing with Rita. Hazel opened her upstairs bedroom window and I whispered

"Let me in please."

"Bugger off from whence you came" she shouted and threw a blanket through the window. Not wanting to wake up the neighbours, I made my way to my office and spent a very cold uncomfortable night in the shaggery. It was not suitable for a lengthy sleep.

Next day I booked into the Grand Hotel where I was equally uncomfortable and most embarrassed, as most of the staff knew me. This called for action and I arranged to meet No. 1 to discuss where our future lay and particularly what was to be done regarding the children. It was then she told me the good news that I was to go ahead and live with my floozy. I could have the three children as long as she could see them whenever she wanted, and that she had met a man who was going to take up an important post in Germany. She wouldn't be able to take our children out of the country at that time so I could have them. What good news I thought. My problem solved, or that's what I thought at the time.

I hastened to Charles Butters the estate agents and asked them to find me a property in the country, on the outskirts of Stoke. They came up with a nice bungalow in Armshead Road, Werrington. Rita was delighted with my plan, but I sensed she was none too happy about taking on three children in addition to Beverley. Can't blame her really! She had arranged for her first daughter Sheryl to stay with Cyril, her husband. We named the bungalow 'The Haven', hopefully thinking that the name might have a bearing on the inhabitants. Wrong!

From the start, I realised that No. 2 was a very jealous person and I had to be so careful when addressing or relating anything to do with my first three children. My eldest daughter Jane was competing in the

Stoke Schools' Swimming Championships. She had won the four events in the past two years and she was going for the hat trick of four wins. She accomplished this with no problem but as we arrived home late, No. 2 flew into a rage and hurled her engagement ring over the garden fence into an adjoining field. Next day I spent hours looking for the bloody thing. Next shock came sometime later when No. 1 arrived at our front door on a dark November Sunday.

"What do you want? I thought you were in Germany^ I enquired.

"No, it's all over between us and I've come for the children." God help us. What to do? Only one thing. In those days the mother could claim custody of any children a couple may have, she was entitled to take them away, which she did.

Some time later, she came up with the crazy idea that it would be better if I bought a large country house and we shared it. She would live upstairs and Rita and I downstairs. Jane, Karl and Lindsey must be sent to boarding school.

"What?" I cried. "Never! Not to those glorified borstals."

But she insisted and that's where they finished up. Jane at Lowther College, a posh school in Bodelwyddan Castle North Wales and the boys at Yarlett Hall, near Stone, Staffordshire.

Our hunt for a big country house was not too difficult and it became a choice between Wetley Abbey and Foxdale, Wetley Rocks. Wetley Abbey was up for auction at Louise Taylors and I arrived there a bit late. I heard the auctioneer accepting bids and as it was around the £2,500 mark I thought they were bidding for a small semi-detached somewhere. I saw Wetley Abbey's owner demonstrating to me and waving his arms about. I thought he was under the influence and waved back likewise.

It was then it dawned on me they were bidding for the Abbey but I was too late. Going, going, gone to Mr. Somebody or other for £3,000. I was flabbergasted and at this point Mr. Swynneton came rushing over to me.

"I thought you wanted my place. It's been stolen." I agreed, as I had been quite happy to have gone up to £10,000. He was none too pleased but the buyer was overjoyed.

No doubt my guardian angel had arranged my late appearance as Foxdale turned out to be a much happier place to have, with much more land and space for stables. That's how it turned out. We bought Foxdale from a Mrs. Walker whose husband had recently died. The house had been built in 1936 for the owner of Elks Biscuits of Uttoxeter. When World War II had started and fearing Stoke-on-Trent would be a target for Hitler's bombs, he fled to North Wales, never to return.

A few major alterations had to be made before we could move in, for instance, one of the four upstairs bedrooms had to be converted into a kitchen and the full sized snooker room converted into a lounge. Downstairs we halved the lounge to make room for another bedroom. Then there were four stables and a tack room to erect. All very expensive, but one's mind boggles at what it may cost today.

All went well to start with and we all settled in amicably. Hazel suggested that when the children were at home from school, we should take it in turns to serve Sunday lunch and we should all eat together.

"Good-o!" I thought. Our first lunch was downstairs where No. 2 served a very nice roast and pudding. Next week it was No. 1's turn and she produced soup, roast, and pudding. The third week, and not to be outdone, No. 2 served up smoked salmon, soup, roast and pudding. The fourth week No. 1 dished up a starter, soup, roast, and two puddings, and so it went on, each trying to outdo the other.

The kids loved it and I was getting fatter all the time. You would have thought Rita's jealousy would have lessened, but in fact, it got worse. The last thing I had in mind was another woman for I had my hands full with her.

If I was going out on an evening's business call, she would drag me into the bedroom before I left to ensure any desire I had was lessened.

"But we only had it this morning" I wailed.

"Don't you love me?" she asked. She certainly knew how to deflate my dongle and I was sometimes hardly in any condition to talk business. Where is it all going to end? I pondered.

Rita's favourite weapon when she attacked me was a letter opener. It was about ten inches long, which gave her a great advantage in our constant battles. I relied on my boxing expertise to evade her lunges to the heart but she very often stabbed my arms. On one occasion, she chased and imprisoned me in our bathroom. I had no way to escape only through the leaded window, which did not open anyway. She paused and I managed to grab her arm and wrestle the weapon from her grasp. I flung her into the bath and got her legs up over her head like a trust-up chicken about to be roasted. I turned on both taps and watched as the water rose higher and higher until it nearly covered her face.

God no, this is a hanging job, so I made the mistake of letting her free. I made off as quick as I could but she was after me like a frenzied dervisher I ran as fast as I could and thought the boat on the lake the safest place, but before I could embark in our rowing boat she was on me and a wrestling match took place. I was jolly lucky and managed to chuck her into the lake.

"I'll get the bitch." I thought and endeavoured to push her under with one of the oars. She was rescued in time by Vic Brown who had arrived to give me a hand in the garden. Vic had experienced No. 2's temper before, as one morning, while we were sitting in the kitchen having a quiet morning break from our toils, the kitchen door opened and No. 2 aimed a large clock at me which crashed through a plate glass window. Vic grabbed his mug of coffee and declared

"I think I'll have mine in the greenhouse, it's safer there!"

It was at this point that I made up my mind to rid myself of this attractive passionate woman who, when one comes to think about it, was in a most uncompromising position.

I decided to find a nice young woman in her teens, who I would dispatch to Switzerland and have her trained to be a competent ladylike housewife. And so my search began for this evasive female. Not for long however, as one Saturday morning I visited the health shop in Trinity Street, and there I saw what I was looking for. A petite blonde with a nice figure and no Pottery accent. I wondered who she was. After she left the shop without a glance at me, I asked the proprietor who she was.

"You know" he answered.

"No," I replied, "If I knew I wouldn't be asking you now."

"It's Aunty Lucy's niece!" Now everyone knew Aunty Lucy, she was a supervisor at the telephone exchange. She and I were great friends. I telephoned her at the first opportunity and mentioned I had seen her niece in the health shop.

"Keep your eyes off her, she's only sixteen."

"Hold a party at your place and invite her along" I insisted.

"I'll have to invite her mum and dad and a few friends"

"That's okay. How much?"

"Let me see. We will need a turkey, wine and a bottle of whisky to start with. Make it two bottles" she added.

I whole heartedly agreed knowing Lucy was very fond of that liquid from over the border and realising she was entering into the spirit of things.

"How about £15?" she continued.

I put the receiver down and put £20 in an envelope and took it across the road to the telephone exchange. The security man I knew, as he frequented my betting shop.

"Just take this to Lucy please" and slipped him the envelope together with a tip for his trouble.

A few days later Lucy telephoned to say she had organised the 'do' for the following Saturday night. I warned Rita I would be late as a couple of my checkers were off sick and there was a big race that day anyway.

"Don't be too late" she implored.

After work on the Saturday I spruced myself up as best I could at the office and proceeded to Larkspur Grove where Lucy's party was in full swing. The first person I sought was her niece. We were introduced, I accepted a drink and started talking to Linda. After a short time, I asked her if she would care for a ride in my Mercedes! She readily agreed.

224

We headed out of Stoke-on-Trent on the dual carriageway and exchanged a few pleasantries. I pulled up at a service station, turned to her and said in the most sincere manner

"Will you marry me please?" She didn't show much surprise but managed to say,

"But I don't know you. I've heard all about you and you are already married!"

"Not for long though, think about it."

"Of course I'll think about it, I don't get proposed to every day." We laughed and returned to the party where the rest of the guests looked very relieved at our return.

Within three months, she came to live with me at Foxdale, and became Number 3. We lived together for thirty years. When we made the decision to live in Spain, we got married at the registry office in Stafford, not telling the family anything. Keith and Ann Hill were witnesses. It was a very touching occasion for me and I wept unashamedly when answering the marriage vows. Linda also cried and so did the registrar. It turned out that both the Hills needed a handkerchief too.

After the ceremony the registrar complimented the bride on her turnout and Linda announced that she had worn the same outfit twenty five years previously and I told the story about her hat, which is as follows.

When we had fixed the wedding date I called at Bratt & Dyke the big stores in Hanley and proceeded to the hat department.

"Good morning Mr. Fear. What can we do for you this morning?"

"I want a hat for my wife to be, we are getting married next week."

"Not again! Who to this time?" the assistant enquired.

"The same lady you know. We have lived together for the past twenty five years.'

"Amazing, and I thought you were already married," she replied. "What sort of hat do you want?"

"I've got a sample of the colour of her outfit." I had thought to cut a small piece out of the seam of the skirt. "How much is that one?" it seemed to be a suitable design.

"£30" I nearly fainted.

"I only want a sodding hat darling, I don't want the shop. Anything cheaper?"

"I'm afraid not."

"Wait a minute," another assistant cried, who had been engrossed listening to our conversation. She rummaged in a large drawer under the counter and produced a very plain straw boater. "You can have this for 50p." she giggled.

"Why so cheap?" I enquired.

"Why? Why because it's got some bird's shit on the rim, we often get a sparrow or two fly into the shop when the windows are open."

"I'll take it. And where is the ribbon department?"

I approached the next floor and asked for a wide multi-coloured ribbon. After perusing many lengths I selected a metre of the one I considered the most suitable. Linda thought how splendid it looked after she had attached the ribbon to her bonnet. As I knew the assistant on the counter, she didn't charge me for the length of ribbon.

"We have had it in stock ever since I have worked here" she assured me. This account of the hat at the registry office broke the ice and our tears were soon replaced with laughter.

The Hills had very kindly booked a table at a very expensive well-known restaurant in the country. We proceeded there and on arrival, we got the VIP treatment, being greeted with glasses of champagne. This was followed by an exceedingly delightful lunch. Jean had looked after the fort that day so we didn't return home until racing had finished. When Dan and Lara arrived home from school, they wondered why we were all dressed up.

"What's been going on?" Lara demanded. I let the 'cat out of the bag' and told them we had just got married. Poor Lara burst into tears and threw herself into Linda's arms. "Is it true, or is Dad telling one of his stories?" she cried.

226

"No it's true." Dan and Tim accepted the news of our marriage with calm indifference, but Jane burst into tears, as had Lara.

Going back thirty years, to the time Linda and I first got together, coincided with the Government's decision to legalise betting. It spelt the beginning of the end of my days of wealth. I suppose the Lord looking down from heaven observed what was going on and declared 'That Ray Fear has got everything – good health, lovely trouble-free children, a beautiful home, money and now a pretty young wife. He can't have everything. We will take away his money'.

I suppose he did me a favour really as money is the least of the problems because it is solved with money. If you haven't got any, get some. I could have been dealt a worse hand, ill health or sick children or insurmountable problems of some sort. I could write volumes about the thirty years, but will endeavour to write about some of the most vivid in my memory.

I set Rita up in a nice semi-detached house in Trentham and agreed not to see her or the two children. I already had Karl, Lindsey and Jane and the thought of the unpleasant encounters with Rita every time I went to collect or return her two, quite frightened me. So for about twelve years I didn't see either Beverley or Marshall.

However, on Bev's eighteenth birthday, I called at her home to take her a present and a ring her grandmother had left her in her Will.

"Hi Dad!" was how she greeted me and, over her shoulder, announced to her mother that I was at the door.

Bev seemed very happy to see me, her mother non-committal. She left us so I could talk privately with my daughter. I said that now she was eighteen she could please herself who she associated with and that I would be very happy if she could visit us at our new home at Fulford. She readily agreed and arranged to call the following Sunday. Marshall was not in and it was some time before he decided to visit us. It was natural that he believed the stories his mother had filled his head with. Bev, who was not so gullible, had realised that it takes two to make a quarrel and Dad was never there to defend himself.

Beverley visited us regularly and got on very well with Tim, Lara, and Dan. She is a natural child lover and turned out to be the perfect mother when she married and had two delightful children of her own.

In the meantime, Hazel had met Brian Mackerness, and decided to leave her comfortable berth at Foxdale. One Sunday, Linda and I travelled to Lowther College in North Wales to visit Jane. I had a premonition that something might happen in our absence so I asked Ray Coomber to chain the gates and stand guard. It so happened that it was Sports Day at Lowther College. I had won the 100 metres fathers' race the previous year and was keen to repeat my success. Imagine my consternation that this year's fathers would have to run with a book on their head. No doubt, this handicap was directed against me and some of the parents' committee had discussed methods to nobble me. However, I won the event comfortably. After the prize giving, an irate father declared

"The race was not fair as you have a square head!" What a pillock! I learned afterwards that he was a prominent barrister in London and later Jane told us his daughter was just as stupid.

On our return home, we found the chain had been cut and the gates wide open. Poor old Coomber was in a real quandary and hastily explained that Hazel and Brian had arrived with a furniture van with driver. I told Coomber he had done his best and to stop worrying. On inspection upstairs, it was to find that the kitchen had been torn out together with most of the best carpets and furniture. The place looked as if experienced burglars had paid a visit. Not much I could do about it anyway but it did at least finalise the 'upstairs-downstairs' fiasco.

Some months later, Hazel, her Solicitor, myself, and Mr. Till, my solicitor, got together at Foxdale to discuss terms for the divorce. It seemed that Mr. Till agreed to all their demands without even consulting me.

On the stroke of twelve noon, he put his papers together and announced that it was his lunchtime. Here I was, fighting for my life, and all he was thinking about was his fat belly. Some years later, Hazel recalled that meeting and said that as she was returning home with her solicitor to Manchester, he had said

"I felt a bit sorry for your husband, he had three opposing him and Mr. Till even made offers I hadn't even thought of!"

Another incident, while on the subject of solicitors, was when Jane's pistol was stolen. The story is as follows:

Jane was training for the first ever Women's Modern Pantathlon Competition. Until then, only men had participated. In this five-event contest, competitors must compete in riding, shooting, swimming, fencing, and running.

I took Jane to the pistol range on Sunday afternoons to practice this skill. On one occasion, I took her pistol from a safe hiding place in our home and laid it on the kitchen table. I went outside to call Jane. She was still on one of her horses practising jumping over a particular jump she had erected.

"Come and watch me" she shouted. I hastened across the garden to the field and watched her jump.

"Come along now or we will be late" I declared. When I reached the kitchen, it was to discover the pistol had gone. I rushed outside and asked Vic Brown who was sweeping the drive if he had seen anyone around.

"Yes," he replied "A man came down the drive on a motorbike and asked if he could fish in our lake. I told him to go to the house to ask Mr. Fear the owner." The so-called fisherman must have knocked on the kitchen door and not getting an answer, had opened the door and saw the gun lying on the table, put it into his pocket and was gone in a flash. I telephoned the police and within a few minutes a plain clothed detective arrived. Although I had never seen him before, he greeted me like a long lost uncle.

"Hello Ray. What's been going on?" I told him what had happened. "Hmm! No problem! Let's get a little statement written down."

"Oh no," I replied. "I've always been advised not to make statements to the police before consulting a solicitor."

"Don't be silly. I don't want to waste our time coming back here. Make your statement and you will hear no more about it."

"Okay" I agreed, "And you're sure this will finalise the matter?"

"That's right" he replied, as he finished off his large whisky.

About two weeks later, I had a summons from Leek Police to the effect that I had not kept my gun under proper supervision and I must appear at Leek Court some days later. 'What a bastard', I thought, and telephoned McKnight and Ryder the eminent solicitors. I spoke to Mr. Till and he said he would get the senior member of the firm to defend me, who happened to be the police prosecutor. I thought this a good move and felt sure, when Mr. McKnight read my brief, I would be discharged without a stain on my character. Wrong again!

I met Mr. McKnight at the court and he greeted me with the news that I had nothing to fear. The magistrate who would try me had just discharged, with a warning, a burglar who had broken into eight houses in the area. He felt sorry for the poor burglar's excuses for stealing and given him a second chance.

Mr. McKnight then sat beside me, opened his briefcase, and took out some papers, which included my statement. He read through it and turned to me and asked

"Modern pentathlon. What's that? Do you mind explaining to me?" I was horrified. Here he was, due to defend me in five minutes time and this was the first time he had read my brief. Solicitors. I have s—t them before breakfast.

We were called before the Magistrate who, after hearing my pleas, declared

"Fined £40 and costs." Mr. McKnight beat a hasty retreat and I never used his company again. Neither did I ever pay the fee he charged for his abysmal defence. It also severed my otherwise friendly association with the Hanley police force.

When the local Bobbie called and asked if I wanted my usual 20 ringside tickets for the Police Boxing Tournament held annually at the Victoria Hall, I told him what had happened at Leek. I asked him if I could speak quite plainly to him.

"Of course you can, Ray."

"Well f—k off out of my office and don't ever come back here scrounging." That saved me £100 a year for years.

Ian Moxons, the city's biggest solicitors had moved to larger offices in Marsh Street, not 100 yards from my betting shop, so it seemed to me the best firm to deal with. The one snag was that No. 2 wife Rita had used them in her dealings with our divorce, and only recently, she had applied for an increase in maintenance through the courts. On the appointed day, I arrived at court and took a seat to await my turn to 'face the music'. Who should turn up but my new solicitor, John Glover.

"What do you want?" I asked.

"I've come to represent you" he answered.

"Not likely!" I said. "I want to win my case. I'll go in alone if you don't mind."

My name was called and after I was sworn in, I faced the judge. Ian Moxon was representing Rita. Things went well and I felt very cool and collected. I had learned from previous visits to court when applying for my betting shops, that the best way to pull yourself together was to take deep breaths, hold them for as long as possible, then breath out slowly. This also gets the sympathy of the judge who thinks you are about to have a heart attack. After my exercise, my brain became clear and I always managed to give the correct answers to suit the judge. Halfway through my questioning, Mr. Moxon, who stood in front of me, asked

"Can you read upside down? Because you're answering my questions before I've asked them." With that, he threw his brief down on the desk and sat down. In his summing-up, the Judge declared

"I think Mr. Fear has been very generous and has been paying too much for too long. Therefore, I do not intend to increase Mrs. Rita Fear's maintenance allowance. Case dismissed." Outside the court, Mr. Moxon came over and shook my hand and said

"You're wasting your time being a bookmaker, you should be a barrister." From then on, I dealt with Moxons and, in fact, John Glover who had worked with McKnights became a junior partner with Moxons and became my personal advisor for many years. We got on extremely well and became good friends.

He came frequently to my home during party times and his wife, Triss, was always good fun. They also came to Abersoch when we were there and I remember well, after a cocktail party I had given, having to wheel Triss back to her chalet in a wheelbarrow. John was legless but managed to reach home without my help. Yes, John was a real nice gentleman and I always told him:

"As a solicitor you would make a better village priest." He was much too nice to be in the legal profession. His judgement was sometimes way out as I will explain in a later chapter.

I nearly forgot! One year, just before Christmas, he said:

"Triss and I would like you to come to dinner on Boxing Day. I've had a brace of pheasants given to me and I know you like game."

Boxing Day arrived and the Glovers greeted us with open arms. After a sherry, he took me into the kitchen to show me the pheasants, which were still in their feathers.

"Do you mind plucking them?" he asked. "I know you're good at that sort of thing." After the plucking came the dressing, and after I had completed these tasks I told him I might as well cook the bloody things.

"Good idea. I'll get the roasting tin" said our host. Triss managed some vegetables but my wife and I were very glad we were never invited again.

Another of our professional friends was Ben Brereton from Barclays Bank. I first met Ben when I dealt with Barclays soon after arriving in the Potteries. He was six feet four inches tall, dark and ugly. He always had a good joke to tell when I arrived daily to collect my night wallets or gain access to my deed box tucked away in Barclays' vault.

After a while, I started to invite him to our house parties and other wild orgies. His presence didn't cost us much as after two sherries he was under the influence and at times during the respectable parties was quite embarrassing. On other occasions, he was the centre of attraction.

I remember one Christmas at Foxdale. Rita had warned him against drinking our Bengal Lancer punch, but to no avail. After a couple of glasses he disappeared. Later on, I enquired where he had gone.

"I think he went outside for a pee." replied one of our guests.

"I had better go and have a look."

So after I had donned my overcoat and armed with a torch, I went in search of our Ben. As I approached the outdoor swimming pool, I heard a faint cry for help. I rushed to the point from whence the cry came, and beheld poor Ben hanging to the icy side.

"I came out for a pee and fell in." he cried.

I managed to assist him from the green slimy water, which had never been intended to swim in as I had decided to convert it into a Japanese sunken garden in the future. Old Ben was nearly frozen to death and I helped him into our kitchen where we were greeted by No. 2 wife.

"Don't bring him in here messing up the place. Dry him off outside."

This done, I told him I would run him home as he was in no condition to drive his own car. I explained to our guests my intention and said I would not be long. How wrong I was. Ben was never allowed a front door key and relied on Bunty, his wife, to let him in. On this occasion he was out of luck for an upstairs window opened and out popped Bunty's head.

"Drunk again. Look at you, you're disgusting." and slammed the window shut. After a lot of shouting from Ben, the window opened again and Bunty reappeared. "Here's the key" she stormed, and flung it into the rose bed. She then turned on me. "As for you, you're always leading my husband astray. I've warned him about you time and time again."

We continued our search for the key, which was no mean task in the dark although we were assisted by a distant street lamp. Finally the key was found and Ben turned to me before entering his home and said

"Goodnight comrade Fear, a true friend."

When I got back to Foxdale all the guests had just gone home when Rita turned to me and said

"I thought you must have had an accident. I was worried to death!"

On the way to my office the following morning, I passed Barclays Bank. Outside was a small gathering of people, including the staff. Ben, who was responsible for opening the Bank, had not turned up yet. Later when I made my daily pilgrimage to Barclays, Ben was behind the counter in his usual place looking as lively as a cricket.

"That was a good 'do' last night, wasn't it?" he said. "But Bunty locked me out of the bedroom and I had to sleep in an armchair. Still, I feel fine now, although I was half an hour late opening this bloody place." I think he told the manager he had been involved in an accident.

At about 7 pm that evening the phone rang in my office. It was Ben. "We've got bowling tonight, and we are £100 short somewhere and can't go home until the shortage is accounted for. We have been here for nearly three hours already. Can you help us out?"

"It's not my account that's wrong" I replied.

"I know, I know, but can you help us out? We want to go bowling"

"OK, send down one of the girls." Five minutes later, I handed over £100 to straighten Barclays' account, never to see it again.

Miss Hawkins was a very attractive spinster in her mid-thirties who had worked at the bank since she had left school. I knew nothing about her love life but what I do remember about her was her beautiful chestnut hair, shoulder length and 'shining like gold'.

"Morning Miss Hawkins. Your hair looks lovely, like a well groomed horse."

If looks could kill, I would have dropped dead. She never spoke to me again. I only meant my comments as a compliment and remembered how fantastic Jane's horses looked after she had groomed them ready for a 'Three Day Event'. Miss Hawkins must have forgiven me however, as she always wishes to be remembered to me when she sends her Christmas card to Ben, knowing he and I are still pals after fifty years.

234

Ben retired early from the bank, sold his home on the Westlands, and went to live in Cornwall. We occasionally exchange a letter but always a card at Christmas. When we came to live in Spain, we invited him annually to visit us, but he always declined, saying he was off to some other part of the world. In 1995, we had a letter from him to say Bunty had passed away and could he pay us a visit.

A few weeks later, he arrived at Alicante airport, eighty years young and looking good. When he saw me, he hastened to climb over the barriers instead of following the normal exit. 'Same old Ben', I thought and indeed, he didn't seem to have changed much. I greeted him with these words:

"Hi Ben. That £100 you owe me is now £2,070 with the accumulated interest." We embraced and exchanged the latest news.

All my family and friends took to Ben. A true gentleman who knew how to behave in company. I learned a lot about him during the next two weeks. His army career was most interesting. He was called up in 1939 and because he had varicose veins, flat feet and other deformities, he was put in the RASC as he was a car enthusiast and owned his own car before the war. This seemed a good move.

He was soon spotted as a potential officer and invited to go before a selection board. He was marched before three officers who fired numerous questions at him. The chairman then asked him why he thought he would make a good officer. After a short pause, Ben came straight to the point.

"I'm buggered if I know, Sir!" The three put their heads together and the chairman addressed Ben once more.

"Well Brereton, we have decided that you need a little more time in the army to settle down. I should apply again in twelve months." Private Brereton then got a cushy job driving a staff car for a very kindly Colonel who treated Ben as an equal. This lasted for two years until the Women's ATS took over these driving jobs.

On returning to duty, an over zealous RSM took an instant dislike to him. He finished up on the Normandy beachhead repairing broken-down vehicles. When peace was declared, he spent a few months in Brussels and Bruges where he had a few romantic encounters.

One in particular sticks in my mind. This happened in Holland around Christmas 1944. A wealthy Dutch family invited two of Ben's company to dine with them. Ben was one of the lucky ones. After dinner, the host's wife asked Ben to come into the kitchen and help her to make the coffee. No sooner were they through the door when the Doctor's wife seized hold of Ben, kissed him with feeling, and tried to take his trousers off.

"What about your husband?" Ben protested.

"Forget about him" was her reply.

"Sorry! I'm rejoining the men." Later in the evening, the doctor invited the two friends to stay the night.

"My wife will sort out your rooms."

Private Brereton was soon asleep in his allocated room but later he was woken up by someone gently shaking him. It was the hostess.

"Come into my bed" she said.

"What about your husband?" Ben queried.

"Never mind about him, he always sleeps in our bomb proof cellar. He's a real coward."

This final statement gave Ben the courage needed and he quickly accompanied this frustrated lady to her bedchamber, where, according to him, he spent the most wonderful, unforgettable night of his life. After breakfast the next morning, he returned to his unit, never again to see the adorable Dutch lady.

For five years, Ben has been visiting us here in Spain, sometimes three times a year and always for a month at a time. He was a good generous guest and as he always says,

"Ray, I'm only repaying the many free-do's I have attended which you put on in your more affluent times." These days he finds travelling a bit too much for him.

Other welcome visitors are Bernard and Nancy Wicklin, a renowned lawbreaker who I would personally trust with my life. I am lucky to have such a friend as Bernard who was born anti-establishment, a bit like myself, but of a more violent nature. He was accused of many crimes and served several terms of imprisonment. This of course enabled him to read, read and read, and educate himself to a high standard. As a well-read man, he was able to communicate with other educated prisoners and prison governors. Some of his stories are unbelievable and many will be revealed in his book 'Through my Window' to be published shortly.

Nearly fifty years ago, he came to my bookmaking office and asked if he could collect bets for me on Shelton Bar, a huge steel works in Etrurea. I readily agreed and gave him a single-race clock bag into which he could put the bets he had collected before the first race. After work, he would bring his clock bag to the office to have the bets checked.

After a while Joe Baddeley and I realised Bernard was winning all too often. Some days, because the results were good for the bookmaker and all the agents were 'paying in', Bernard would win.

When we jokingly reminded him of this, he would roll his large blue cow-like eyes round like a frightened black man and say

"The luck will change." It never did! We caught him out one day when the first race was won by a non-probable, that is to say, a horse that wasn't included in the morning paper's list of starters. The horse won at 20-1.

When I opened his bag and saw that two or three of his slips included the 20-1 winner, I immediately knew there was a fiddle somewhere. We checked his bag, paid him out and I said

"That's it Bernard. If you want to continue as an agent, you will have to bring the bets to the office before racing starts. I am withdrawing your clock bag."

"Okay pal," he said, "that's it then."

Later that evening the telephone rang and a strange voice informed me,

"Someone's been getting into your clock bags. It's easy, and if you meet me at such and such a place (I forget where), I'll explain how it's done. It'll cost you £10"

"Bugger off" I replied. It's a racing certainty it was our ex-agent up to one of his tricks.

Some years later when we became friends, he told me without admitting his own guilt how the single race clock bags could be fiddled. On Shelton Bar, there were large magnets that were so strong they could easily move the hands of a watch or clock in either direction. So it was easy to get the result of the first race, pop it in the clock bag, and adjust the hands accordingly.

Sometime after he had finished as an agent, he called at the office and asked Joe and I if we wanted to earn £200 in a week. We were interested!

"Lend me £200" he said "and next week I'll give you back £400" I thought it was a con and at first refused him. But he persisted and rolled his large blue eyes round in his normal fashion.

"Okay, just this once" I agreed. The following week he came and plonked £400 on the counter.

"There you are boys. How's that?" He visited us frequently asking for cash ranging from £200 to £500 with a 100% profit in a week or two. It was very good business and Joe and I were very sad when he landed in jail. Nancy was a wonderful loyal wife and stayed by his side no matter what he got up to. Looking back on his life recently, he said

"It is funny that men turn to crime when there are so many legal ways to be dishonest!" One of his favourite tales relates to me.

As I could get no sense relating to odds from the other local bookmakers, I decided to sell my head office to Ladbrokes who were branching out into the world of betting shops. I had sixteen shops before they ventured into this type of betting. Ladbrokes, together with William Hill, advertise 'No limit' on all their betting and this is what the punters wanted.

I couldn't afford to go 'No limit'. I could have opened a clock bag at 7 pm one evening to discover a yankee bet with four winners which would have fetched so much I would have had to sell my house, car and put my wife on the streets to pay out. No go! I kept limits and lost at least 50% of my business. I had endeavoured to get all the local bookmakers to follow suit, but to no avail. In a very short time, most of them sold out to the big firms or went skint. That is why I sold to Ladbrokes and tried to cut my losses.

Cyril Stein, head of Ladbrokes, came to see my shop and discussed the price he was willing to pay. He came with one of his managers to Foxdale where we had lunch. On viewing my property, he said:

"You must have made a lot of money with your runners. My home outside London would fit inside your garage, and it cost me £250,000"

We struck a deal and I moved my HQ to the Cobridge office, which incidentally I had taken over from our old friend Bernard Wicklin. He had been suddenly arrested on some charge or other.

Back to one of his favourite stories. I was in the habit of taking my greatly reduced night safes to the bank each evening after business. Bernard related that a band of villains came from Manchester to waylay me. Without my knowledge of what was going on, I left the first night from the front door. They were waiting for me with bludgeons at the back entrance. Next night for some unknown reason, I left at the back door and they were waiting for me at the front. On the third night I had a bit of crumpet upstairs awaiting my services, so I didn't go out until very late. In the meantime, they gave up the ghost and returned to Manchester and, seemingly, never to return, certainly not to relieve me of my night wallets. I sure was lucky, as Bernard will confirm.

Another case in which Bernard was involved was a Mrs. D. who lived in a nice country house on the outskirts of Stoke-Leek. She had advised the Leek Police of her intention to go on holiday and would they keep an eye on the place. In no time at all local villains knew of Mrs. D's absence and raided the place. This was unknown to me.

One day, friend Bernard arrived and said

"I know I owe you £600. Keep this jewellery for me and I'll repay you in a couple of days"

My reply was (and I was only guessing),

"It's bloody stolen. I don't want it. Bugger off"

"No Ray, it's okay. Just keep it for me and I'll pay you back the money I owe you." I reluctantly agreed.

The goods were in an old sock. I turned the contents out to discover a large gold cigarette case, a necklace, a diamond ring, a pearl necklace and one or two other items. I hastened to Jane's manure heap and carefully buried the sock and its contents. Next day I received a telephone call from Inspector Barnes of the Leek Police. Although I had never met the gentleman, he addressed me by my Christian name.

"I would like to see you please Ray. Can you come now to the station?"

"No" I replied. "I am busy and it's Christmas in a few days"

"It's rather urgent, and will only take a few minutes of your time" he replied.

"Okay, I'm on my way, see you in ten minutes." I had guessed it might be in connection with the jewellery I had received from friend Bernard.

In the Leek police station, I was shown into Inspector Barnes's office. He indicated to another plainclothes detective to leave the room.

"Hello Ray" he said, and shook my hand. After a few pleasantries he addressed me as follows. He spoke in the third person:

"If I was a man who was well known, lived in a lovely home with a nice wife and family, had a very good business, that man would be a fool to get involved with stolen jewellery. Don't you agree Ray?"

Although my legs turned to water, I remained outwardly calm and replied:

"Buggered if I know. I don't know what you're talking about."

"If I was that man," he said, "I'd get a registered letter and post it to Inspector Barnes, Leek Police Station.

"Yes, I suppose that is what this guy should do. Is that all you wanted to see me about?"

"Yes, and a happy Christmas to you and your family" he replied.

On the way home I called at the local Post Office and purchased a size 'H' registered envelope. I retrieved the sock from the dung

240

heap, washed the jewellery carefully, and made sure to remove any fingerprints. I carefully packed the valuables into the registered envelope and posted it from the busy main post office in Hanley. I had been tempted to retain the diamond ring but in my haste, I thought I'd better get rid of the lot. Knowing what I know now, I would have kept most of the valuables.

After a very stress-free Christmas, dear old Bernard turned up with the £600 he owed me. I was waiting for him to ask for the jewellery, but he never did, and I didn't mention it either. I was only too happy to have the £600 safe in my pocket. He also gave me a Royal Doulton dinner service as way of interest. It adorns our table to this day on special occasions.

Sometimes, months or even years would pass before I would see Bernard, and it was two years before he called again.

"Hi Bud. Can you lend me £2,000?"

"No I bloody well can't" was my immediate reply.

He then went to great lengths explaining that he was working on an oil refinery and employed several men. The bank had refused to give him any more credit, and despite the fact that the job was nearly finished, they still wouldn't loan him another penny.

"I need the £2,000 to pay the men's wages. They need their wages and in a couple of weeks I'll be paid for the work we have done, and I'll pay you back then, Ray," and he held out his arm. "I'll cut this off if I don't pay you back in two weeks."

"Wrong," I replied. "I'll cut your f--king head off!" I gave him a cheque and he disappeared as quickly as he had arrived. Two weeks later he returned with my £2,000 together with a gift which was his usual practice. Dear old Wicklin. Salt of the Earth.

1962-1963 was a very severe winter with three months of hard frost throughout the UK. There was no racing. Having no idea when racing would start again, I continued paying my staff who manned the Betting shops. All the other bookmakers had told their staff to 'sign on' and get paid dole money, which was about half their usual wages.

The bad weather continued week after week and I still kept hoping. Paying thirty staff for twelve weeks ran away with a lot of money, besides my own overheads, which included two wives, a girlfriend, and numerous children to support. At one point, I had to sell the 500 gold sovereigns I had accumulated when I first started bookmaking.

I had always had a good relationship with the banks I dealt with, but when things started to go wrong they soon became uptight. I remember one manager saying he would like to have a look at my garden at Foxdale, when I knew the only reason for this visit was to check on my collateral.

I arranged to pick him up from Hanley and had him walking round the grounds within fifteen minutes.

"Isn't it beautiful" he declared. "I didn't know you had a lake. Any tadpoles?"

"Of course" I replied.

"May I have some for my young son?"

"Certainly" I replied. I got a 2lb jam jar, tied some string around the top to make a handle for easy carrying, and netted a few hundred tadpoles. I drove him back to Hanley and about a quarter of a mile from his bank I said

"I am off to Stoke. Do you mind getting out here? He looked none too pleased and certainly looked a sight manoeuvring through the crowds in his bowler hat, rolled umbrella and brief case, not forgetting his large pot of tadpoles. As I drove away, I laughed to myself. 'That will teach you, you Clever-Dick!'

Foxdale had been on the market for two years and in spite of advertising in the national press, no-one wanted an estate of six acres and a very large house. In the London area, no problem, but in North Staffs, very difficult. We finally sold it to a dentist who, after I was committed to another property, dropped his price, even though he had agreed to pay my asking price. My new property was a gift! Tim Cooper phoned me one Saturday lunch time and said

"I have just the property you are looking for."

"I am just off to Abersoch for two weeks holiday. I'll have a look at it on our return."

"It will be sold by then" Tim answered.

"Okay" I said. "I'll pop in and have a look on the way to Abersoch."

"Good luck. I know you will buy it" said Tim.

When we arrived at the new house, I thought to myself, 'This is it', but God knows how much they will want for it. I knocked on the door and was greeted by a very nice young woman.

"Is it convenient to have a look round?"

"Certainly. Come in." Within five minutes, my wife and I said we would like it, but how much?

"You had better have a word with Bagshaw"

"But it's 3 pm on a Saturday afternoon, they will be closed"

"No" replied the lady. "I've just spoken to Mr. Bagshaw, he's in his office." She rang the number and handed me the receiver. After a few pleasantries, I asked him how much the house was.

"£10.500" he announced. I thought to myself that it was about as much as I could afford. I thought it was dead cheap.

"I'll give you £10.000" I said.

"Make it £10,250 and it's yours."

"Done" I replied, "but I have a problem. I'm off on holiday for two weeks."

"What's your name?" he asked. I told him. "That's okay Mr. Fear, I know of you, and a bookmaker's word is his bond. I will contact Tim Cooper and take it off the market. Have a good holiday."

We were overjoyed. The property had originally been two cottages, which the previous owners had knocked into one. On one side was a large cowshed, which could house four cars. On the way to Abersoch we discussed what we could do to improve the property. Upstairs where there were four bedrooms with no bathroom, we decided to convert one of the bedrooms to a large bathroom and the cowshed would make a shower room, one bedroom, an office, and a toilet. There was ample room for the four stables and tack room which the buyer of Foxdale wanted removing. The stables could be erected in front of half a dozen pigsties, which ran across the rear of the house.

"What shall we call it?" asked Tim, our only child at the time. I had thought about this for a long time and suggested we call it Kandahar, after Mother's first husband's great uncle, Field Marshall Lord Roberts V.C. of Kandahar.

In his life, he had been created an earl, viscount, baron, and baronet. My mother's first husband was a great nephew of this great soldier. He won his V.C. recapturing the company colours during the Indian mutiny. He was made famous with his march to Kandahar - encircled by the rebels. He covered, with his army of 20,000, 320 miles of mountainous terrain from Kabul in 28 days. The siege was raised very quickly, hence his title 'Roberts of Kandahar". At 82 years, he commanded all commonwealth troops at the commencement of the 1914-18 conflict.

While visiting his beloved Indian troops in the frontline, he contracted pneumonia and died three days later. The whole nation mourned and even the enemy sent their salute.

The entire German press unanimously expressed esteem for Lord Roberts:

'Even in war there are moments when the warrior salutes the enemy with his sword instead of striking with it, and such a moment came with the death of that gallant warrior Lord Roberts.'

The Victoria Cross is the most enviable of a soldier's decorations. To think his only son earned this award trying to save the guns at Colenses in the South African war. It's the only instance where a father and son both earned this coveted recognition of personal valour. Roberts was made a field marshal the day he heard his son had died of wounds sustained trying to save the guns. Next day he was dispatched to South Africa in command of the British Army.

The King attended Lord Robert's state funeral, which was as large as Churchill's. Buried in St. Paul's, one can see to this day, set in a block of stone, simply 'Roberts 1832-1914. Only four paces away is the Duke of Wellington's tomb. Below in the crypt where he was laid to rest is a bust of Roberts, not four paces from where Nelson lies.

Lord Robert's father, General Sir Abraham Roberts G.C.B. was 90 years old when he died and his fortune went into chancery for 99 years. He was of the Plymouth Brethren religion and consequently, his money couldn't be handed down to anyone, hence, 99 years in chancery.

After a certain amount of research, it was discovered that my eldest brother Jim was the only remaining male to the vast fortune that had accumulated in the past 100 years. Jim spent many months trying to prove his claim but unfortunately, records in both Bristol and Waterford, Ireland had been destroyed by the Blitz and fire, and as he said

"What's the good of so much money to me? I'm happy with my life as it is."

What happened to the fortune? The 'powers that be' opened Robert's Homes for ex-servicemen up and down the country. At least the money didn't fall into the hands of the politicians. Relating this story to tradesmen and bank managers, mother was able to acquire credit far beyond her means. Good old Ma!

Linda agreed to call our new home Kandahar. I was able to get the two father-in-laws to do the alterations as they were both builders by trade. Hazel's father, Sam, had retired and came to live with us while he did his part of the alterations. He got on well with wife No. 3 and her father Cliff. I had set about the garden long before we moved in and was able to transplant many of my azaleas, rhododendrons, conifers, and such, from Foxdale. I made a very attractive herbaceous border stretching some sixty yards. Within a couple of years, it was a showpiece and cars would slow down to view such beauty as they passed the house.

Moving the stables was no problem and we settled in very quickly. We were right out in the country but only eight miles from Stoke. We were ideally situated and could get to the Peak District, Buxton, Alton Towers, Derbyshire, Cheshire, and Shropshire, all within half an hour.

I had retired from bookmaking although I retained my bookmaker's permit. I had rented out a few of my shops and the income from those shops, together with the money I earned from Vernons Pools as their main agent in Stoke-on-Trent, we were able to keep the wolf from the door! However, the income from the Betting shops soon dried up as none of my ex-managers who rented them were able to make a go of it. So I sold them off very cheaply and wondered what I would do next. While I was on holiday with friend Jack, he suggested I should start taking bets again from home.

"You mean under the counter?" I enquired.

"Exactly" he replied. Now the customs people were very hot in those days, and were always on the watch for betting tax dodgers. The tax at the time was 8% and you had to guess your week's takings and pay it in advance.

"I would have no difficulty getting many of my old credit clients together who would welcome a chance of tax free betting."

"Well, get cracking" Jack said.

Within two weeks I had three more phones installed in my office and had contacted a good few of my oldest and most reliable punters. When I told Jean who ran my Pools office on Fridays, she was thrilled and readily agreed to help us on Saturdays and other busy days.

"You'll probably finish up in jail" I assured her.

"As long as it's with you I don't mind" she laughed.

So I started the business which was to run for several years, that is until we were betrayed by Jane's husband who turned dirty guts when she unloaded him. He reported me to the Customs and Excise office. Fortunately, I had an anonymous phone call one day, the voice said

"They are on to you Ray and will raid you tomorrow." In spite of the fact that he had tried to disguise his voice, I recognised the caller as a customs official who I had befriended and indeed shared my political views.

"Who is speaking?" I enquired.

"A friend" and rang off. I was naturally very surprised and thought I must get organised straight away. My first thought was how to continue my business legally without losing any customers. After giving it some thought I made up my mind what to do.

246

First, I telephoned the customs office and asked to speak to the bossman. I was put through to the manager who I remembered well, as he was one of the customs men who visited my office when I was operating legally years before.

"Hello Ray, what can I do for you?" He asked.

"I want to start bookmaking again and I shall be operating a credit business from my home."

"What, again?" he said sarcastically. "When do you intend to start?"

"Tomorrow" I answered.

"Tomorrow! That's not giving us much notice is it?

"I've got my bookmakers permit and there's no law against me taking bets anytime."

"I had better send up Mr. Cadigan to complete the details" he continued.

"No, I should like you to come along personally if you don't mind. It's important we get off on the right foot" I insisted.

"Okay, tomorrow morning at 10.30" he concluded.

In the meantime, I hid anything that may have given away my past misdeeds. Then as our clients came through with their bets that afternoon I explained what had happened. The general opinion was that 'We've had a good run for several years, we will stick with you Ray'. I must admit that with dear Jean's help, the accounts we sent out weekly were first class and every bet we took we returned to the client so there was no argument. Claims were unheard of. Where applicable we sent S.E.A. and commission was generous to the agents we employed. Mostly publicans who were only too eager to keep their customers in the close proximity of the pub rather than losing them to the nearest betting shop.

Mr. Cadigan and the manager arrived on time next day. It was the first time I had met Mr. Cadigan. A real softy, a bachelor who lived with his mother in Stone. His sole interest in life was his cat, of which I was to hear all about at a later date.

"Let's have a look at your new office" said the manager. When he saw the four phones, the first thing he asked was "How long have you had four phones?"

"About six years" I replied.

"Why so many?" I had expected this question.

"Well you see, I have over 300 football Pool agents who in turn have 20,000 clients. Every Monday I have dozens of calls and when I only had one phone, there were so many complaints that the agents couldn't get through, I had to have more lines installed."

I bet he was thinking 'Bloody liar'. However, nothing more was said and while we were having a cup of tea, I asked him if he remembered the first time we had met.

"I do indeed, and I often relate the experience when friends think I have a cushy job when I am called upon to make an after dinner speech." Our first meeting had taken place years before when my H.Q. was at Cobridge. I had an early call from two custom officers.

"What do you want?" I asked.

"We have come to monitor your phone business" they replied.

"What do you mean?" I asked.

"Well, when your phones ring we will answer them, make a note of the client's name, then hand the phone to you or one of the clerks. After the call we will see if you have a client on your books by that name and compare the type of investment he makes."

"What do you mean?" I asked again.

"It's quite simple. We are first establishing that you have a client by that name and he bets in £1 or £10 or £100. The idea being that you aren't attempting to defraud Customs and Excise."

He asked to see the current ledgers where we keep a list of all clients' weekly transactions, their winnings or losses, whether they owed money or were in credit. Fortunately, every bet we took at that period was above board, as I couldn't trust all the clerks that I employed. If I had been doing elicit business, they (the clerks) would always have you over a barrel. As I had no doubts that all my business was straight, I became very bold.

248

"Okay, yes, that's fine. Tell me something. Is there anything in your laws to say I have to provide chairs for you to sit on?"

"No" came the answer.

"Well you can f---ing well stand up all day. If you want a piss, there's a public shithouse along the road, and Harry, when you make the tea, if you give these two people a cup, you will be sacked on the spot. Furthermore gentlemen, I am retiring to my private office to inform my clients that you are here." With that, I stalked off to my office slamming the door. I spent the morning on the phone talking to old girlfriends and the likes.

"Yes" the manager said. "It always raises a laugh when I tell them about Fear of Piccadilly Racing."

Some time later, I had another even more frightening experience with the customs inspectors. It was a nice sunny Saturday afternoon and my wife and three children were all set to go to Abersoch as soon as racing had finished. Jean and Gay were to finish off business so we could be away on our three-hour journey to our chalet on the Warren.

We had been fairly busy and I was gathering together a few of the larger bets taken from a few of my most trusted clients whose bets I was not going to record, when suddenly a car pulled up outside the front and two large men jumped the nine foot long farm gate that we always kept locked during racing. They rushed to the front entrance, rushed through the entrance hall, through the kitchen and clashed with me in the passage leading to the office. They had obviously been briefed as to the layout of my home.

One of the two men shouted out 'Customs! Special Branch Chester,' and hastened into the office where the two girls continued with their work, quite oblivious of the two intruders. I had tucked my tax-free bets down the front of my shorts and hoped that Jean had gathered up any other questionable bets. Needless to say, she had.

"What do yer want?" I asked. "I am off on holiday, and I am just about to take a shower, so help yourself."

"We want to see the bets you took from your agent in Blythe Bridge who collected in the Duke of Wellington Pub last Saturday week" and he gave a date.

By law, we have to keep all bets for three months so it was no problem locating the envelope containing our agent Roy Heath's bets. I guessed what they were after, because on that day when I was checking the bets that Roy had phoned in, there were a few new non-de-plumes and two or three £10 bets. Normally I would have hidden the £10 bets but on this occasion I was a bit suspicious and telephoned Roy and asked for an explanation.

"I was going to ask you about the guy who came into the pub dressed as a painter and decorator. He asked if he could get a bet on and someone directed him to me. He bet very funny. Sometimes in 50p, sometimes in pounds and then those £10 bets. Sounds like a set up don't it?"

I agreed and put through all his bets for that day, and it's a good job I did. What happens is that the customs send in some of their employees dressed as everyday workmen who have above average bets hoping the bookmaker hasn't disclosed them. Then there is a huge fine, as the customs say, 'We think you have been doing this for several years and we reckon you have defrauded the customs of so many thousands of pounds in customs duty.' You are fined there and then many thousands of pounds and in some cases your licence is objected to at the next annual sitting of the licensing committee.

The bookmaker can argue as much as he likes and declare the figures are much exaggerated, to which the customs reply 'Prove it', which of course is impossible. Yes, the customs people are a law unto themselves and have much more power than the police. In fact, they are an older body than the original Bow Street Runners.

A couple of other incidents worth recording regard two other bookmakers. Garry Franklin, son of Neil Franklin, the former Stoke City and England centre half, who incidentally, after the English season had finished, decided with Mountford to go and play for a Colombian team in South America. 'How awful', 'What a bounder,', 'What a cad', were some of the comments from the press and F.A. officers alike. Poor Neil never played football again. Not that he would have missed the £5 a game he earned for playing for England. I've told him on several occasions he should sue the F.A. for taking away his livelihood. He was the forerunner of things to come. The latest Portuguese player Figo, exchanged teams for thirty million pounds.

Back to Garry. His office in Snow Hill was raided and as always, the first thing the customs do, is sweep the office to collect up any scraps of paper which might reveal some under-the-counter transactions. They also empty the dustbins into plastic bags which they take away to scrutinise. As one of the officers was doing this, Garry innocently asked him how long he had worked for customs.

"Twelve years" came back the reply. To which Garry retorted,

"Twelve years, and you finish up emptying f--king dustbins. Great! That's just great!"

The second bookmaker was in an outlying district of Stoke-on-Trent and he was raided. On the floor on the customers' side of the counter the custom's guy found a slip of paper with £100 EW on a particular horse running that day.

"Where is it recorded on your daily take?" he asked the bookmaker.

"Oh that was old so and so. It was just a joke"

"Explain!"

"Well old so and so is an OAP and is always first in the shop. He bets 10p each way as a rule and has a 10p yankee on Saturdays. Well today he came in and slipped me a betting slip with £100 EW on it. I nearly fainted. I am only a small bookmaker and anything over £5 gives me the jitters. 'I am only kidding', said our comedian, 'I thought I would give you a fright.' You silly old bugger, I said, you nearly gave me a heart attack"

"If you tell me the truth you'll get a lighter fine" announced the inspector.

"It is the truth" replied the bookie.

"You'll be hearing from us in the near future. Good afternoon" said the Gestapo. The bookmaker was indeed fined. How much I can't remember but he closed shop so the fine must have wiped him out.

251

I was always lucky when dealing with the income tax collectors and customs officials. I never felt guilty at deceiving them. I considered it revenge.

Another close shave I had with the income tax bodies in the 1970s must be recorded here. The government had realised that the only way the working class could keep their heads above water was to work hard all day and then seek a part-time job elsewhere. This was known as 'moonlighting'. The government labelled it 'The Black Economy'. They introduced a new body of investigators stationed in Newcastle-on-Tyne. Stoke-on-Trent was one of their first ports of call.

I was one of the first to be investigated. The phone rang in my office and I was invited to call at their new office in Newcastle-Under-Lyme, at 10 am in a couple of day's time. I was informed that it was my Pools agents they were interested in. As a bookmaker for 40 years, I didn't panic, but got to thinking on how to hoodwink this new form of Gestapo. It would be fatal to reveal the names of my collectors. They had all been advised when I signed them up that their commission would be tax-free, so they would not take too kindly to having to pay tax on their hard-earned pittance. I envisaged losing at least one third of my business if the names were revealed.

As I had over 600 callers calling at my office and receiving commission, I decided to register them as agents, so instead of claiming I had 320 sub-agents, I claimed I had 1,020. These divided between the £25,000 weekly take averaged £25 when it was really £80. I made up my mind not to reveal anyone.

I arrived half an hour late which they accepted without a murmur. I spent the next hour talking about my past and kept the three investigators fully interested. As it was getting close to their lunchtime I thought I had better start talking about the business in hand. I was quite firm in the information I gave them and said I could not tell them the names of any of my subs. They were most sympathetic and said I must tell them the names of my biggest agents.

"I'll check up" I said "and see you tomorrow."

I made off home and they to their lunches. Next day I arrived one hour late and explained that I had been searching through my thousand odd agents and there were few earning over the stipulated amount which they were interested in. I said I would work on it if it took me all night, but I would furnish the names tomorrow, which happened to be a Friday.

"Yes, that's alright Mr. Fear, but we want all the names tomorrow as we move on to Nottingham next week." That's what I wanted to hear, and explained I may be a little late as my wife was expecting her third child. "Oh, congratulations" they cried.

Next day I had a lay-in, took my time over breakfast, did a little gardening, and then set off to complete my business with the taxman. I had listed six of my 320 agents who had agreed for me to declare their earnings. One was a newsagent and five were ex-Littlewood collectors who had always been instructed to declare their earnings by a very unsympathetic manager.

"Where have you been?" was how I was greeted, as it was 11.45 am. "We have sat here for nearly two hours waiting for you."

"I'm dreadfully sorry" I replied. "I have just come from the hospital, my wife had a little boy not two hours ago. Both are fine." Congratulations were the order of the day and one of the chaps even suggested we sent out for champagne.

"No! We have got to finish the business with Mr. Fear. What have you got for us?" The bossman asked.

"Here are the biggest earners" I replied. They glanced at my list.

"What's this? Only six? That's ridiculous!"

"No it's not. They are the only ones I am prepared to disclose. I cannot afford to lose any of my collectors now I have another mouth to feed." They did laugh and on parting, the bossman said

"Goodbye and we hope we never have to meet you again." A close shave, I thought, as I drove back to see my wife and six-year-old baby!

Chapter 11

The Cattery

In spite of earning enough to enjoy a reasonable lifestyle, I was always short of money and in the late 1970s managed to earn a large overdraft which seemed to worry the bank manager more than it did me.

I'm not joking. One morning at 8.15 am there was a knock at the front door. Who should be on the threshold? None other than my old friend the bank manager.

"You're early, what do you want?"

"I'd like a few words with you" he answered. "I pass the end of your road every morning and thought I would take this opportunity to discuss (I knew what was coming), your overdraft and what you intend to do about it."

"I am busy getting breakfast for Lara and Dan (Tim had already gone to work). You'll have to come into the kitchen. Follow me." From the kitchen's picture window, I had a nice view of the rear of the property including the four large stables and tack room.

"Well, what are you going to do about it?" asked the bank manager. What was I going to do? At that precise moment, I had no idea what excuse I could make. Then I aspired.

"The empty stables. I'm going to convert the stables into something."

"What?"

Again my mind was a complete blank and then Dandy, our black cat came to my rescue as he passed the window. "I'm going to open a place to keep cats when their owners go on holiday" I announced.

"You mean a cattery?"

"Yes, that's right. A cattery." So that's what they call them, I thought. When we went on holiday, we left Dandy to his own devices, to survive as best he could, a rat here, a rabbit there and an occasional hare. He never came to any harm, lived until he was fourteen, and earned me over £1,000 on one occasion. How come?

Every morning my first act on descending the stairs was to open the front door to retrieve the milk before the bluetits had pecked through the foil to get a free drink, and to let in the cat. I always greeted him in the same way.

"Hello Dandy. Had a nice rat have you?"

However, on the occasion of the 1983 Grand National, I was looking through the list of runners and saw one of the runners was called 'Hello Dandy'. I thought to myself, 'I'll have a fiver each way on that one', as it was ridden by Doughety, a very good jockey indeed. To my delight it finished 4th at 66:1 so I won about £75.

When the list of runners was published for the following year's Grand National, I saw 'Hello Dandy' was entered again but had to carry 4lbs more. I had followed his career since his 4th place and noted he always ran in the longest of races and never won. Out for an airing I always felt.

When Ladbrokes first published in the press for the Grand National, 'Hello Dandy' was quoted at 33-1, so I had £20 each way at 33-1. From then on his price continued to drop. I had a few more £5 each way at various prices. On the big day, he finished up at 14-1. As a bookmaker, people always thought I was in the know and could give them a good tip, particularly on the Grand National, when the once a year punters were hoping for a winner.

This year I was confident and told all and sundry 'Hello Dandy' would win. The Grand National is the bookmaker's busiest day of the year and I was so busy I didn't have much time to think of my wager. On my Book, 'Hello Dandy' would be a good result but my fortunes rested on the placed horses. As the prices are so high in the National, the bookmaker is virtually paying out on four winners. The oaf who introduced paying out on the 4th horse home in handicaps of 14 or more runners wants a bullet up his backside. Many a good day has been spoilt by having to pay out on the 4th horse.

Needless to say, 'Hello Dandy' ran a brilliant faultless race and won by several lengths at 14:1. Yippee! I was a very happy man and

255

so were my friends who listened to my advice and had backed the winner.

Back to my unwelcome visitor, the bank manager.

"I shall get sorted as soon as possible" I assured him.

I discussed the idea with my No. 3 and she was most enthusiastic and offered to run the business. My first port of call was at Stafford where, by chance, the largest cattery in Britain was situated, and had been shown on TV recently. I arrived on the pretext of boarding my cat and asked the very offhand owner if I may have a look at the cages where Dandy would be housed.

"I am off but I'll get one of the gals to show you round" she replied.

A very nice young lady appeared and asked me what I would like to see. I slipped a £5 note into her hand and said

"The lot."

If she had guessed what I was up to, I will never know, nor did she question my actions when I took out my tape measure and made notes of the sizes of the different constructed pens and what they charged per day for boarding. Finally, she showed me the expensive suite, which was the size of a small room with one or two homely features. I'll better that, I thought.

"That was an Aston Martin your boss lady was driving, wasn't it?" I enquired.

"Yes" replied the girl, "she has two." It was indeed a big cattery but the setting was not very impressive and I made up my mind to do something better.

I started the construction straight away. The tack room we decided would be an office and with a bit of imagination we very soon had it looking very pleasant. I knocked out the dividing walls of the four stables and constructed a double row of thirty cages. At the back of the stables were a row of pigsties and the first thing I did there was to build my 'Executive Suite'. During our second year in business, I constructed another forty cages in the former piggery.

I carpeted the floor of the executive suite, put in a table and chairs including an armchair, electric fire, pictures on the walls and an old TV. We had leaflets printed and advertised in the local papers. We decided to charge £2 a day for the normal pens and £5 for the executive suite. That was the going rate in the 1980s.

When people telephoned to make a reservation for their cat, I always insisted they called first to have a look at our work of art. I did this for two reasons. One I could see the type of person we were dealing with and secondly they could see for themselves, the accommodation their animal would be housed in. When showing a prospective client around, I always reserved the executive suite until last and can imagine when they told their friends about the 'Kandahar Kattery' they would say

"Fantastic place, even got a TV in the pens. My parting shot to our prospective clients was "If your cat doesn't look better when you fetch him or her home than when they arrived, there will be no charge!" Not once did an owner take advantage of my offer.

We soon were well established and our returns were above expectations. We boarded over 100 cats during the Potters' fortnight holiday and averaged 20 cats a week the rest of the year. We only wished we had started the cattery 20 years earlier when the bottom fell out of Bookmaking.

Each pen contained a large washing-up bowl in which was placed special wood shavings. A litter tray was also installed. However well groomed the cats were on arrival, their coats were 100% cleaner when they left. In the bottom of every sleeping bowl was a pile of dust and dirt. Before sleeping in their bowls, cats always circle around and around and automatically groom themselves. If the cat looked a bit scraggy, I would give it a good combing the day before its departure. Irrespective of the owners' instructions regarding feeding their pet, they all got the same diet, a good quality dry food, and water. Never milk; it's the worst thing one can give a fully grown cat.

Apart from holiday periods, it only took an hour in the morning and an hour in the afternoon after racing had finished to tend to the work involved. A cat is a scrupulously clean animal and it will always use the litter tray.

Linoleum was on the floor of each pen, which made it easy to clean out once the pen had been vacated. Tago was sprayed about the place daily, which resulted in an illness-free cattery. Not once did we have to call in a vet for our feline guests. The annual inspection, when we had to renew our licence, was always satisfactory and the inspectors all said it was the best cattery they had ever visited. It's surprising what half-a-dozen free-range eggs will do!

One dear old lady had not been on holiday for eight years as she couldn't trust anybody to look after her three babies. After several inspection visits she booked the executive suite for two weeks. The three cats duly arrived and I was warned that one of them was very excitable and hated strangers. I was given instructions on how and when to feed her three prizes, and how to deal with the excitable cat. I discussed it with my wife and decided the best thing was to starve them for three days. I visited them regularly and entered their room several times a day.

The wild cat was indeed wild and flew around the room like one possessed with the devil. I groomed the other two and made a fuss of them. By the third day, the excitable one and I were pals too. I was able to groom him and treat him like the others. When I took them their first feed, they were most grateful and from then on tranquillity reigned. I soon got the wild one to sit on my shoulder or lay round my neck like a fur collar.

Would you believe it, their owner returned home four days early and telephoned us to say she had been so worried about her cats she decided to cut short her holiday and could she collect her family?

We had ten minutes to give the finishing touches to the three cats. I made a point of being in the executive suite when she arrived and had old 'Wild Willy' sitting comfortably around my shoulders.

"Hello my little darlings, come to mummy" she said. None of her prize possessions made a move towards her. In fact, they practically ignored her.

I explained to her that her fears of the past eight years were unfounded and her cats would have always been happy in her absence, because like dogs, cats only love the hand that feeds them. She was astonished and declared that they all looked five years younger. She insisted in paying for the full fortnight's board. Furthermore, she made up for lost time by going on holiday twice a year from then on.

Keith Hill approached me one day and said a friend of his had a little poodle she wanted to board and wasn't very happy with the kennels she had visited. Having heard from Keith what a nice 'home from home' place we had, he would deem it a great favour if we would make an exception and take the dog for a couple of weeks.

"Not bloody likely" I said, "Our clients wouldn't like it if we had dogs about the place.

"I'm going to send the lady along so you can sort it out" he replied. She turned up a couple of days later and as usual, I fell for a pretty face, she was an Olivia de Haviland type. The poodle was little, as Keith had indicated, and quite likeable if you like that sort of thing, but the owner was in a class of her own. She assured me that her Fe-Fe didn't bark and would be very happy in one of our cages.

The following Saturday our poodle arrived together with a supply of large prawns and fillet steak, to be fed alternate days. It seems prawns and steak was Fe-Fe's favourite food, as indeed it was also my idea of a good scoff! Mrs. X took a good ten minutes to say goodbye to her little pet. As soon as she had gone, the dog started whining and then barking.

"For God's sake, that's all we need on our busy day. Cats will be arriving by the dozen any moment now," Linda declared. "What shall we do?"

I had an idea. Dear old Tim had gone on a two-week holiday the night before so his bedroom on the ground floor was vacant. We could put her in the bedroom. We dispatched Fe-Fe post-haste into Tim's room. After this had been done, the telephone rang and Mrs. X was just ringing to ask if Fe-Fe had settled in all right. I assured her that her little doggie was very happy indeed. I told her that we had been having second thoughts, and decided she would be more contented in our home.

"Oh Mr. Fear, you are an angel. How kind of you. I shall go on my holiday very happy now." I popped my head in Tim's bedroom to see how the hound was getting on, only to discover she had done a large dollop, not in the tray we had provided but bang in the middle of the bed. I shouted at the dirty little bitch and cleared up the mess. All the bedding had to be removed and I covered the mattress with a waterproof sheet. Bloody dog! No food for you today my girl. That evening our homemade soup, the prawns and fillet steak went down very well indeed.

Fe-Fe was very fussy about her eating and didn't like cat food or the popular brand of dog food. I said to myself, 'You'll eat anything when you get hungry.' After a couple of foodless days, the little poodle started eating. I found out she liked a slice of wholemeal bread with butter and that is what she lived on during her stay.

When I worked in the garden I took her outside with me, tied her with a length of string to a tree and allowed her to have freedom of movement. We became good friends. On the Friday before she was due to go home, my wife suggested I gave Fe-Fe a shampoo.

"What the hell? I've never shampooed a stinking dog in my life!" I retorted.

"Now's the time to learn" she answered.

I got an old baby bath, filled it with warm water, and proceeded to wash the poodle to the best of my ability. She did look a mess, like a drowned rat.

"You had better get the hair dryer on her" Linda suggested. This I did and whilst I was drying her, I thought to myself, 'I've worked my balls off for forty years and finish up washing f--king dogs. Something went wrong somewhere!'

After the hair drying and a good combing, Fe-Fe looked a real winner. I rubbed a little olive oil around her eyes and paws, a trick I learned from Jane when she was preparing her horses for horse trials. I polished her collar and thought she looked a real picture. No sooner had I finished than the telephone rang. It was Mrs. X's daughter. She had returned from her holiday a day early and thought it would be a good idea if she collected Fe-Fe now, so it would be a surprise when her mother returned on the following day.

An hour later, the daughter arrived and the first thing she said was:

"Doesn't Fe-Fe look fantastic? How much do we owe you?" I had the good sense to tell her that I would sort it out with her mother. The next day the phone rang. It was Mrs. X.

"Oh Mr. Fear, I want to thank you for looking after Fe-Fe. She looks marvellous. How did you manage to look after her so well with all the other work you have to do?"

"Oh, it's nothing" I replied. "By the way, I've discovered that her favourite food is wholemeal bread. Very good for humans and animals alike. But please be sure to butter the bread on both sides"

"How much do I owe you?" was her next question.

"Well we charge £2 a day for cats, which amounts to £28"

"I'll send you a cheque today, you won't be disappointed. Goodbye Mr. Fear"

Two hours later La Margarets pulled up outside and the driver, who I knew, got out with a huge bouquet of flowers. As it happened, one of the Webster daughters next door was getting married and I shouted to the driver,

"It's for next door, there's a wedding on"

"No Ray," he said, "It's addressed to you"

"Blimey. I've got a secret admirer" I joked. When I read the card I was knocked over, for it read:

'To dear Mr. Fear who has looked after me so well - love Fe-Fe.'

What a charming lady. I couldn't wait for the post on Monday. As predicted, Monday morning in the first post, a sweet smelling sky blue envelope arrived and inside was a short note and a cheque for £150. I couldn't believe my eyes. I hastened to send an acknowledgement and assured Mrs. X that her little Fe-Fe would always be welcome at Kandahar.

The following Christmas, Mrs. X arrived with appropriate gifts for every member of my family living at Kandahar. Fe-Fe immediately recognised me and greeted me like a long lost friend. I was rather relieved as I had feared she may have remembered the odd kick up the backside and rush to take cover.

Another odd happening while we were running the cattery was when a customer asked if beside her cat, we would look after two tortoises. Good God, what next!

"Would that rabbit hut be okay?" I asked. "Perfect" she said.

When they arrived, I heard the whole history of Bill and Betty. The owner had had them for years and for the winter months, they were housed inside her home. They were the two largest specimens I had ever seen. The male quite ten inches long. After explaining what they liked to eat, she said

"Do look after them. I would die if anything happened to them"

"Don't worry darling. I'll take good care of them" I replied. After a couple of days I thought, 'Poor things. The rabbit hutch isn't big enough for them', so I constructed a pen in the paddock at the back of the house. The enclosure was easily constructed with eight railway sleepers, two high all round, making a height of about a foot. Plenty, I thought, to keep them from escaping. How wrong I was for the next day, Bill was missing.

"That's all we need," said Linda. "I told you to keep them locked up"

"We will soon find them" I replied. Wrong again! The paddock was about half an acre and overgrown at the bottom, so together with Linda, Lara, and young Dan, we searched for hours without any sign of the damn tortoise.

"I've had an idea. Dan, please run down to the village and knock on all the doors and ask all the school kids to come up and help search for Bill. Tell them I will give £10 to the one who finds him."

One hour later Dan returned empty handed. He couldn't find any volunteers despite of my generous offer.

"What shall we do?" wailed Linda. "We are ruined"

"Well I don't know about you" I said, "but I'm hungry. Let's have our dinner."

"How you can think about eating at a time like this. I'll phone the police" she cried. She got in touch with our friend Bevington who suggested we phone police HQ at Stafford where they train police dogs. After a brief conversation with Stafford, Linda put down the telephone and repeated what the dog trainer had told her.

"Well madam, we have dogs that can hunt criminals. We have dogs that can track escapees. We have dogs that can detect explosives. We have dogs that can detect drugs, but I am sorry madam, we haven't any dogs to detect the whereabouts of tortoises. Good night."

We all laughed and ate our dinner. After our meal, I took command and as Tim had arrived home from work, there were five of us. "We will operate in the same way we did mine clearing in the army" I said. I gave my orders and we began our organised search, instead of bayonets, we used sticks. I kept my eye on the team and saw Dan had wandered off to a pile of rubble overgrown with stinging nettles.

"What the hell are you doing? Come out of there, you won't find him there." Wrong again.

Dan ignored me and within minutes held up Billy.

"Got him, Sir" he shouted.

Yes indeed he had, right in the middle of the rubble. Can't imagine what Billy saw in such uncomfortable surroundings when he had the whole field to go at. "What about my £10" Dan cried.

"I'll pay you later" I assured him. I never did and fifteen years later, he constantly reminds me of the fact. I returned Billy to the pen and watched carefully to try to discover how he had got out. I hadn't long to wait for within minutes he was nearly out again. How he escaped was easy, all he did was get Betty to stand alongside a sleeper and he clambered onto her back and over the parapet. I soon had them tucked up safely in the rabbit hut. When I related the incident to the owner, all she said was:

"You shouldn't have gone to such trouble." I wonder what her real reaction would have been if I had announced that we had lost one of her pets. She was very generous and said she would pay the same price that we charged for cats, plus the £10 I said I had to pay the finder. I never told Dan about the payment. One of these days when my money tree blooms, I will pay him double.

Chapter 12

Vernons Pools

As I have already told you in a previous chapter, I was a main agent for Vernons' Pools for over thirty years, during which time I built up the business to a take of well over a million pounds a year to become by far their biggest main agent. Organising 320 sub-agents and arranging the collection of 90% of these agents' coupons every Friday night was no mean task. Originally, I did all the work myself but as business grew, I employed clerks and drivers as and when it became necessary.

I opened an office where people could bring their individual investments each week, and to encourage this, they were allowed a 12.5% discount. Very soon, not only was I Vernons' biggest main agent, but their biggest sub-agent too.

Mr. Wilburn ran this office until his retirement, then my illustrious secretary Jean took over and ran it successfully until the end. There are many funny stories about my years in the pools and I'll relate but a few.

While we were operating the pools from Marsh Street, the clients would bring their coupons to the betting shop, which had three clerks behind the counter, Mr. Bradley, Mr. Stanford and David Scrivens. One Monday morning, a gentleman came bouncing into the office with a broad grin on his face.

"I've won the pools" he announced. "I've got 24 points" the maximum at the time.

We advised him that as there were only nine draws on the coupon on Saturday, the pay-out would be excellent.

"I know, I know. I've already been in touch with Liverpool and they have confirmed that the pay-out would be in the region of

Finally after a few more weeks, the message was 'Don't come again. I haven't got time to fill in football coupons', and at no time was there a mention of his big win or a thank you for his services.

I was luckier. On one occasion when one of my sub-agents won a considerable amount, he was overjoyed to see me and said it was a syndicate of eight, which he organised and held one share. He suggested to the other participants that as I collected his pack personally every Friday night at 11 pm,. I should be rewarded. Mr. Key had suggested £10 from each participant but they felt that was too much and agreed to £5. So I copped £45, as Mr. Key contributed £10, the amount he originally suggested. I don't think £10 from the others out of the £12,000 they each won would have broken them, still I was pleased with my windfall.

During mid-winter I was very concerned with weather forecasts and dreaded the days when snow had already fallen or was forecast for the coming Friday evening. My drivers could cope with the town calls albeit an hour or two late, but collecting from the sub-agents who lived in the country and moorland areas was a nightmare.

I owned a Landrover for some years so I would relieve the regular driver and do the collecting myself. I also had a good chum who lived in the village who would loan me his Landrover when two were needed. Not once in thirty years did we fail to get our three kit bags full of coupons ready to be collected by Securicor at the given hour, usually 2 am on the Saturday morning.

I remember on one occasion when the whole country was under several inches of ice and snow, HQ at Liverpool telephoned me and asked if I could get hold of half a dozen Landrovers as they had heard I used this means of transport during bad weather. I thought for a moment, 'Why should I go to all that trouble? No. F--k 'em, let them get their own Landrovers. Bloody cheek!'

It turned out that on that particular week, some of the main agents didn't get their coupons in until late on the Monday night. I blame HQ for this. What a shower! Couldn't organise a dog's dinner.

The only way the top dogs seemed proficient was by hassling the main agents to make an even greater effort in their desire to become as big as Littlewoods. The job was bestowed on the collectors' service manager, who drove the regional managers, who endeavoured to get the area managers, who threatened to sack the district managers if they didn't get more effort from us main agents. I was supposed to drive my sub-agents to greater effort but I never did. I treated them all with kid gloves and quickly realised that most of them were content with the size of their round and didn't want any more calls - or the possibility. There were a few exceptions who were content to collect from their clients three nights a week, but they were few and the majority wanted to finish their collecting, do the bit of clerical work to finalise the coupons they had collected, and get down to the Labour Club or pub, to spend their hard earned pittance.

Years earlier when I had established a good relationship with Mr. Bethel the Collectors Service manager, I told him that Vernons' had best put up the sub-agents commission before the government stepped in and put the betting tax up from 20%. I was told no way could the government do this. But they did. The government put up the tax to 25%. I pointed out that each week the Pools companies had to declare their expenses for that particular week which was around 33%. The tax was 25%, the main agent's 15% (of which 12 ½% went to the sub-agents), that's a total of 73%. This left 27% to be paid in winnings to the poor unsuspecting clients. The fact was that the pools companies were not declaring the full extent of the expenses. Tax was a dirty word and never mentioned. If they declared the real figures, I am sure many people would have realised they were being 'ripped-off'.

I begged HQ again to pay the subs more before the conservative government raised the tax once more. Their response was 'No'. Soon after, at the next budget, up went the pools tax to 30%. I made a final plea, but to no avail. I had pointed out that if Vernons' expenses were 33%, agents' commissions 15%, tax 30% which made a total of 78%, if you raised the commission to shall we say 20%, that would be 83%, leaving only 17% for dividends. Even the woodenheaded chancellor would see they couldn't tax the Pools anymore as the companies wouldn't have anything left to pay the dividends with. As I had forecast, up once more went the tax, this time to an all time high of 33%.

So instead of paying the agents who did all the work trudging around the houses on a Thursday or Friday night in all weathers, the stupid peasants who ran the pools preferred to pay the politicians, those band of half-wits who's only reason for applying for the job was that it was overpaid, and apart from when they have to canvass their constituency for a few days during a general election, kiss snotty nosed children, pat old ladies on the head and promise the earth, they do nought of any consequence.

Even the genuine ones have to toe the party line or out they go. Like our once great hope, Enoch Powell, on reviewing the Common Market declared,

"An anti-soviet block concocted by the Yanks" and did his best to get his views known to the voters.

I was a bit disappointed in Mr. Powell for not trying to take power. I am sure that if there had been a referendum in Britain at that time, he would have been voted the most popular politician of all time. Greater than Churchill who, although a great orator and wartime leader, was to say the least a trifle insincere. For instance, while campaigning as a liberal in Dundee in 1908, he told his electors

"We know what to expect when the Tories return to power, a party of vested interests, banded together in a formidable confederation."

The trickery of tariff jugglers; the tyranny of a well-fed party machine; sentiment by the basketful; patriotism and imperialism by the imperial pint; dear food for the millions and cheap labour for the millionaires. Churchill then made another miscalculation regarding the mentality of the British electors when in a 1945 election speech broadcast on the radio he said,

"I declare to you from the bottom of my heart that no socialist system can be established without political police. No socialist government conducting the entire life and industry of the country could afford to allow free, sharp, or violently worded expressions of public discontent. They would have to fall back on some form of Gestapo!"

Churchill had so often decried the 'Nazis' and 'Gestapo' in his wartime broadcasts. Now he was suggesting a Gestapo run government headed by that very sincere, mild mannered man, Clement Attlee. The public were not amused and not taken in by Winnie's remarks. The socialists won the general election with an overwhelming majority. They kept to their word and the welfare state was born.

The lot of the working class certainly improved and if it hadn't been for the billions of pounds wasted on defence, things could have been a lot better. Defence nonsense. Defence against what? Those dreadful Russians whose wealth is untold? More gold, diamonds, oil, and other minerals than the rest of the world put together. Can you imagine them invading Britain, a hornet's nest? No! The Russians have always been our ally, defeating Napoleon in 1811/12, inflicting more casualties in the battle for Smolensk on his way to Moscow than were inflicted on the French at Waterloo. In the First World War, the Russians sustained five times more dead fighting the German-Austrian armies than we and our entire Empire.

Enough about politics for the time being, let us get on with my experiences with Vernons' pools. Sorry, I mean Vermins' pools!

When my number 3 decided that we should come to live in Spain, I naturally had to give thought as to what I would do with my businesses; bookmaking, pools, and the cattery. The cattery could be included with the sale of Kandahar and my credit bookmaking could very quickly be turned over to Keith and Ann Hill, our bookmakers and social friends. As for the pools business, son Tim decided to take over. As he had been involved with pools since he was a schoolboy, it would be easy for him to follow in his father's footsteps. I was confident he could do the job well, and with a young man's enthusiasm, which I had long since got weary of.

When I first started in pools everything was left to me and I was never badgered or hounded in anyway, but in time things changed and eventually the country was split up into areas. Regional managers, area managers, district managers, most of them had one thing in common, they knew very little about pools or the downtrodden collectors who collected them. I can say in all truthfulness, that in all the many years dealing with these hard heads, they never once got me one sub-agent of any consequence, lots of red herrings and Chinese restaurants where they had recently taken their lunch and kidded the owner into becoming an agent for Vernons' pools. On interviewing the owner and wasting valuable time, I was told not to bother to call, as they were not interested in earning a few pence a week.

However, in August 1989 the regional manager, our Don McLean, took Tim and me to Liverpool to introduce Tim to the Collectors Service Manager and some of the directors of the firm and confirm our April agreement. I told them I would only retire to Spain if they agreed to reinstate me if Tim, for any reason whatsoever, finished as the main agent. This they all readily agreed to, thereby ensuring the continuation of their biggest collectorship and an income for myself.

All went well for three years, Tim did well, and in-fact increased business. To enable us to continue our life style he agreed to send us £80 a week from his adequate commission. However, a new managing director was employed and the dishonourable nincompoop Mr. H decided to split up the bigger main agents thereby hoping to increase business.

When Tim was here in Spain for his annual two weeks holiday, Mr. H thought it a good time to do the dirty and he got all the area managers in the country to converge on Stoke-on-Trent and instructed our 320 agents to deal from henceforth with one of the new six main agents employed to take over his round. To cut a long story short, I asked a firm of solicitors I'll now refer to as 'M's' to have a go at Vernons'. After six years of buggering about, M's failed to complete our case and the six year time-limit elapsed. I was advised by the Law Society to contact the Offices for the Supervision of Solicitors, the O.S.S. After a two year investigation, they found M's guilty on nine counts of irregularities and they had to pay me £2,500 within seven days.

The O.S.S. couldn't deal with negligence, a much more serious charge, so I sought a new solicitor to eventually take M's to the high court on a charge of negligence. Knowing what a bunch of incompetent rogues most solicitors are, I sought the help of a life-long friend Tim Cooper, whose father and mother were also good friends of mine. He gave me the name of Neil Chadwick whom I contacted. I sent him my brief, and as I write this chapter, he is pursuing justice and claiming £250,000 compensation from M's. Before I finish this book, I may have had a verdict, but I doubt it!

The regional manager, Mr. Don McLean, who was under threat of dismissal if he didn't carry out the director's orders, also resigned and consequently was free to tell the truth as to what really happened. In his statement, he confirmed that Tim was a good agent and that if his area was split up, Vernons' would lose a great deal of business. His advice was ignored and in-fact his predictions were worse than even he predicted. After six months, not one of the six new main agents remained and what was left of the once great area fell into the hands of the daughter of one of my sub-agents. She endeavoured to regain the lost business but after two years, Vernons' closed down their collector service and sacked a staff of 4,000 in Liverpool. That's what happened when they so thoughtlessly employed a whiz kid who thought he knew more about pools than people who had been in the business for over thirty years.

To quote Len Wright, a lovable main agent from Derby;

"Not having to deal with those Vernons' arseholes should be worth an extra decade of living for each of us. W and F etc. would have been dangerous adversaries had they been issued with a brain instead of being the programmed robots they are. They surely would not have hoped to outwit you and I. Trusting you have given them a good slagging in your book. Absolute wankers the lot of them. Most of them of doubtful origin up at Mount Vernon." My sentiments entirely!

M's and their insurance company, knowing my financial position, will be hoping I will not be able to finance a high court case but thanks to the help of a friend and son Dan, I've been able to employ a barrister who has advised M's that we are prepared to go all the way to gain a satisfactory result. With this information, a settlement out-of-court will probably be the outcome.

CHOLMONDELEY CASTLE
MALPAS, CHESHIRE

TEL: CHOLMONDELEY (082-922) 202

20th October, 1987.

Ray Fear, Esq.,
Kandahar,
Crossgate,
Nr.Fulford,
Stone,
Staffs.

Dear Ray.

Thank you so much for your letter and the enclosures which I was very pleased to have.

I stick to a very healthy diet these days, with no animal fat, and plenty of fibre. I eat a lot of poultry and fish. The good old 'Baron of Beef' which we used to have at the Association Dinner is definitely out!

When I am a bit better organised, I would very much like to meet you again, so will keep in touch.

Best wishes.

Yours sincerely,

Cholmondeley

A letter received from the Marquess of Cholmondeley M.C. confirming receipt of food parcel sent to His Lordship by the author

Bill Tellwright after winning the Grand Military Gold Cup for the third time. With Her Majesty The Queen Mother

Yeoman Warder Bill Callaghan and Yeoman Warder Steve Froggatt in the Beauchamp Tower - 2004

The Casemates, where the author was conceived. With daughter Natasha and Yeoman Warder Fiddes

The author, aged 65, given number 1 as the only foreign entry in his 9th Potteries Marathon

Sylvia and author on Saint George's Day 2004

The author, out with the North Staffordshire Hunt

brought his bet to the house every morning. As Mr. Webster Senior lived next door, he sometimes entered through the back garden gate so poor John didn't see Mr. Webster approach, only heard him knocking on the window waving a bit of paper which John mistook for a summons. Panic set in!

"The Customs are here. What shall I do?" He soon realised his suspicions were unfounded when he noticed that Mr. Webster was in his pyjamas. John insisted that for the rest of the week, Mr. Webster phone in his bets, thus preventing Dear John from having a heart attack. Pat says her husband has never been the same since his experiences as an illegal bookmaker. John's comment to me was,

"Please don't ever, ever, ever, ask me to do this job again."

Another good pal was Roy Heath of Blythe Bridge. We spent many a happy hour discussing chickens and their ability to lay large brown eggs. Roy was a character. An honest Bernard Wicklin who took bets for me, illicit or otherwise, for a number of years. One December, as Christmas was approaching, he said to me:

"You have always been good to me Ray, so this Christmas I am going to give you a nice fat turkey for your Christmas dinner. I'll go to Uttoxeter market, you can get a whopper very cheap."

"If you insist" I answered. As Christmas approached I was wondering if indeed his offer was forthcoming so I telephoned him to enquire if he had indeed managed to get a whopper.

"You'll be well pleased" was his reply. "Come tomorrow morning I shall have him plucked by then." Come the morrow I called at his home. Mrs. Heath answered the door. She was in a state! Feathers in her hair and a most unpleasant smell greeted me.

"He's in the bloody lounge plucking your bloody turkey."

Her hostile greeting was so unlike her. We had always been on the best of terms until now. No wonder she was in a mood. When I entered their front room it was to discover Roy sitting on the hearth with this enormous turkey plucking away merrily and throwing the feathers on the open fire. Most of them missed the target and floated around the room like a snow storm.

"Good God!" I exclaimed. "What ever are you doing?"

"Won't be long" he said. "I'll drop it off at your place when I've finished." I beat a hasty retreat, apologising to the irate Mrs. Heath.

"Happy Christmas" I called out to her.

"Happy Christmas my foot" she bellowed back.

A few hours later dear Roy arrived at Kandahar with the bird. It was like an ostrich and weighed 32lbs. Me thinks I won't get it in the oven, but I didn't mention this to my benefactor.

"How kind of you" I remarked. "Stop and have a drink" to which he readily agreed. "Your wife didn't sound too happy" I said.

"Oh she's okay, and thinks the feathers stuck on the Christmas tree will give a natural effect." I wonder!

I was right about one thing, the turkey was far too big for the oven so I carved it in half, did a few operations on backside and leg, and got it to fit in the oven. We started cooking just before we retired on Christmas Eve and by lunch time next day it was ready to be devoured. It was delicious and the other half we had at Easter. I've always kept in touch with Heath and, in fact, he is the only needy person I have instructed my family to give £1,000 to when my time comes. He will certainly benefit if I come into money in the near future which I am certain will happen, one way or another. Roy is the salt of the earth. Poor - yes - but a happy man.

Going from one extreme to another, I must mention another good friend, the Marques of Cholmondeley, a title he inherited from his father. In the army he was Lord Rocksavage. Living at Malpass Castle midst 6,000 acres of Cheshire was poles apart from Blythe Bridge, but like Roy Heath, he was a generous good friend. We first met when he was president of the North Staffs Comrades Association. I was the vice president. He was also president of my North Staffs Modern Pentathlon Club. He sponsored some of our events without question and if I had a bad run on the racing, could always rely on him helping me out. I sometimes wondered why this man, the Lord Great Chamberlain of England chose to befriend me. He who walks backwards, in front of Her Majesty the Queen at the State Opening of Parliament. I think he admired me because of my fitness and healthy outlook on life.

He telephoned me one day and announced he had had a slight heart attack and what would I recommend for his recovery.

"That's easy," I said, "change your diet."

"Tell me more" he said. After some explanation I said I would send him a food parcel. As I remember, I sent him some Bio Salt, Soya bean flour, dark maple sugar, brewers yeast and an assortment of vitamin pills with full instructions on how his cook should administer the contents of the parcel. I am afraid my advice came too late for he died soon after I departed to Spain, in March 1990.

I first heard of his death in a newspaper I rescued from a park bench, (I never buy English papers in Spain.) It read, and I quote:

'And to my moneybags son, I leave £118 million. Peer makes record Will, topping the previous highest of £92 million left by Dorothy de Rothschild.'

To think of it, I was sending one of the richest men in England a food parcel, free of charge of course.

Prior to my departure to Spain, I telephoned His Lordship and told him I was departing to sunnier places. He seemed quite sad at hearing the news and said the country would be the poorer at my departure. He asked about Jane, (he always enquired about her since she had won the Open Senior Horse Trials at Malpass Castle some years before). I told him that Dan was in the Staffordshire Junior Tennis squad but I didn't think we would be able to carry on with his coaching as the advanced tennis coaches were very expensive, as indeed was membership in the local tennis club.

"When you get settled in let me know and I'll be able to help Dan financially with his tennis" His Lordship said. Now that was a great gesture on top of what he had already done for me in the past.

As particulars as to the new Marquises whereabouts were disclosed in the paper, I thought a letter might be in order. After passing on my condolences, I mentioned the conversation I had with his father relating to sponsoring Dan's tennis. In a very short time I had a personal letter back saying he was very happy to receive a letter from his father's good friend, but at the moment all his money was tied up but he would consider a grant next year.

Twelve months later I wrote reminding him of his suggestion but he promptly wrote back to say no cash was available. I politely answered his letter and finished by telling him I was sorry he couldn't see his way clear to carry out his father's wishes. I heard no more. To think a man who owns a four-thousand acre Norfolk Estate and the world's biggest herd of 1,000 head of White Fallow Deer next door to Sandringham, and who had just inherited £118,000,000, was unable to help promote son Dan's tennis, was beyond me. No wonder he was affectionately known in the south of France, not as Lord Rocksavage, but as Lord Rocksausage. Which reminds me of the time when his father was attending a dinner we held in honour of the achievements of the swim kids, the S.O.T. team that had swum the English Channel both ways, Cardigan Bay, Loch Ness and the Irish Sea, all in the space of six weeks.

After a very fine dinner, speeches were made. In response to a toast to the guests, Captain Hookes, a staunch Welsh lobster fisherman who had helped us with his boat in our training at Abersoch, began his response by acknowledging the presence of His Lordship the Earl of Rocksalmon. There was a hushed silence for a moment until the Earl burst out laughing. I explained later to Lord Rocksavage that the error was intentional, and that Captain Hookes was a supporter of Home Rule for Wales, and he disliked the English, the up-classes in particular. He always said I was the only Englishman he tolerated, probably because my father was born and bred in Aberyswyth. The Earl made light of the incident and made a point of having a lengthy conversation with Captain Hookes after the presentations and speeches.

Besides John and Mandy Howle, there were many other good friends and characters amongst the hunting fraternity. Ray and Judy Allman must top the list as hard working members of the North Staffordshire hunt. 'Ray One', as I always referred to him. He was a little older than me, was a staunch 'Queen and Country' man and an ardent conservative. We had many a heated conversation during the

284

lulls whilst out hunting. I couldn't understand why a man of humble background could support the regime that had kept his parents in such servitude.

Judy, on the other hand, who had been born into middle-upper class surroundings, tended to support my views, when carefully explained to her. Judy was, I think, my most intelligent punter. She could relate or take a bet with the precision of the most experienced bookmaker's clerk. She bet with me for over forty years and we never had one dispute. Now I live in Spain, I always telephone Judy with any betting I require on the big races.

I always remember one Saturday when we hunted from 'High Fields', we did a point of some twenty miles. At the end only three of us were in contention. Judy, Major Friend and myself. At this point the master called it a day and we trudged back to our boxes. 'Ray One' died a couple of years ago but dear Judy battles on relentlessly.

Mr. Jack Baker of Highfields was a real character. A born actor and brave as a lion when hunting. His horse, like mine, was nothing special to look at but would jump anything in sight. I never saw Jack on the floor.

I remember one of his escapades. He dressed up as a woman and booked into the Newcastle-Under-Lyme Ladies Turkish Baths. He sat there quite undisturbed reading 'The Times', when one of the wealthy oversized ladies sitting beside him asked if Jack would mind rubbing her neck. Unfortunately, while carrying out this operation his towel fell from his breast, revealing a hairy chest. There were screams and the police were called and Mr. Baker was locked up.

In court Mr. Baker pleaded guilty, but said he had done it for a bet. 'Case dismissed' announced the magistrate who happened to be a hunting man. I met Jack and his charming wife recently. They are like a couple of newly-weds and he is 87 years old, and still hunts on special occasions.

Together with J.S. Bourne, Bill and Jane Tellwright were joint masters of the North Staffordshire Hunt in 1963-67, the period when, together with daughter Jane, I started hunting. A most enjoyable sport. I have partaken in many sporting activities but the one I enjoyed most was in the saddle for three or four hours hunting the great county of North Staffordshire.

I was out hunting one day when Bill Tellwright approached me and asked if I was indeed Mr. Ray Fear. I answered in the affirmative but was flattered that the master would approach me in the middle of hunting.

"Come back to Betton House after we call it a day" he said. "We can have a chat over tea and crumpets."

I accepted his invitation and finished up worn out, covered in mud in his spacious kitchen. After tea and crumpets had been served he came to the point of my visit.

"Look here Ray. I've heard all about your sporting activities and the success you had with the Channel swimmers. Now you're into the Modern Pentathlon and the Pony Club Triathlon" (the Triathlon consisted of riding, shooting and running). "My boy Kirkland is a good rider but needs some coaching on the other two events. Will you take him for a couple of weeks during his coming holidays?"

"You mean for me to house him for two weeks?"

"Exactly" he responded.

"He can bring his pony too" I said. "We have plenty of stabling"

"Good idea."

Kirkland was duly delivered with pony and suitcase at a later date and there began a trial of personalities. A very well mannered boy, as one would expect who was a pupil of Marlborough College, where he was a boarder and used to being away from home. He accepted my discipline without a murmur and the fact that we rose at 6.30 am each morning and were racing round the Greenway Hall golf course by 7 am didn't alarm him whatsoever.

The shooting was no problem as I had a range set up on the one-time bowling green at Foxdale. It's there all my team learned to shoot to a very high standard. Kirkland, who had brought his own pistol, soon mastered the technique needed for hitting a five-second exposure turning target. He went riding with Jane and she schooled him over her own cross-country fences.

At the end of the fortnight, he looked a different lad, he was fit as a fiddle. He made our team the same year. North Staffs won the Pony Club National Championships for five consecutive years. A feat that has never been equalled.

I remember at one competition, Kirkland was riding Jane's 'Cufflink', a brilliant 16.2 hands horse. She had won the Open at Chatsworth a couple of years previous and had high hopes for the Badminton Horse Trials.

The owner rider Miss Judy Bradwell had found it difficult to train Cufflink because when she was well-fed on oats needed for the strength-sapping thirty odd miles they have to do on the second day of the competition, it went to her head and she went a bit crazy. Feeding her on hay and bran was fine, but oats was fatal. However, come the first day's dressage, Cufflink managed to jump out of the dressage arena much to the horror of Judy and the thousands of spectators. Elimination was declared by the three judges and Judy, in tears, shouted to her father:

"I'll never ride that bloody horse again!"

That's when we stepped in. Jane and Judy attended Captain Goldman's Academy at Holmes Chapel on refresher courses and it was there I met Mr. Bradwell who asked me if I would be interested in buying Cufflink.

Yes please, Dad" Jane said. A price was agreed which was very cheap for those days, and Cufflink was duly delivered to Foxdale.

She was a beautiful chestnut and when fed on hay, very quiet to handle until of course, when she was in competition and facing a fence. She was absolutely fearless and would jump anything. It was fatal to point her at any jump you didn't intend her to jump, for she would be off and over, come what may. Jane won many cross-country competitions with her but never entered her in the three-day events, knowing her past history in that quarter.

I hunted with her once and that was enough for me. We were having a splendid day jumping everything in sight, until we came to a five bar farm gate, which several of the leading horses refused to jump over. 'Ah', I thought, 'Pinky Thursby Pelham jumps everything, I'll follow her'. I had turned Cufflink's head away until I saw that Pinky was well on her way. For the first time I can remember, Pinky's horse refused and turned sideways to the gate. But it was too late! I was on my way and Cufflink not only jumped the fence, but Thursby Pelham's horse as well. I had only flown once before, but felt a great thrill as we sailed up and over the astonished Pinky. The news soon got round and Bill Tellwright came alongside and said he would like to have a ride on Cufflink sometime.

This was later arranged and the particular meet was held at Bill Tellwright's home at Betton House. I took the two horses there and was very happy to rely on my dear old Chatter and pass Cufflink to my more experienced friend. On this particular day, Bill turned out in a bottle-green jacket instead of his normal pink. He played a very low profile at the back of the field, as he got the feel of Cufflink.

We hadn't been hunting for more than ten minutes, when we came to a gate, in front of which was a great patch of mud, at least six inches deep. Alongside the gate was a five-foot hedge straggled with barbed wire.

"Let the fox see the rabbit" bellowed out Bill, and tore at the barbed wire fence. His take-off was the same as the gates which didn't help Cufflink's brave effort. She did well but caught a hind-leg in the wire and down she came. By this time the gate had been opened and I hastened through, not giving Bill a glance for fear of some reprimand or other. This was to come later. The irate Mr. Tellwright caught me up. I could hardly recognise him, his face, like the rest of him, was covered in mud.

"Ray, Ray. I thought you told me the f--king horse could jump barbed wire." I felt like telling him that nobody in his right mind would have attempted such a jump, but I held my tongue and said nothing. We had a good day and Bill and I arrived back at my horse trailer together. I've never seen anything so comical in my life, for by now the mud had dried, and Bill now looked like some mad scarecrow.

Removing his topper, his hair stood up on end to add to the fiasco.

288

"Did you enjoy riding her?" I managed to say.

"You bet. She's a wonderful animal. Never ridden a better. In fact I had quite a lovely time jumping in all directions. I didn't follow the hunt you know, and in fact, about half way, I went over the point-to-point course at Muckleston. Come in for tea and crumpets."

We made our way back to the kitchen and what followed will stay in my memory until the day I die, and probably after! As we entered the kitchen a large white African parrot flew from somewhere or other and landed on Bill's shoulder, and for all the world he looked like a dirty version of Long John Silver from the book 'Treasure Island".

"Jane, Ray's here. Get the crumpets organised" my host yelled out. How he managed to eat his crumpets and drink his Earl Grey remains a mystery as his face was set solid.

My fourth tale about Cufflink concerns young Kirkland. We were competing in a triathlon competition, and Kirkland as the most experienced rider in our team, agreed to ride Cufflink. She flew round the course but on coming out of a wood and down a steep bank, she should have turned right alongside the railway track. But no. Kirkland was unable to change direction in time and Cufflink went straight ahead confronted by the barbed wire fence that protected the line. Every bit of six feet, she jumped right over and onto the lines. How Cufflink never fell, or however Kirkland stayed in the saddle, I'll never know.

Kirkland quickly regained his composure and as I had positioned myself at this point, he shouted for instructions as to what to do.

"Jump back over" I yelled. At this point one of the jump judges who had witnessed the goings-on ordered him to carry on along the line where he would find a gate. This of course would have taken a lot longer and jeopardised our chances of winning the team event. "No" I bellowed. "Jump back here." Without hesitation this is what he did, completing the course without fault in the time allowed.

The jump judge came up to me and said,

"You're mad, completely mad. I shall report you to the stewards." The jump judge must have had second thoughts for when the North Staffs team received their rosettes and trophy, nothing was said. As we were boxing our horses, the judge came up to me to apologise for his outburst and said,

"That horse could win the Grand National!"

I must relate two business transactions I had with the Tellwrights, both father and son. To earn a little pocket money, Kirkland bred some very fine bantams. I was most interested and ordered ten. I was extremely happy with my purchase and received the following bill a few days later. I quote word for word, the contents of his typed letter.

Cadman and Tellwright Ltd.
Poulterers to Nobility and other Rich Classes,
Head Office: Cotton House,
Marlborough College,
Wiltshire
14th May 1973

Dear Sir,

Your esteemed order for ten of the purest bred astronomically high quality miniature old English game bantams has been dispatched; and the birds are now assumed to be affording their owner much pleasure.

The company has satisfaction in presenting its customer with the bill for the aforesaid transaction. Our modest fee of £0.65 per bird will, we are sure, be greeted as excellent value for money, and the company looks forward to further transactions. It is thus with much pleasure that the company presents the bill for £6.50.

The nominal charge of ten guineas has been waived in view of our esteem for our most respectable customer.

Eagerly awaiting payment.

Yours faithfully,
Israel Tellwright

P.S. The company would like to take the opportunity of advising its customer that recent tests have shown conclusively that the production of eggs by the XXII strain of bird is greatly increased by the addition of honey, vitamin concentration and a light sprinkling of caviar to the mid-afternoon and late evening meals.

How many twelve-year-old boys educated in a normal council school could have dictated such a letter? It just shows the difference being privately educated. Needless-to-say, thirty years on Kirkland has followed in father's footsteps and done very well for himself. At this moment he is clerk to the course at Haydock Park Racetrack.

One afternoon in the middle of racing, Bill Tellwright called at Kandahar.

"Hi Ray. Can you loan me ten grand?" was how he greeted me. "No, I'm not joking. I've a touch of the shorts. I am having difficulties with my bank manager. He is a real peasant."

"I know the feeling" I replied, as I had had problems with a certain Mr. Ainsworth.

Lucky enough I had transferred my overdraft from Barclays to the National Westminster where Mr. Phyl Brown was manager. Mr. Brown, an old naval officer of World War II and I got on like a house on fire. I suggested that Bill did the same as I had done and change his bank. This he did and his current difficulties were soon sorted out. I explained why I couldn't lend Bill the ten grand and mentioned that one of my clients had won a considerable amount on a yankee bet only yesterday and I was wondering how I could raise the money to pay him the following Monday when our accounts were sent out.

Without hesitation Bill offered to lend me £500 there and then which I gratefully accepted. What a guy. Called on me for a loan and finished up parting with £500 of his own money. There were not many like him about.

Bill Tellwright was a fearless horseman, competing in the Grand National and the Grand Military Gold Cup at Sandown Park. He won the Gold Cup on three occasions so you can judge for yourself as to his riding capabilities. In 1985, Bill was exercising a young horse he had recently purchased, when he met a local farmer and asked if he could pop his horse over a couple of hedges on the farmer's land which he happened to be passing.

"By all means Mr. Tellwright. You're welcome. Go ahead" he replied.

Bill opened a gate to gain excess and cantered up to a low hedge. As he jumped, the horse stumbled and brought its head right back, cracking poor Bill squarely on his head, breaking his neck. He died instantly. Hundreds of people attended the memorial service.

It would not seem fitting if I didn't relate Jane Tellwright's experience when riding Cufflink, who had found a new home with the Tellwright family.

Out hunting one day in unfamiliar country, she very unwisely pointed Cufflink at a large hedge entwined with barbed wire - a jump she had never encountered before. While flying through the air, she realised that there was a huge drop on the other side of the fence. Too late, only to hope for the best.

Fortunately, the horse didn't fall but must have sustained an injury, for Cufflink never hunted again. So impressed was Jane with the horses effort she very uncharacteristically did something she had never done before; next day she measured the drop and was not surprised to find it was just over 10 feet, which made it bigger and certainly more dangerous than Beechers' Brook on the Grand National. Forty years on, the now Mrs. Jane Stoddard recalls the account with clarity and states,

"Cufflink was the bravest horse I'd ever ridden. But quite mad!!"

Amongst my closest friends are Peter and Sheila Toft, affectionately known throughout North Staffordshire as Tofty. Tofty, like David Scrivens, would bring his father's clock bag to the office and wait for settlement. He was a likeable boy but as he grew older, got a bit too big for his breeches. One afternoon after an affray, I got hold of him by the coat collar and told him he was going to join the Army.

"Okay, don't get excited" was his reply. Much to my surprise he accompanied me to the recruiting officer.

"He wants to join the guards" I told the recruiting sergeant.

"Not tall enough" he replied.

"I would like to join a light infantry regiment if you don't mind." Tofty piped up.

I left them to it. After a while Tofty disappeared from the scene and I didn't see him again for some three years. But when he paid us a visit I was really pleased to see he had developed into a very smart young man. He had finished up a corporal in the King's Shropshire Light Infantry KSLI, and while he was in Germany, had taken a course in ladies hairdressing. He was also a talented joiner. In no time at all he was well established with a very tasteful hairdressing salon employing twelve hand-picked girls. He also opened a pub, The Forest Inn.

Unfortunately, during a scuffle he injured a guy who had been causing a disturbance. Malcolm Bevington, head of C.I.D. in Hanley, who had been his friend, turned on him and prosecuted Tofty. He was heavily fined and ordered to keep the peace. He was endeavouring to keep the peace when the fight took place!

He opened a racing account with me and I have referred to his goings-on in an earlier chapter.

In 1981 it was decided that the Potteries would hold their own marathon the following year. When I learnt that Tofty was going to enter, I decided to follow suit. Starting training again at 57 was hard work and I often wondered as I pounded the roads and byways, whether I had bitten off more than I could chew.

Nevertheless, Father's Day 1982 arrived. I hadn't heard much from Tofty but I thought with his twelve year advantage, he would beat me by an hour. There were posters erected at the start with times for the runners to form up on the approximate time they thought they would take. I had decided to line up with the four-hour group. I didn't see anybody I knew amongst the 4,500 starters, so decided to try and locate Tofty. He wasn't at the three-and-a-half hour marker, nor the three hour. I finally located him up front with the two-hour 15-minute runners.

"What are you doing up here?" I politely asked him.

"Piss off and mind your own f--king business" he snorted. I thought he looked a bit tense and not his normal self.

I made my way back to the four-hour post to await the pistol shot. My intentions were just to finish. After halfway I was wondering how my agitated friend was getting on. It was easy to follow his progress as nearly everybody knew him. I started asking various friends amongst the quarter million spectators lining the route.

"Where's Tofty?"

"About two miles in front of you"

A little later I asked another spectator where Tofty was.

"About half a mile ahead. He's walking"

Ah walking! I'll catch the bugger now. As all long-distance runners know, if you start walking you're lost and will take at least an hour longer than one's best time. Three miles to go I spied Tofty's dad.

"Where's Peter" I cried.

"Just up there" he shouted. "He's walking." I hurried along and caught up with him.

"What's up?" I asked. He looked knackered and replied,

"I went too fast to start with. I should have listened to you"

"Anyway, start running now, come on alongside me" I shouted.

"I can't. I can't"

"Yes you can. Start now. Everyone is looking at you walking, you won't be able to live it down." With that he broke into a trot and kept up with me.

I encouraged him and kept him running. As we approached the finish with about 200 metres to go, he suddenly started sprinting. Away he went. It was impossible for me to catch him and he won by about ten yards. As we went up the funnel to the recording table, we both stood there together and the young lady asked who was first.

"Me" Tofty yelled. "Me"

"For God's sake" I said to him. "We've just run twenty-six miles, does it matter who's first?"

"Does it matter? Course it does. How can I tell my friends that an old bugger like you beat me?"

"Thank you very much" I replied.

Son Dan met me with my change of clothing and I very quickly changed in the marquee provided for that purpose. The first person I saw after getting dressed was poor old Tofty laid out on the grass as if dead. He was surrounded by his wife and friends.

"Hi! How are you feeling?" I jeered at him. He answered me the same way as he had four and a half hours earlier.

"Piss off, Fear!"

Later that night Tofty telephoned me to explain quite calmly his findings on the marathon.

"You know Ray," he said. "I haven't had a proper night's sleep for over a week. I've been so worried about today's run and I've decided never to run twenty-six miles again." He kept to his word but ran several half marathons, one of which sticks in my memory.

It was the same year. The start was at Sneyd Green. As was my custom I looked around for Tofty but he was nowhere to be seen. After a few miles I ventured to ask a friend if he had seen Tofty.

"Yes" was his reply, "he's a little way ahead of you."

'What's his game? Where was he? At the start?' I pondered. Halfway up Litchfield Street and two miles from the finish there were several tables with drinks of various types for the runners. I didn't stop for a drink as I was keen to try and catch my opponent. I had caught a glimpse of him earlier on, some 100 metres in front. He was hard to pick out with so many runners bunched together. I lost sight of him and ran on as fast as I could manage. En-route we had to pass Peter's pub, the Forest Green, and standing outside were his staff and customers.

"Seen Tofty?" I shouted out.

At that very moment a voice cried out in my ear,

"Yes I am bloody well here" and with that Tofty tore off past me in a virtual sprint.

"The bugger." I thought. "Tactics, tactics!"

When the results were published, he had beaten me by three minutes. That evening he telephoned me to tell me how he had hoodwinked me. At the last refreshment table in Lichfield Street, he had knelt down and waited for me to pass. Then he was up and ran comfortably a few paces behind me. He said that had I looked in the large windows of Lewes Department Stores, I would have seen him

296

quite clearly. So he reckoned he had beaten me twice. On reflection he must have held me in the greatest esteem to go to such lengths to get his nose in front.

Not only did Tofty like to keep his nose in front in our running days, but also during his weekly betting with us. He only bet when the meeting was being televised. We always knew his call as it was always after the race had started and the horses had settled down after the first couple of furlongs. This sometimes gave him the advantage but not often.

I remember him having a couple of pounds each way on a horse that was at least twenty lengths in front in a three mile steeplechase. It fell at the sixth. The phone rang.

"That's Tofty" we all cried.

"To be sure, stick me two pounds each way," and he named the horse that had leaped into the lead. It fell at the next fence. The race was coming to its climax and the firm favourite had taken over the lead. It was going very smoothly and looked a certain winner. The phone rang once again and Tofty bellowed out his instruction,

"£5 on the favourite."

Jean looked at me and I answered her enquiring glance.

"Take it" I cried.

With two jumps to go I thought to myself that I shouldn't have taken that bet, it was ridiculous. But luck was with me however for the favourite fell at the last. A deadly hush descended on the office.

The phone rang. It was Tofty. "Tell your boss I'm never ever going to have another f---ing bet in my life" and he banged down the phone. But he was back on again half an hour later, up to his old tricks.

I remember him coming on in the Two Thousand Guineas Classic. The race was half run and he backed the horse in front that eventually won. When Jean wrote out his account, she only paid him evens instead of 2/1. When he telephoned with his complaint, she said,

"You had your bet when the race was half over, so we only paid you half the odds."

He went berserk until we assured him we were only kidding. Tofty has visited us a couple of times here in Spain, but more about our card schools in my next volume.

Chapter 14

A Day in an English High Court

CLAIMANT
F.R.
(Litigant in person)
-Versus-
DEFENDANT
Legal Muggers
(Elite of the British legal system)

On the day of the trial, both the claimant and defendants congregate in the Court chambers. The defendant's barrister, a man who would not be hard to recognise in any crowd, makes himself known to F.R. Pleasantries are exchanged. The claimant is a litigant in person, representing himself. The defendant has an unmistakable barrister and 6 retained solicitors, who are ushered into the courtroom, where both sides lay out their stalls and prepare for action.

The judge enters and, for some unknown reason, everyone has to bow. The judge looks as though it is a long time since he's seen a barber, gives a few instructions, and signals for battle to commence.

F.R. wants to answer the defendants' 'Skeleton Legal Argument' before continuing, but the defendants' say there is no case to answer, and give 12 reasons. F.R. is refused permission to question the barrister, explaining that the judge has a copy of their reasons.

F.R. insists on his answers as he knows they refute the defendants' defence with convincing reasons. The first reason should end the case there and then. The defendants claim F.R. cannot establish an alleged claim against Shermans, and it has negligible chance of success.

F.R. answers:

"I contend I have a case because the defendants rated my case to the Legal Aid Board as having an 80% chance of success. That rating is very high. This was also later strengthened by another qualified member of the firm who said, at a later date, 'our client has a very excellent chance of success'."

There is silence from judge and barrister. F.R's argument falls on deaf ears, and no comment is made.

There is further confab in the courtroom as to the best way to proceed. F.R. wants to call and question the defendants' witness, but this is denied. F.R. wants to get on with presenting his case and is invited to the witness box. Before doing so he asks the judge if he can take his notes with him, but is told there are copies in the witness box. After taking the oath, F.R. is confronted with two huge ledgers containing one thousand pages of the defendants' exhibits, and is then subjected – a man of 78 years – to a 5 hour ordeal of constant cross-examination, the bulk of which has nothing to do with F.R.s case of professional negligence.

The bulk of the ledgers contain correspondence between the two contenders of 12 years earlier. F.R. is asked by the barrister about previous appearances in court, referring to appeals with respect to refusals to grant betting shop licenses. He also reads a letter dated 1995, which relates to what F.R. had told the defendants, reading as follows,

'My Barrister told me I had made a good witness, as F.R. could look the judge in the eye, tell him what he wanted to hear, and look like a choir boy.'

The Judge then listens to a constant barrage of cross-examination relating to letters and statements made more than 10 years earlier, and asks why F.R.'s statements vary so much, first mentioning one witness, then three, then none, and never mentioning the most important witness - Tim; why is this? 'Now turn to page so and so; and the saga of cat toying with mouse, continues for five hours.

By now, it is plain to see that the close-to eighty-year-old claimant is getting rattled, mentioning several times to the court that this line of questioning has nothing to do with the case. The case is F.R. verses the defendants, not F.R. verses the firm that the defendants should have sued for breaking a verbal agreement.

(Earlier, the Judge had referred to F.R.'s earnings and questioned how much income tax F.R. had paid. F.R. reply "Not much with four wives and eleven children to support" brought a smile even to the stony-faced Judge)

F.R. says there had been two meetings held that confirmed the verbal contract, and four witnesses could be called to attest to that fact, but the barrister says the first of those meetings never took place, and further asks why, in all the previous statements, there is no mention of the prime witness. He then goes on to claim that it was because the witness had never been at the meeting. So the witness is judged to be a would-be perjurer without ever being able to get as far as giving evidence.

The barrister questions F.R. on his unsigned contract, and it is confirmed that F.R. did have a verbal contract with ITP Pools, back in the 1960s. Then the taunting starts:

"Why didn't you ask for your job back?"

"If you didn't have a contract, only a verbal agreement, they could have reinstated you, and then sacked you"

"Why did your statements vary? It's apparent you had little chance of success."

By this time F.R. is getting frustrated but has been warned never to argue with the judge or the defendants' barrister. F.R. is finding it difficult to answer so many irrelevant questions without raising his voice, and informing the whole lot of them what a load of wankers they are, and that there wasn't any justice in that f***ing court.

Half an hour before the close, F.R. is allowed to call his first witness but is promptly hauled over the coals for leading the witness. Their barrister starts on F.R's witness but the clear and concise nature of his answers seems to rattle the lawyer. While these important proceedings are taking place, the judge gives an excellent imitation of someone who has fallen asleep. The witness is dismissed and told, in advance, that he will not be needed on the second day.

The judge begins gathering his papers and says the case will continue the next day at 10.30 am. Everyone bows. F.R. is taken aback when, having closed the proceedings for the day, the judge addresses him and tells him that the most he could expect from Shermans' will be four weeks wages in lieu of notice, and that he would be wise to consider the mounting costs (£30,000). F.R. gathers his documents and joins his two witnesses in the foyer, where the barrister invites them to join him in an ante-room. There, he tells F.R. that he has no chance of winning the case. An offer of settlement to the court prior to the start of the case had been made, and F.R. asks whether it is still on the table.

The barrister leaves, then returns to say that his clients are prepared to pay their own costs of £34,000 provided that F.R. withdraws from the case, and warns that if the judge were to make an order for costs against F.R. he would have to sell his house. F.R. asks how much his clients are prepared to pay if he withdras his claim, and pointed out that his home had never been in his own name, but had been bought and registered in the name of his son.

The barrister and his sidekick, a cheery fellow who closely resembled Happy, as in Snow White and the Seven Dwarfs, scurry from the ante-room, scenting victory. F.R. for his part, confers with his two witnesses, who point out that if F.R. wins the case, and is awarded compensation, both sides will most likely have to share the costs, meaning that F.R. would have to dig deeply into his own pocket!

With this threat in mind, F.R. has to make a decision. The barrister and Happy return and said they are authorised to offer X pounds and would pay their own costs, provided FR signs a confidentiality agreement'.

F.R. is exhausted by this time, and to avoid the ordeal of further battle with the enemy on the next day, and together with his companions leaves the battle-ground to head for home, asking himself 'Did we win - or did we lose?'

The witnesses, on the way home, consoled F.R. with the thought that he hadn't lost. If he had, he'd have money to pay, and nothing to come. Even being urged to 'Get on with life and forget the bastards that conned and sabotaged you' was of little comfort.

F.R., feeling a great load had been lifted from his shoulders, slept well, and woke - as usual - at 6 am, pondering how and why he had been treated so scandalously by the barrister, judge and the 'British Legal System' in which he had naively placed his trust. Justice is easily recognised - a fool can see it clearly, but the law was concocted to confuse us peasants and keep us firmly in our place, whilst keeping the barristers and judges rich, but of course, that was its intention all along.

The case of the previous day was held in their exclusive domain, not fit to be adulterated and invaded by some dammed old-age-pensioner without the necessary qualifications to compete. The judge, barrister, and defendants joined forces to create a formidable foe, with the sole purpose of quietening F.R., who dared to question their law, and in their domain.

F.R. reflected on what had gone wrong - and why? The court timetable outlined the procedure.

Day one: Opening and skeleton arguments, claimant's evidence and claimant's supporting witnesses.
Day two: the remainder of the claimant's evidence and the defendants' submissions and or evidence.

F.R. had been denied the opportunity to cross-examine the defendants in the opening skeleton arguments, and forced to act as claimant and lawyer at the same time. The claimant was denied his opening evidence and was unable to present his case of negligence. In fact, negligence was never mentioned. Throughout the day, upon asking the barrister if he could question the defendants, F.R. was told that they were not going into the witness box. F.R. entered the witness box, believing that it was from there that he would present his case, and fell into the trap that 'The System' - and those who abuse it - had laid for him.

FR. had asked the Judge if he could take his evidence into the witness box and was told 'No, everything is there already'. F.R. entered the witness box thinking he was about to present his case. None of his papers were there, only the barrister's two huge ledgers, containing 1,000 pages of correspondence that F.R. had sent to his solicitors during the first 6 years of dialogue with them, and another 6 years to bring them to that day. A total of 12 years.

Most of the correspondence criticised the barristers who were asked to deal with the complaint and had missed the plot from beginning to end. The rest of the time was spent cross-examining F.R.

"Turn to page so and so"

"Now turn to page 560"

"Now turn to page 29"

"What you say is different on both occasions, why?"

The process went on and on, never ending! The events had occurred 10 years or more earlier, and the letters were written two or three years apart and, more to the point, the letters were written believing they were 'confidential' and written to F.R's solicitors, who were, at the time, on his side!

'Mr. F.R. you write that you want a barrister who is on your side and will come up with the right answers, what do you mean?

The judge suggested that perhaps F.R. wanted a bent barrister. This nonsense went on, despite protests from F.R. The judge never intervened to curtail the line of questioning. He seemed always ready to criticise F.R. and, towards the end of the day, suggested that if F.R. was reinstated by Shermans, they could sack him with one months notice and one month's wages.

To sum things up, F.R. had no chance of an honest settlement from the start, and how would it read in the press? 'Eighty year old pensioner defeats seven wise men'. Hence the defendants insisting upon F.R. signing a confidentiality note before leaving the court. Gagged during the debacle of rigged court proceedings, and gagged afterwards, as well.

304

Chapter 15

Lessons of Life

Now in my 79th year, I look back over my life and wonder what it's all been about. What have I learned? What have I accomplished in more than three quarters of a century? Compared with the rest of the world, I suppose I have been very fortunate indeed.

First and foremost, my good health and energy that all my family have also enjoyed. Call it 'luck' if you will, but come to think of it, a lot of thought has gone into accomplishing good health.

From an early age I read as much as possible about sensible eating. Meeting Doctor Gordon Marsden, the so-called 'Australian Quack' set me on the right road. Feeding the family correctly was a good grounding for their formative years. Being keen on sport I was able to assist my children who were interested, in their selected sports.

The constant moving around the country, whilst children, with all its ups and downs, could only have given us boys an insight and broader view as to how the rest of the country survived. We were not born poor, far from it, but in the early thirties - after father had commuted and spent his pension - we lived in some right hovels and, occasionally, went to bed hungry. It was a great experience which engraved into our characters the old saying 'Waste not, want not'. Until recently I would rummage in the dustbin and root out scraps of food my wife had thrown away. Upon observing him, she soon came cured of her extravagances.

World War II changed the future for all the young people of that generation. It messed up our education and, in my case, any possibilities of attaining proper training for an athletic career. On the other hand, it enabled me to join the Guards where I met so many different types, and made life-long friends. The officers, because of their background, wealth, better education and feeding, were better behaved than the rank and file, who with their humble backgrounds produced some real unpleasant characters. During my service I had several articles of value stolen by my roommates. The only thing I stole was a pair of boots for Jack Francis, choosing stealing to a good hiding. I shall keep quiet as to what I purloined from the Huns.

From the cradle to the grave we are 'conned' on two counts. One, the English weather, and two, the politicians. We live in hope that things will get better but they seldom do. Take for instance what happened when the 'war to end all wars' was over. Soon after World War II, America rewrote history and, as usual, their dishonest politicians got it all wrong.

In 1945, Joseph Stalin – 'Uncle Joe' as he was affectionately known throughout the world – was the most popular man in the world. 'We cannot allow this', thought the hierarchy that ran the States. So many millions of dollars were spent on anti-soviet propaganda. Just as today, the bulk of the nation believes what it reads in the papers, be it right or wrong. So they swallowed all the lies and half-truths that were spread.

The receptivity of the greater masses is very limited. Their intelligence is small, but their power of forgetting is enormous.

After Churchill's resounding defeat in the general election of 1945, and although he retained his seat as a Tory MP and received wages as such, he took it upon himself to clear off to 'Yankee land' for several months holiday, followed by a lengthy stay in a lovely villa by Lake Geneva. Lucky him.

Whilst in the States in March 1946 he visited Fulton, Missouri, and lowered the so-called Iron Curtain.

"From Stettin in the Baltic to Trieste in the Adriatic, an Iron Curtain has descended across the continent of Europe."

I can hear him now. The countries that fell under the USSR's influence were mainly the countries that fought Russia during the war. These countries were our enemies too. Austria, Bulgaria, Hungary, Rumania. The USSR government's idea was to have buffer states in case they were invaded again as had been the case for centuries.

The spheres of influence were agreed at Yalta between Churchill, Stalin, and Roosevelt. So the Russian part-occupation of those countries was agreed by Great Britain and the United States. Today we would call them a peace keeping force.

Stalin's answer to Churchill's ill-timed outburst was broadcast to the world on Moscow radio. Nothing relating to Stalin's reply was reported in the British press. Stalin said Churchill's was a dangerous act, calculated to sow seeds of discord amongst allied governments and hamper their cooperation. Churchill was accused of rudeness, lack of tact, shameless libel, and blatant distortion of facts.

Like Hitler, he was letting war loose by a racial theory. He and his friends considered that the English-speaking nations, because they thought they were the only fully valuable nations, should rule the rest of mankind. I'm inclined to agree with Stalin's words.

When Russia's great patriotic war against the Nazi invaders ended in May 1945, the soldiers of the Soviet Union went home to rebuild a country devastated by the Huns.

The USSR had lost 1,710 cities, 70,000 towns and villages, 31,850 industrial enterprises, 1,974 farms, 65,000 kilometres of railways, 84,000 schools and other educational establishments and 43,000 libraries.

Do you think a country so devastated would be interested or have intentions of starting another war? The USA, on the other hand, had no war damage or civilian casualties. Not one bomb was dropped on American soil

The USSR had 20,000,000 dead and millions of the population were seriously injured. Questioned recently about World War II, 90% of English children thought we fought the Russians, thus revealing the power of propaganda.

To think that the blood bath could have been prevented had our short-sighted politicians listened to Russia's pleadings, to sign an Anglo Franco Russian pact (as before the 1914-18 conflict) that if Germany transgressed in any way they would put 200 divisions in the field, together with the French, equally large, army, would soon have crushed any of Hitler's ambitions. The British navy would have command of the sea. Stalin had read 'Mein Kampf' and Hitler's aim to have the Ukraine as Germany's bread basket. All Stalin's proposals were in vain. France was in agreement, but Britain would have nothing to do with those 'Wicked Bolsheviks!!'

Only recently, Tony Benn wrote to me, and stated that in the thirties, western governments actually supported Hitler and rejected the Russian offer of an alliance against Nazi Germany; which might have averted the war. If the west had taken a more positive attitude to the USSR, I think the necessary democratic developments there might well have transformed the history of the World and averted the Cold War. Whatever one thinks of Tony Benn, he was an honest politician, popular with both sides of the House of Commons, and his integrity is without question.

At the beginning of this chapter I asked what I had learned during my life. One thing is certain: I don't trust the Yankee politicians and believe, as Enoch Powell declared, that the United States has a powerful and quite illegitimate influence on the internal affairs of the United Kingdom.

Again, in January 1979, Powell forecast a future in which Britain would become the ally of Russia and Japan against the might of the United States, China, and United Europe. Britain will revert back to its historic mistrust of European Power Blocs. He argued that, in the past, Russia had been the ultimate guarantor of Britain's survival as an independent nation: 1812 Napoleon; 1914 against the Kaiser; 1941 against Hitler. Time will tell if his forecasts come true.

Although I have never been involved with politics or politicians, I have always taken an interest in their tactics. As a young man in Churchill's days, and knowing virtually nothing about parliament, I suppose I was conservative, but as the years rolled by I read many books and came to realise that all was not well in our so-called 'democratic country'.

I have read English, German, American, and Russian versions on the particular subject. From the four accounts, if one has a pygmy-sized brain, one can glean a little of the truth. As for our 'press' they all print different accounts of a speech made by some personality or other, adding a bit on, or leaving a bit off.

I was staying at the Russell Hotel in London on one occasion and went outside to buy an evening paper. The newsvendor had sold out and the only paper left on his rack was Soviet Weekly.

"Try this mate, it's the only paper that prints the truth" was all he said, and gave me a copy. Free - if you please.

Back in my hotel room I read the paper cover to cover and was so impressed that I sent an annual subscription to receive a weekly copy through the post, which I maintained for over 30 years. If Mrs. Thatcher made a speech it was printed word for word, nothing added or taken out, even if it took two pages. Soviet Weekly was always a refreshing read. I was sad when the paper ceased to exist in 1991.

To shock people and aggravate others, I always claimed to be the only communist bookmaker in England, never realising that the world's biggest bookmaker William Hill was as left-wing as anyone could be. He was a close friend of Harry Pollit, the only communist party Member of Parliament.

As a young man, William Hill's bible was Karl Marx's 'Das Capital' and although a multi-millionaire, he always remembered his humble upbringing.

He was extremely angry that faceless men, whose only concern was their profit, reducing families to near starvation, attributed all injustices to those on the Right. What infuriated him most was by the accident of birth the sons of the rich were automatically entitled to the best jobs, while those who had been born in the slums were doomed to spend their lives performing the most menial tasks. I could not voice my own feelings better. Democracy? Hypocrisy, more like it.

It's hard to imagine the size of Hill's organisation. In Hill House in Blackfriars, he had 400 telephone lines and a staff of 2,000 to handle his credit bookmaking alone. I thought I was doing well with my four phones. However, I had 20 betting shops before William Hill started. He was always against betting shops and did all in his power to prevent them from being legalised.

After the shops were legalised, it was three years before he ventured into this type of business. He advocated that all betting shops should close during racing hours. As we know, the opposite of his ideas have come about. TV is now on view at most betting shops and these shops command 90 per cent of total betting turnover.

As discussed in my synopsis, my future lay in meeting the right people at the right time. There is no doubt that my encounter with Kenneth Webb and his demand for an immediate answer whether to accept his offer for me to take up the position he offered in Stoke-on-Trent, was the turning point in my life.

That was in 1952. How things have changed these past 50 years. I fear for the worst in many ways. Who is to blame for this situation? Liberalism, political correctness? The declining birth-rate and the fact that in my children's lifetime 10% of the population will be over 80 years of age.

The politicians, mindful of this, have allowed uncontrolled immigration from the third world, to increase the number of tax-payers. I think immigration must be curtailed and illegal immigrants mercilessly deported whence they came. Those that are allowed to stay must be completely immersed in the language and culture of our homeland.

Seeking political asylum is a nonsense. Seeking a greatly improved lifestyle at our expense, more likely. As things stand today, and unless things change immediately, by 2050 the ethnic population will outnumber the English. The only hope is 'Cometh the hour - cometh the man'. The hour has come, but where is the man? No one in sight. I'm afraid that, in the future, the problem will prove so great it will be impossible to rectify it with peaceful means. I am sure our grandchildren will not accept the destruction of their civilisation as tamely as we have done. My advice to my wife is instead of taking our seven-year-old daughter to flamenco lessons, take her to the Rifle Club and teach her how to handle a useful weapon. God forbid, but it will surely come to bloodshed in little Natasha's lifetime.

Now, what of the EEC? The United States of Europe. The German-French coalition will rule the roost. The United States of

310

Europe, dominated by two of our greatest historical foes. Signing the Union Constitution will be the last straw. It means the end of our control of our armed forces, the right to make treaties with other states. Laws passed by our ancestors during the last one thousand years, over-ruled at the whim of some bureaucrat in some other country, who knows nothing of our English ways, and cares even less. It would be better if we became a state of America, or had entered into a pact with The Third Reich in 1940.

Had Napoleon or Hitler invaded us, we may have thrown them back from our fields and beaches, but cannot beat the United States of Europe. They are too many, too powerful, and too rich. They would take over without actually invading or firing a shot.

What of the monarchy? I had thought at an early age it would be a good idea if Her Majesty presided over her government and, together with a dozen ministers, ruled the country. The foreign secretary would be an educated man who would speak several languages. The most imminent doctor, Minister of Health. An experienced farmer, Minister of Agriculture, and so forth.

Unfortunately, Queen Elizabeth II, unlike Queen Elizabeth I, is happy to go along with whatever government promises to leave Her Majesty and her family in the lap of luxury, to which they have become accustomed. If only Her Majesty had taken on the government on behalf of her People? Alas, too late now.

Our only hope is for a strong opposition party, with a strong leader, who will make a complete withdrawal from the European bureaucracy. We don't want them interfering in our daily lives, and certainly don't want their troops based in our gracious land. To once more quote Enoch Powell, at the outset of our joining the common market in 1967, 'An anti-soviet bloc concocted by the Yanks." Now there is no Russian threat (there never was one, anyway), let's get the hell out of the EEC.

Now I reside in Spain, I've been very happy to accept the Spanish way of life. They are a proud nation and will not take too kindly to any stupid laws that Brussels makes. If the do-gooders endeavour to stop bull-fighting, I am sure the Spanish would simply ignore such a ban. Cruel - they say. Well, at least the bulls get three or four years of life, where they enjoy freedom and the best of treatment. On the big day they get a chance to kill their butcher. When the reader sits down to his Sunday lunch of roast beef and Yorkshire pudding, just remember the next mouthful of meat come from some poor animal cramped up in some sort of factory, force-fed, and hit on the head at 1 year old, or less. If I were a bull, and I've sometimes been described as such, I would sooner choose the former life - and death.

As I was toiling in my garden yesterday, I thought to myself, here I am, purging away, condemning all and sundry. What good have I ever done? Not much, I am afraid. It's all been about securing happiness for myself and family. Self! Yes, that says it all. I've had four wives and four families. My ex-wives have all done very well for themselves and enjoyed happy relationships with their chosen partners. One of my ex-wives is a millionairess, who declined my request for a loan to pay the cost of publishing this book.

Apart from paying gas and electricity bills for some of my old agents' wives, who came begging to my office for financial help, and one who wanted to visit her family in Yugoslavia, yes, and a couple of my permanent staff who wanted new cars, I've little else to be proud of.

Come to think of it, I did buy a new church bell for St. Phillips Church, Werrington, Stoke-on-Trent. How come? I was getting a little fed up with the Sunday morning clatter of the church's old bell, so consulted with the vicar and asked him if it would sound better if he acquired a tape recording of one of the countries most favourable chimes, and play it over the appropriate loud-speakers? I had heard of it being done in other churches.

"No" he said, but come to dinner, and we can consider the alternatives. My number-one and I received the invitation at a later date. The only thing I can remember about the occasion was the starter we had for dinner. It turned out to be thinly sliced boneless kippers, which our host assured us was difficult to distinguish between kippers and smoked salmon. Not having tasted smoked salmon at that early point of my life, I wholeheartedly agreed with him.

312

I remember the vicar as a young, underpaid gentleman with a wimpish sense of humour, who traversed the neighbourhood on an ancient bicycle. He said the church bell was cracked and the only remedy was to get a new one. Not realising what I was letting myself in for, I said,

"I'll pay for a new bell." He seemed very surprised and said he would make the necessary enquiries.

A while later, he informed me that we must go to Loughborough in Leicestershire, the venue of one of the world's most eminent bell makers, who incidentally, it was claimed, had made the bells for the Notre Damn in Paris.

At a later date I took the vicar to the Loughborough bell makers and we were shown round this most interesting workshop. The thing that struck me most was the size of the bells. Most were in excess of six feet in height.

The Vicar had very sensibly taken measurements of the existing bell, which amazed me, as from the road it looked about a foot high. Wrong, nearer five feet. "How much?" I enquired. I had thought in the first instance that ten or twenty pounds would have secured the best bell available. I was way out, and nearly fainted when told £500, which would include transport and installation. £500 in 1956 would be equivalent to £7,000 or more, today.

"Go ahead" I said

The manager said they could put an inscription on the bell for no extra charge. I thought for a minute and said

"Dedicated to the birth in this parish of Jane, Karl and Lindsay Fear, 1956" The manager assured me the engraving would last for 1000 years.

I told the vicar on my way home my gesture was to be anonymous and no one must know who the donor was. I didn't want the taxman nosing into the affairs of the 'generous man of wealth'. To my request, the vicar readily agreed. I didn't live long in the area to hear the much improved sound of the new bell, summoning the villagers to church.

It's Thursday 20th January 2005. It is 6.45 am and I have just finished my first cup of tea here in bed, and ponder how to finish my narrative. I wonder why it has taken so long to write this book. The truth is, I have been too busy with other things to really sit down and get on with the job. When I have had the time, the writing has been easy, as I've a very good memory and everything I have related is true.

I do tend to exaggerate on occasions - but who doesn't? I have only dealt with my experiences up until my exodus to Spain in 1989. The events from then on will be published in my next volume 'Pawn Shop Dick in Spain' which I hope to complete by 2007. That is, of course, if I have not been extradited to England to face charges of one kind or another. In Spain, no one is sent to prison who is older than 70 years of age - that is the law. 'Muchas gracias'. These last 15 years have been every bit as eventful as my life in the UK.

To finish my story, I have included a letter from two yeomen warders from The Tower of London, where I was conceived. I thought the letter fitting, their humour great. They discreetly refer to my driving and mental collapse. They had come to Spain in 2004 as the guests of honour of The Royal Society of St. George. They spent the day after the banquet as guests in my villa, or should I say, in my garden. It was a most beautiful day.

My answer to the beefeaters' jibes about my age is simple:

Age is a quality of the mind.
If you have left your dreams behind,
And hope is cold,
Then you are old.
But if you live your life with zest,
And give to life your best,
Then you are young, young man.

314